RACE CLASS AND POWER IN BRAZIL

Library of Congress Cataloging in Publication Data
Main entry under title:

Race, class, and power in Brazil.

   (CAAS special publication series, ISSN 0882-5300; v. 7)
   Papers first presented at a symposium held in 1980.
   Bibliography: p.
   Contents: Race and class in Brazil / Thomas E. Skidmore — Race and socioeconomic in-
equalities in Brazil / Carlos A. Hasenbalg — Updating the cost of not being white in Brazil
/ Nelson do Valle Silva — [etc.]
   1. Blacks — Brazil — Congresses. 2. Brazil — Race relations — Congresses. 3. Social
classes — Brazil — Congresses. 4. Power (Social sciences) — Congresses. I. Fontaine, Pierre-
Michel, 1938-   . II. University of California, Los Angeles. Center for Afro-American
Studies. III. Series.
F2659.N4R24   1985   305.8'96'081   85-19543
ISBN 0-934934-22-3
ISBN 0-934934-23-1 (pbk.)

Center for Afro-American Studies
University of California, Los Angeles

Library of Congress Catalog Card Number: 85-19543
ISBN 0-934934-22-3
ISBN 0-934934-23-1 (pbk)
ISSN 0882-5300
Printed in the United States of America

Designed by Serena Sharp
Produced by UCLA Publication Services Dept.
Typography: Freedmen's Organization

RACE CLASS AND POWER IN BRAZIL

Pierre-Michel Fontaine, Editor

CENTER FOR AFRO-AMERICAN STUDIES
UNIVERSITY OF CALIFORNIA, LOS ANGELES

Center for Afro-American Studies
Claudia Mitchell-Kernan, Director

CAAS Special Publication Series
Volume 7

Publications Committee
    Margaret Washington Creel
    Baruch Elimelech
    Pierre-Michel Fontaine
    Lewis Langness
    Claudia Mitchell-Kernan
    Richard Yarborough
    Robert Grant, Consultant
    Dianne Pinderhughes, Consultant

CONTENTS

CONTRIBUTORS

ANANI DZIDZIENYO teaches in the Afro-American studies program and the Center for Portuguese and Brazilian Studies at Brown University (Rhode Island). His research interests cover Blacks in Brazilian society and politics, as well as the relations between African and Latin American countries. His publications include *The Position of Blacks in Brazilian Society* (1971, 1979) and "Blackness and Politics in Brazil" in *Politics and the African Legacy* (1984), Rhett Jones, editor.

PIERRE-MICHEL FONTAINE, formerly an associate professor of political science at UCLA, is assistant representative for legal affairs of the United Nations High Commissioner for Refugees in Thailand. He has taught and written widely on Caribbean and Brazilian politics and political economy and is completing a major study entitled "Race and Class in Brazilian Politics and Society."

LÉLIA GONZALEZ is professor of Afro-Brazilian studies of the Visual Arts School for the State of Rio de Janeiro and professor of popular Brazilian culture in the department of arts, Catholic University, Rio de Janeiro. She is the co-author, with Carlos Hasenbalg, of *Lugar do negro* (1982).

CARLOS A. HASENBALG is professor of sociology at the Instituto Universitário de Pesquisas do Rio de Janeiro (IUPERJ). He has published *Discriminação e desigualdades raciais no Brasil* (1979), is the co-author of *Lugar do negro* (1982), and has written several articles on race relations and racism in Brazil.

MICHAEL MITCHELL is director of the Afro-American studies program at St. Peter's College in Jersey City, New Jersey. He has done extensive field research on Blacks in Brazil and has written articles on several aspects of Afro-Brazilian society and politics. He is presently doing research on the impact of race on the formation of the modern state in Latin America.

CLAUDIA MITCHELL-KERNAN is professor of anthropology and psychiatry and director of the UCLA Center for Afro-American Studies. She has conducted sociolinguistic research in the United States, Belize, and Samoa, and has written numerous articles on sociocultural aspects of language use among Afro-Americans. Chapters of her monograph *Language Behavior in a Black Urban Community* (1971) have been widely anthologized; and her co-edited book *Child Discourse* (1977) is widely cited. Her most recent book, co-edited with Gordon Berry, is *Television and the Socialization of the Ethnic Minority Child* (1982).

NELSON DO VALLE SILVA is senior researcher at the Laboratorio Nacional de Computação Científica, Brazilian National Research Council (CNPq), and was recently Fulbright visiting professor at the Center for Latin American Studies, University of Florida, where he taught a seminar on "Comparative Racial Stratification: Brazil and the U.S." He has published many journal articles in Brazil and abroad and has written widely on Brazilian racial and social stratification. He is completing a study entitled "Trends in Class Structure in Brazilian Society."

THOMAS E. SKIDMORE is professor of history and director of Ibero-American studies at the University of Wisconsin. In *Black into White: Race and Nationality in Brazilian Thought* (1974) he analyzed the rise of the "whitening" ideology in modern Brazil. His *Politics in Brazil: 1930–1964* (1967) has been translated into Portuguese and widely used in Brazilian schools and universities. Most recently he has co-authored (with Peter H. Smith) *Modern Latin America* (1984).

J. MICHAEL TURNER is a visiting research fellow at the African Studies Center, Howard University, and in the African studies program, Georgetown University. He is also a consultant in the West Africa regional division of the World Bank. From 1979 to 1984 he was a program officer in the Rio de Janeiro field office of the Ford Foundation, during which time he worked with Afro-Brazilian social, cultural, and academic groups as a part of his program assignment. He has written on various aspects of Africa's historic linkages with Brazil and is conducting research on contemporary relations between Latin America and Africa.

FOREWORD

As civil rights legislation in the United States progressively eradicates most forms of juridical and overtly violent racism and racial discrimination, the character of race relations in this country becomes more and more comparable to that of Brazil. When the legal base of discrimination and segregation erodes, the attitudinal and behavioral bases go underground.

Scholars of race relations in Brazil and in the United States have begun to see class, rather than race, as the foundation of the socioeconomic and political structures that perpetuate the marginalization of people of African descent. Nevertheless, there are authorities on the subject, some of whom are represented in this volume, who remain convinced that race is still the designator that marks off many Blacks for relegation to the underclasses.

It cannot be denied that modernization and industrialization have wrought profound changes in the social structures of a number of New World societies. The decline in the legal underpinnings of racial stratification is one example. Despite such changes, however, certain disturbing constants require examination. The research presented in this volume focuses on the shadowy infrastructure of Brazilian race relations, as well as the local movements that are attempting to unveil it and bring an end to racial discrimination in Brazil.

The study of Brazil's race relations presents complex problems. The official view of Brazilian society by its government, which until recently was one of the most repressive military dictatorships in the New World, has been one of "racial democracy." The irony of such an appellation in an otherwise authoritarian regime aside, most Brazilians have upheld this view for decades as a matter of national pride. The fact that racial discrimination and segregation have been outlawed in Brazil is seen as proof that any racial problems were eliminated with the stroke of the legislative pen. It is noteworthy that a parallel mystique has developed within the field of comparative slavery.

It was once widely held, and is still debated, that the Latin version of plantation slavery was more humane than that practiced in the United

States. This view rests in part on the existence in Latin America of legal codes which recognized slave marriages, protected slave families from being separated through sale, and made more generous provisions for manumission than were characteristic of the United States. Both the over-representation of African descended people among the Brazilian underclass and the high mortality rates of slaves in Brazil suggest that neither the contemporary situation nor the historical picture can be adequately apprehended by reference to civil rights legislation and laws granting slaves' "rights."

The Thirteenth, Fourteenth, and Fifteenth Amendments failed to guarantee the political rights of Black Americans between the 1870s and the 1960s. Nor did this legislation undermine the variety of practices that subordinated Blacks to whites in the labor market. Not only was racial subordination in the political and economic arenas the order of the day, but these disabilities were further exacerbated by the presence of such terrorist organizations as the Ku Klux Klan, which showed its grim determination to uphold white supremacy through violence and intimidation. The juxtaposition of these facts of history against the aforementioned constitutional amendments and the "separate but equal" doctrine articulated in *Plessy v. Ferguson* in 1896, not successfully challenged until *Brown v. the Board of Education of Topeka, Kansas*, in 1954, strikingly emphasized the gulf that can separate jural norms from custom and accepted practice.

Brazilian Blacks continue to predominate in the lowest economic strata of their society. The unequal start that freed slaves had in 1888 when compared to their better-trained white rivals in the labor force has frequently been tendered as the reason for this. As the works of Afro-Brazilian historian Manuel Querino document, however, many enslaved Africans were far from unskilled, being proficient in such crafts as metallurgy and mining before being taken to Brazil. As Brazil nears the centennial of its Abolition, the last in the New World, this claim becomes untenable. It seems that Blacks were able to adapt to the labor needs of the eighteenth and nineteenth centuries, but lag behind in the twentieth. The fact that Brazil's "economic miracle" bypassed the majority of the population has only worsened the plight of the Black underclasses, giving them less hope than ever of escaping their privation.

It is clear that a significant basis for socioeconomic inequality of the races in Brazil is to be found in the relegation of African descendants to pariah status. Denied access to education and with only a modicum of political representation, what can we expect the effect to be upon Black peoples' aspirations and belief in the possibility of social and economic betterment? While the subject of race and racial stratification seems to assault the sensibilities of many people today, racial and ethnic stratification are significant social problems in the modern world. Indeed, they are of sufficient magnitude to cause civil strife and prolonged human suffering. We cannot afford to seek refuge from these facts by denying their existence, however. Such a strategy is likely to exacerbate existing problems by suppressing the means to voice and seek remedies to grievances.

In the face of government discouragement of studies of race relations or of the Afro-Brazilian community as an ethnic group, scholars work in far from ideal conditions. As Nelson do Valle Silva discusses in his contribution to this volume, even census gathering techniques have been adjusted to make demographic studies difficult. Nevertheless, as the research presented here attests, it is still possible to produce significant and insightful studies of this complex area.

Scholars who have contributed to this book have used a variety of approaches in the study of race, class, and power in Brazil. They present Marxist, quantitative, and anti-class analyses covering many aspects of the Brazilian situation. Dr. W. E. B. Du Bois identified racial stratification as the problem of the twentieth century. It now appears that this situation will continue into the twenty-first century. A first step to solving the problem is to admit its existence and to understand its complexities and ramifications. When confronting a Hydra, only Herculean labors can prevail. A simple stroke of a lawmaker's pen will not suffice.

The papers comprising this volume derive from the Center for Afro-American Studies 1980 symposium, Race and Class in Brazil: New Issues and New Approaches. Time has diminished neither the prominence of the issues nor the validity of the approaches. We gratefully acknowledge the co-sponsorship of the symposium by the UCLA Latin American Center and the Black Students Alliance. The support of the Ford Foundation, which supplied travel grants to our Brazilian participants, and of then-Chancellor Charles Z. Wilson and the Council of Comparative and International Studies was equally indispensable. Pierre-Michel Fontaine, who conceived the symposium and took major responsibility for bringing it about, has generously helped in bringing its results into publishable form, with the collaboration of CAAS managing editor Marcelle Fortier. Sabrina Gledhill, a Brazil scholar herself, ably copyedited the manuscript and developed the glossary. Finally, I express my personal appreciation for the unfailing cooperation and patience of all the contributors to this work.

Claudia Mitchell-Kernan
Director
Center for Afro-American Studies

University of California
Los Angeles

INTRODUCTION

PIERRE-MICHEL FONTAINE[1]

The papers gathered in this volume arise from a symposium given at UCLA entitled Race and Class in Brazil: New Issues and New Approaches. The topic and orientation of that meeting expressed a conception of Afro-American studies which is both comparative and international. The symposium was undertaken on the premise that, despite the variations created by differing historical and socio-ecological experiences, there are fundamental similarities in the conditions of African peoples in the Americas, whether in the United States, Jamaica, Ecuador, Cuba, Argentina, or Brazil.

The issue of race in Brazil and its relations to class and other socioeconomic and political issues have generated considerable controversy (Fontaine 1980). As symposium participant Carlos Hasenbalg pointed out, the history of the study of modern race relations in Brazil can be broken down into three stages or schools of thought. The first stage began in the early 1930s, when Gilberto Freyre (1946) rejected the blatantly racist interpretations of Oliveira Vianna and others, but introduced in their place the concept of "racial democracy," alleging the absence of racism and racial discrimination. In the second stage, Donald Pierson (1942) and others studying the Brazilian Northeast during the 1940s and 1950s argued that whatever prejudice could be found was class-related and that factors such as education, occupation, and wealth were more important than race in the determination of social rank and class interaction.

The third school of thought appeared in São Paulo in the 1950s and 1960s and focused on the Center-South and South of Brazil. The dominant influence was that of Florestan Fernandes (1969, 1972, 1977) who, as Hasenbalg has pointed out, substantiated the significance of racism and racial discrimination in industrial and capitalist Brazil, but saw them as an aberration, an archaic survival from the seigneurial, pre-capitalist, and pre-industrial past. It must be said, however, that Fernando Henrique Cardoso (1962) and Octávio Ianni (1962, 1972, 1978), the other two prominent members of the São Paulo school, have not upheld this "anachronism" argument. They emphasize the adaptation of racism, having been engendered by the system of slavery, to the structural characteristics of industrial capitalism.

This point was developed by Hasenbalg (1979) who, while rejecting the interpretation of race as an epiphenomenon of class, conceptualized racial ascription as relating principally to the subordinate aspect of the reproduction of social classes. In other words, race is an important determinant of one's location in the class structure. Race then becomes a powerful subsidiary means of maintaining and reproducing the capitalist system, an instrument to be used by those who dominate the means of production.

The topic of race and class is controversial in Brazil. Unlike most other issues of social research, disagreements over the study of race in that country are not merely academic matters. UNESCO has embroiled itself in this controversy on two occasions. The first was in the 1950s, when it sponsored the research that constituted the third stage mentioned above. To the surprise of everyone, including UNESCO, it showed that Brazil was not quite a model of racial harmony. The second time was in 1972, when UNESCO reported to the United Nations General Assembly on continued discrimination against Blacks in Brazil's luxury hotels, restaurants, and other public places, based on research conducted by the Brazilian Center for Educational Research in Rio de Janeiro. The Brazilian delegate to the U.N. sent a telegram of protest to the Secretary General attacking the reliability of the Center's research (Azevedo 1975, 54–55).

Others have faced varying degrees of opposition when they have attempted to conduct or to support non-congratulatory research on Brazilian race relations. It did not help matters much, on the eve of the military overthrow of the Goulart government in 1964, that the writings of three of the members of the São Paulo school were strongly influenced by Marxism. This ideological influence was not lost on Freyre (1968b), who had been a supporter of ARENA, the party of the military government. Eventually Fernandes, Cardoso, and Ianni were all forcibly retired from the University of São Paulo and *cassados* for ten years in the post–1964 era.

In 1969 Brazil's National Security Council identified studies and reports on racial discrimination in that country as subversion (Azevedo 1975, 53, n. 27). In 1977 the Nigerian government, allegedly under pressure, rejected after first accepting a paper submitted by Abdias do Nascimento (1978) to the Second World Festival of Black Arts and Cultures (FESTAC '77) on the theme of the genocide of Blacks in Brazil. Similarly, in that year, considerable pressure was reportedly brought to bear on a well-known United States foundation to terminate its funding of a Black awareness project in Brazil. In 1978, the foundation decided not to fund any research on race in Brazil. By 1979, it was reportedly not supporting research on Brazil at all in order to avoid controversy.

In spite of such obstacles, a fourth stage of research — not mentioned by Hasenbalg — appeared in the 1970s. It is more heterogeneous than its predecessors and, therefore, more difficult to characterize. The seminal thinkers of this stage were political scientists Bolivar Lamounier (1968) and Amaury de Souza (1971), whose contributions have not yet had their full impact. The very disciplinary training of Lamounier and Souza is in itself a novelty, as to this day the field is dominated by sociologists and anthropologists.

Also instrumental in stimulating the development of the current stage of research in Afro-Brazilian studies is the Working Group on Themes and Problems of the Black Population in Brazil, which is part of the National Association for Postgraduate Studies and Research in the Social Sciences (ANPOCS), based at the University Research Institute of Rio de Janeiro (IUPERJ), Candido Mendes University. Carlos Hasenbalg, Lélia Gonzalez, and University of São Paulo anthropologist João Baptista Borges Pereira (1967) are among the principal animators of this group, founded in 1979, which has generated a good many papers on specific themes of the Afro-Brazilian condition characterized by a great variety of approaches, methods, disciplinary orientations, and levels of quality.

Afro-Brazilian studies have also been enriched by the efforts of several research bodies, the most prominent of which is the Center for Afro-Asian Studies (CEAA) of Candido Mendes University, led by its executive director, José Maria Nunes Pereira Conceição, and historian Joel Rufino dos Santos (1980). As in the case of Afro-American Studies in the U.S. the current wave in Afro-Brazilian studies is strongly influenced in some of its parts by the Black movement itself. Most provocative and expressive of this mood is the work of Rio de Janeiro Federal Deputy Abdias do Nascimento (PDT-RJ), the titles of whose writings speak for themselves (1978, 1979, 1982, 1983). Also noteworthy in this regard, but with a class orientation, is the work of Clovis Moura of the Brazilian Institute of Africanist Studies (IBEA) (1976, 1977, 1981).

The scholars represented in this volume, several of whom are members of ANPOCS, throw significant light on the complex relationship between race and class in Brazil. Among other issues, they discuss the meaning of the concepts of whiteness and blackness in Brazilian society, as well as of the intermediate categories of color; the changing levels of racial identity;

the use of quantitative methods in the study of such phenomena; the relevance of rural-urban disparities to race-related socioeconomic differentials; and the opportunities offered to Blacks by the process of *abertura*.

Most, if not all, of the contributors to this volume hold two premises in common. One is the perception that the Brazilian racial condition can best be studied through a comparative perspective rather than as a unique phenomenon. The other is a refusal to interpret the issue of race as a mere epiphenomenon of the class issue, or seeing racial consciousness as false consciousness. Hasenbalg assesses such an approach as inadequate and proposes a plausible explanation of the relationship between race and class, in which race is subordinate to class without being submerged by it. Gonzalez, too, rejects the "reductionism" that has resulted in the Brazilian Left's conservatism vis-à-vis the racial question, its insistence that the racial problem can be effectively subsumed under the issue of class.

Another important topic is the very definition of race in the Brazilian context. Despite the proliferation of skin color terminology in Brazil, Hasenbalg and Silva find it more realistic and analytically useful to employ a white-nonwhite classification rather than white, Black, and mulatto. In fact, one of the two major hypotheses that Silva tests in chapter 4 is Degler's "mulatto escape hatch," which suggests that the mulatto suffers less discrimination than the Black (1971). Silva concludes that this hypothesis is implausible, and that the treatment and socioeconomic conditions of Blacks and mulattoes are basically similar.

Silva also disagrees with Degler's other major hypothesis—that race plays no significant role in social mobility and that the socioeconomic differentials between whites and nonwhites at the time of Abolition explain current disparities. Instead, Silva finds nonwhites to be consistently "much less efficient" than whites in transmitting their achieved socioeconomic status from generation to generation. Whites generally obtain higher marginal rates of return on experience and schooling, and the difference tends to increase with higher levels of education. All of this is consistent with Hasenbalg's finding that, as well as achieving lower levels of education on the average than whites, racial discrimination subjects nonwhites to a "cycle of cumulative disadvantages," the result of which is that income improvements yielded to nonwhites by additional years of education are much less than those accrued by whites.[2]

Also discussed in this volume are changes in racial attitudes which Dzidzienyo, Gonzalez, Mitchell, and Turner have detected, primarily in the Center-South and South. Dzidzienyo contrasts the Brazilian attitude toward Africa, which he terms "frozen Africanity," with the "dynamic Africanity" of U.S. Blacks. At the same time, Dzidzienyo shows the regional differences within Brazil by contrasting the cold reception the

Asentehene (leader of the Ashantis of Ghana) received in Bahia with the enthusiasm shown him by the Black population in São Paulo during his visit to Brazil in 1978. On the whole, however, Dzidzienyo notes a growing interest in contemporary Africa on the part of Afro-Brazilians, which parallels the growing interest of both government and business in African trade.

The issue of increasing racial identity is further explored by Turner, who sees Afro-Brazilian university students in Rio, São Paulo, Porto Alegre, and Brasília as having evolved from perceiving themselves as brown in 1971 to proclaiming in 1978 that they are Black. Significantly, he sees this evolution as having been influenced in part by the Black Rio or Black-Soul movement among unemployed and underemployed Black youths in Rio which began in 1976 (Fontaine 1981). Mitchell confirms the significance of the Black-Soul movement, among other phenomena, in the development of racial consciousness. That movement is not without its limitations, however, since, according to Mitchell, it lacks the structure to channel the feelings of racial identity into constructive political action, a point with which Gonzalez agrees.

This volume also demonstrates the relevance and importance of the political analysis of race relations in Brazil, especially in the chapters by Dzidzienyo, Fontaine, Gonzalez, and Mitchell. Black political mobilization is a major subject of discussion. Mitchell analyzes the implications of *abertura democrática* for Black progress in Brazil. He argues that the current political restructuring is a major determinant of the levels and styles of Black political activism. However, Blacks can also influence the abertura by "redefin[ing] racial issues for political debate [and] rais[ing] the stakes . . . by increasing the demands [in return] for their allegiance."

Gonzalez describes the nature and style of this Black political activism in her analysis of the structure and activities of the Unified Black Movement. Founded in 1978, it is currently the most salient Black collective action effort in Brazil. She compares it favorably to the Brazilian Negro Front (FNB) of the 1930s and the Negro Experimental Theater (TEN) movement of the 1940s and 1950s, both of which were, in her view, paternal, overly personal, and authoritarian; they failed to go beyond racial integration and deal with the larger issue of system integration. The new movement is seen to have avoided these pitfalls and to have adopted a strategy of class action as well as racial action, internationalism, and ecumenism, while avoiding paternalism, cooptation, and the cult of personality. At the same time, it is seen to be the true offspring of the FNB and the TEN.

The political implications of race are further considered in my discussion of the notion of power as applied to Blacks in Brazil in chapter 5.

There, I suggest that, while tempting, it is not very useful to think of Blacks in Brazil as being powerless, and that their complete helplessness is a rather implausible proposition. It is more fruitful to examine the following areas critically: (*a*) interstitial power—such as electoral and bureaucratic politics in the *favelas*; (b) residual power, as in Black political sub-patronage and patronage; (*c*) incremental power, like that which may result from occupational, educational, or social mobility; and (*d*) unorthodox channels to power, as in political mobilization efforts such as the Unified Black Movement.

This volume appears at a critical period in contemporary Brazilian history, a time when Brazilians are poised on the brink of "redemocratization." For some Blacks, the question is whether the new democracy will be both political and racial. This is not a reference to the vaunted "racial democracy" of yore which, at the height of military rule, Azevedo correctly identified as "constitut[ing] the major source of national pride" (1975, 7–8). As he saw it, "there is nothing that is invoked more frequently and with so much emphasis, as proof of the absence of prejudice and of tensions in our society. It constitutes probably the most sensitive note in the moral imagination of Brazil, cultivated with insistence and with intransigence" (my translation).[3]

The achievement of true racial democracy will, of course, depend on the achievement of political democracy. The ability of Blacks to pursue this objective by political means will depend on their ability to place the issue on the broad political agendas at federal, state, and local levels. On the eve of the inauguration of Tancredo Neves in March 1985 as the first civilian president in twenty-one years, the political position of Blacks did not appear very promising. In the Federal Congress, there was still only one visibly Afro-Brazilian senator albeit a very prestigious one, Nelson Carneiro (PTB-RJ), who has spent a lifetime pursuing social democracy in general, being the most consistent defender of the rights of women and the poor. He was the author and prime mover of the divorce law, which took some two decades to bring into being. Another fruit of his labors was the law on the status of common-law marriages. His latest victory at this writing was the unanimous passage by the Senate in an emergency session of his bill outlawing discrimination against women (December 1984).

In the lower chamber there are now only two Afro-Brazilian deputies where there were three before March 1983. These are singer Aguinaldo Timóteo (PDT-RJ) and writer and Black movement leader Abdias do Nascimento (PDT-RJ). Timóteo won one of the largest numbers of votes in the November 1982 elections (some 500,000 votes), based on his popularity as a singer, but he has since broken with the leadership of his

Democratic Labor Party (PDT) and given his support to the losing government candidate for the presidency, following a series of bizarre incidents. Abdias do Nascimento failed to be elected at first, having obtained only about 15,000 votes, but he was able to take office through the use of Brazil's *suplente* system, which allows the person with the next highest number of votes to substitute for the elected candidate and so on down the line, whenever the incumbent is incapacitated, or is appointed or elected to another office. During his first year in office, Nascimento produced a series of speeches and bills focusing on racial discrimination, including a bill on compensatory racial quotas which exemplifies the strong American influence on his thinking (Nascimento 1983).

In the state of Rio de Janeiro, out of dozens of Black candidates, only one state deputy and one Rio de Janeiro municipal councilwoman were elected in November 1982. The former is José Miguel (PDT-RJ), a Baptist preacher and volunteer social worker with a nonracial constituency. The latter is a *favelada* nurse, Benedita da Silva (PT-RJ), who has complained of discrimination against her in the Municipal Council itself. A large number of Black candidacies in the state of São Paulo produced only one state assemblyman and one São Paulo city councilman. Previous to March 1983, there had been four Black São Paulo municipal councilmen, including the president of the Municipal Council, and one Black state assemblywoman. The new municipal councilman is José Maria Rodrigues Alves (PMDB-SP), whose popularity is based on having been a star soccer player with the Corintians team. The new state assemblyman is Benedito Cintra (PMDB-SP), a leader of working-class movements, which form his power base. The only Black state governor is João Alves Filho in Sergipe, whose racial background appears to be of little salience.

The vote for Black candidates, if not the Black vote, appears to be very weak. In the two major states of Rio de Janeiro and São Paulo, Black candidates have won only when they have been able to appeal to a nonracial or multiracial constituency, generally a class constituency, such as workers, favelados, and inhabitants of the urban peripheries. The candidates with a strong racial appeal generally lost in the 1982 elections, even when, as in the case of Lélia Gonzalez, they also made a strong working-class appeal. There are several factors which can explain this phenomenon, and the matter has been furiously debated within the Black movement in Brazil (Ferreira and Pereira 1983). Aside from such aspects as the higher level of illiteracy among Blacks in a country where illiterates are not allowed to vote (whereas voting is compulsory for the literates), the inexperience and lack of material resources of many Afro-Brazilian candidates, or the alleged lack of support from the parties, a fundamental factor seems to be the relationship of class to race in the Brazilian context and the resulting social and political perceptions. As the lower and working classes — to which most Blacks belong — are fully integrated in the same conditions of poverty, the racial appeal is limited in its impact, especially as it must counter the powerful ideology of racial harmony so pervasive in Brazilian society.

In the state of Rio de Janeiro, Governor Leonel Brizola (PDT) has expressed his commitment to racial democracy, not only by engineering Abdias do Nascimento's access to incumbency, but also by appointing two Black state secretaries, both of whom were defeated in the 1982 elections. In São Paulo State the winning party, PMDB (Party of the Brazilian Democratic Movement), has not found it necessary or expedient to follow suit, in spite of formal promises allegedly made before the elections. In both states, however, the Black movement appears to have been seriously, if only temporarily, disrupted by its involvement in electoral politics, a fate which seems to have befallen most of the other minority or grassroots movements which appeared to be so vigorous at the turn of the decade, such as those by women, homosexuals, workers, and church movements. As a result of trying to influence the political parties to further their own aims, these movements were smothered by the more powerful, more established, and more experienced political organizations. Formerly mechanisms of social-political mobilization, they became vote-collecting instruments and their specific goals were lost in the general struggle for political power.

For the São Paulo Black movement, dismal electoral defeat resulted in a total inability to influence the parties, including the winning PMDB party with which Blacks had most closely identified. In Rio de Janeiro, some of the leaders of the Workers Party attributed the party's poor electoral performance to an allegedly over-intimate association with minority movements. In March 1983, as the PMDB was taking over the state government in São Paulo, Black movement leaders were locked in a pitched, but losing, battle with it over political appointments. In fact, all the energy of the movement seemed to be focused on making the PMDB live up to promises of jobs, the fulfillment of which the Black leaders were no longer in a position to demand.

What was needed in the circumstances was an understanding of the meaning of race in Brazilian society, and its relation to class and power. Although the Black movement simply repeated in 1982 the mistakes committed in the 1930s and 1950s (Ferreira and Pereira 1983), there now appears to be a learning process at work. Even at the height of the fight for political jobs in São Paulo, a few clearly understood what was going on under the rubric of "opening a space for Blacks" in the state government, and some even denounced the *empreguismo* being displayed. Many realized that political power is not given on a silver platter and has to be taken, and all began to analyze the causes of the defeat.

NOTES

1. Formerly Associate Professor of Political Science at UCLA, Pierre-Michel Fontaine is now Assistant Representative for Legal Affairs of the United Nations High Commissioner for Refugees in Thailand. Neither institution is responsible for the views expressed here or in chapter 5.
2. The quantitative methods used by both Hasenbalg and Silva in arriving at their conclusions are just as important as the findings themselves. These methods are far more elaborate than those used by other students of racial inequalities in Brazil, with the possible exception of Oliveira, Porcaro, and Costa (1980), also members of the ANPOCS group. Hasenbalg and Silva were the first to use the racial data generated by the 1976 PNAD conducted by the Brazilian Institute of Geography and Statistics (IBGE).
3. There are those who claim that no one has advocated the thesis of racial democracy in the past two or three decades. However, the psychological and material bases on which the myth rests are still very much present. Freyre (1978a) continued to emphasize what he saw as the color blindness of Brazilians — their consciousness of being beyond race — which he considered to be socially, economically, and politically democratizing, shortly before he lamented the fact that Blacks are severely underrepresented in positions of power or status in Brazil (1978b). Similarly assimilationist views were expressed from a slightly different perspective by novelist Jorge Amado when he received the Tomé de Souza medal for his contributions to literature on 30 November 1984 from the Municipal Council of Bahia. It was a ringing endorsement of race mixture which is worth quoting at length:

   It is necessary to repeat that there exists only one solution to the racial problem and that is the mixing of the races. Anything else, whatever it may be, leads irrevocably to racism.... It is here, in this city of Bahia...that the Brazilian nation began its formation. Our city was the immense bed of love where the races, the bloodstreams, the cultures mixed to produce the birth and growth of our *mestiço* race, our mulatto culture, and affirmation of our originality as a people (*Jornal do Brasil*, 1 December 1984) (my translation).

BIBLIOGRAPHY

Azevedo, Thales de 1975. *Democrácia racial*. Petrópolis, Rio de Janeiro: Editora Vozes.
Bastide, Roger, and Florestan Fernandes 1959. *Brancos e negros em São Paulo*. São Paulo: Companhia Editora Nacional.
Cardoso, Fernando Henrique 1962. *Capitalismo e escravidão no Brasil meridional*. São Paulo: Difusão Europeia do Livro.
Cardoso, Fernando Henrique, and Octavio Ianni 1960. *Cor e mobilidade social em Florianópolis*. São Paulo: Companhia Editora Nacional.
Degler, Carl N. 1971. *Neither Black nor White: Slavery and Race Relations in Brazil and the United States*. New York: Macmillan.
Fernandes, Florestan 1969. *The Negro in Brazilian Society*. New York: Columbia University Press.

———— 1972. *O negro no mundo dos brancos*. São Paulo: Difusão Europeia do Livro.

———— 1977. *Circuito fechado*. 2d ed. São Paulo: HUCITEC.

Ferreira, Yedo, and Amauri M. Pereira 1983. *O movimento negro e as eleições*. Pamphlet No. 1. Rio de Janeiro: SINBA, Instituto de Pesquisas das Culturas Negras (IPCN).

Fontaine, Pierre-Michel 1980. Research in the Political Economy of Afro-Latin America. *Latin American Research Review* 15(2): 111–141.

———— 1981. "Transnational Relations and Racial Mobilization: Emerging Black Movements in Brazil." In *Ethnic Identities in a Transnational World*, edited by John F. Stack, Jr., 141–162. Westport, Conn.: Greenwood Press.

Freyre, Gilberto 1946. *The Masters and the Slaves*. New York: Alfred A. Knopf.

———— 1978*a*. O brasileiro como uma alem-raça. *Folha de São Paulo* (May 21).

———— 1978*b*. Brasileiros de origem afro-negra. *Folha de São Paulo* (August 1).

Gonzalez, Lélia, and Carlos Hasenbalg 1982. *Lugar do negro*. Rio de Janeiro: Editora Marco Zero Ltda.

Hasenbalg, Carlos 1979. *Discriminações e desigualdades raciais no Brasil*. Translated by Patrick Burglin. Rio de Janeiro: Edições Graal Ltda.

Ianni, Octávio 1962. *As metamorfoses do escravo*. São Paulo: Difusão Europeia do Livro.

———— 1972. *Raças e classes no Brasil*. 2d ed. Rio de Janeiro: Editora Civilização Brasileira.

———— 1978. *Escravidão e racismo*. São Paulo: Editora HUCITEC.

Lamounier, Bolivar 1968. Raça e classe na política brasileira. *Cadernos Brasileiros* 8(3): 34–50 (May–June).

Moura, Clovis 1976. *O preconceito de côr na literatura de cordel: tentativa de analise sociológica*. São Paulo. Editora Resenha Universitária.

———— 1977. *O negro: de bom escravo a mau cidadão?* São Paulo: Conquista.

———— 1981. *Rebeliões da senzala*. 3d ed. São Paulo.

Nascimento, Abdias do 1978. *O genocídio do negro brasileiro: processo de um racismo mascarado*. Rio de Janeiro: Paz e Terra.

———— 1979. *Mixture or Massacre? Essays in the Genocide of a Black People*. Translated by E. L. Nascimento. Buffalo, N.Y.: Afrodiaspora.

———— 1982. *O negro revoltado*. 2d ed. Rio de Janeiro: Editora Nova Fronteira.

———— 1983. *Combate ao racismo: discursos e projetos*. Brasília: Centro de Documentação e Informação, Câmara dos Deputados.

Oliveira, Lucia Elena, Rosa Maria Porcaro, and Tereza Cristina N. A. Costa 1980. O "lugar do negro" na força de trabalho. Paper presented at the Fourth Annual Meeting of ANPOCS, October, Rio de Janeiro.

Pereira, João Baptista Borges 1967. *Cor, profissaõ e mobilidade: o negro no rádio de São Paulo*. São Paulo: Livraria Pioneira Editôra.

Pierson, Donald 1942. *Negroes in Brazil*. Carbondale: Southern Illinois University Press, 1967.

Santos, Joel Rufino dos 1980. *O que é racismo?* Coleção Primeiros Passos. São Paulo: Livraria Brasiliense Editora.

Souza, Amaury de 1971. Raça e política no Brasil urbano. *Revista de Administração de Empresas* 11(4): 61–70. (October–December).

2

RACE AND CLASS IN BRAZIL: HISTORICAL PERSPECTIVES*

THOMAS E. SKIDMORE

Our understanding of modern-day race relations in Brazil rests primarily on research done between 1945 and 1965. To appreciate the context of that work, we need to look at the history of sociology and anthropology in Brazil. Before 1945, both disciplines were in the early stages of development, centered largely in São Paulo, with clusters of researchers in Rio de Janeiro and Bahia. The 1930s had seen an influx of influential foreign scholars, such as Donald Pierson, Roger Bastide, and Emílio Willems. All played important roles in the development of graduate faculties at the University of São Paulo (USP) and the Escola Livre de Sociologia e Política, both in São Paulo.[1] One of the most significant publications of this era was by the U.S. scholar, Pierson, whose *Negroes in Brazil* remains an outstanding research work on Bahia and the Northeast, although its conclusions are now generally rejected.[2]

With the end of World War II there was a renewed surge of foreign interest that reinforced the efforts of the small community of Brazilian researchers. Prominent among the non-Brazilians were North American anthropologists, especially from Columbia University, and French scholars. Most knowledgeable among the latter was Roger Bastide, who had been in Brazil since 1938 and had already won USP support to begin a large-scale survey research project on race relations in São Paulo. Key Brazilian scholars included Florestan Fernandes (University of São Paulo) and Thales de Azevedo (Federal University of Bahia). Among those who distinguished themselves in the study of race relations were Charles Wagley, Marvin Harris, Costa Pinto, René Ribeiro, Oracy Nogueira, Fernando Henrique Cardoso, Octávio Ianni and Arthur Ramos. We largely

*Reprinted, with changes, from the *Luso-Brazilian Review* 20, 1 (Summer 1983), 104–118, by permission of the author and the publisher. Copyright 1983 by the Board of Regents of the University of Wisconsin System.

owe our present knowledge to these researchers and their collaborators.

Several themes have emerged from this body of scholarship.[3] Most relevant for our purposes is the direct, at times explicit, challenge to the long prevailing view of Brazil as a "racial democracy." In its more extreme form, that belief held that race and skin color make virtually no difference in Brazil. Vianna Moog, a prominent Brazilian writer, has stated, "the highest, most significant and most edifying aspect of our culture is racial brotherhood."[4] If there are few dark-skinned Brazilians at the higher levels of society, it simply reflects past disadvantages — poverty and the lack of education which inevitably accompanied slavery. The belief held by the elite was well stated by the president of the National Congress: "In Brazil, access to society depends upon individual effort, intellectual ability, and merit. . . . We have all inherited common attributes, and what we are building — socially, economically and politically — proves the correctness of our rejection of the myths of racial superiority."[5] If race does play a part in stratification, this view holds, it is small. Brazilians may not give the benefit of the doubt to a darker person, but the frequency is not great enough to alter the fact that Brazil is substantially free of racial discrimination.

How did Brazil reach this supposedly harmonious state? The answer, say believers in its "racial democracy," is to be found in Brazilian history. Almost in spite of themselves, the Portuguese created a multi-racial, slave-based society with a large free colored population. Portuguese colonization seemed somehow immune to racial prejudice. In the words of the Congress president, "In our land the three ethnic groups interacted to produce the union of which we are the expression and synthesis."[6] The Portuguese male was crucial in this process. At home he had known the charms of dark-skinned Moorish women, and thus it is not surprising that in the New World he succumbed to the Indian, and later African, women. This trend was reinforced by the absence of women among the Portuguese explorers and colonists. The inevitable outcome was miscegenation.

Most important for future race relations, according to this view, was the fact that Portuguese men had guilty consciences, as well as strong libidos. As a result, they often manumitted the mixed-blood offspring they had sired by their slave women. Affectionate weakness for the illegitimate progeny of miscegenation led directly to the sharp contrast between the fate of people of color in Brazil and the U.S. This simplistic idea was well expressed in the 1940s by Waldo Frank, a minor U.S. literary figure who often traveled to Latin America: "Why is the difference so great between the exploited Negro of Brazil and the exploited Negro of the United States? Because the latter have known lust and greed of their masters; the former, lust and greed no less, but tenderness also."[7]

The belief in "racial democracy," whether it fitted the historical facts or not, has been the operating racial ideal among the Brazilian elite since at least 1920. It accompanies an equally fervent faith in "whitening," the result of the elite's struggle to reconcile Brazil's actual social relations—the absence of a clear line between white and nonwhite—with the doctrines of scientific racism that had penetrated Brazil from abroad. It also implied that the inexorable process of whitening would produce a white (or light tan?) Brazil. Thus, the legacy of the Portuguese libido would "solve" Brazil's race problem. This remained the elite view through the Second World War—despite the fact that "scientific racism" had become discredited in academic circles by the 1930s.[8]

The 1930s were the decade that elsewhere saw the application of one of History's most vicious racist dogmas, anti-semitism. In the aftermath of 1945, Europeans looked abroad for models of interracial peace. Hadn't Brazil for years been disproving the racist shibboleths about miscegenation? In 1950, UNESCO decided to study Brazil's harmonious race relations and share Brazil's secret with the world.[9] International teams of scholars, primarily anthropologists, undertook field research around the country, pursuing common research goals. Such international recognition greatly reinforced the Brazilian elite's belief in their "racial democracy." In fact, however, this and succeeding research raised serious questions about, and partially discredited, this image of Brazilian society.[10]

Other factors were also eroding the image. An important element in the definition of Brazil's "racial democracy" had always been the contrast with the United States.[11] The phenomena of segregation and racial violence, such as urban riots and lynchings, were unknown in Brazil. Even if there had once been onerous barriers to Black advancement, Brazil had never been infected with the race hatred so evident in the U.S. Whatever the precise explanation for the difference, Brazilians could say that their country had the distinction of representing man's best future. Hadn't UNESCO said as much?

But the U.S. was changing. The Supreme Court decision of 1954 sounded the death knell for racial segregation, and subsequent legislation closed virtually every loophole sought by the die-hard racists. Where once the law had been used to segregate, it was now a force for integration. Both uses assumed a clearly defined bi-racial society. Both stemmed from the assumption that race is a fundamental, perhaps the most fundamental, characteristic of North Americans.

From the Brazilian viewpoint, it might at first appear that the U.S., by finally eliminating legal color bars, was merely catching up to Brazil in the early nineteenth century, when its few color bars, remnants of the colonial era, disappeared. The difference in the U.S., however, was the militancy and organization of nonwhites. In the non-violent resistance movement, led by Southern clergymen such as Martin Luther King, Jr., Blacks forcefully claimed their "rights." Brazilian nonwhites had not shown a comparable degree of initiative since final abolition in 1888. U.S. society, the major point of reference for Brazilians when describing their "racial democracy," had changed in a basic way.

Another shift in the Brazilian elite's foreign points of reference occurred in Africa. There, as in Asia, the Second World War brought in its wake a cry for decolonization. The remaining empires of Britain, France, Holland, and Belgium were now an unpleasant reminder of the era when white Europeans, using racist language, had taken control of much of to-day's "Third World." In Africa, the departure of the empires and their ruling whites paved the way for the appearance on the world scene of na-tions totally governed by Blacks. This trend contradicted one of the cen-tral assumptions of the Brazilian belief in "whitening": the closer to his African origins, the less civilized the man of color. Indeed, faith in "whitening" was based on the assumption that the superior racial element, that is, white, was prevailing. Now Africa had, not white, not even mulat-to, but Black nations. These new peoples wanted no part of "whitening," a doctrine that assumed assimilation, if not the extinction, of African iden-tity. As in the case of U.S. desegregation, History was removing the very landmarks that had helped anchor the Brazilian elite in its racial beliefs.

Brazil's relations with Africa were further complicated by the fact that Portugal was the last European power to relinquish its African colonies. It was a Brazilian, Gilberto Freyre, who had spelled out the most am-bitious doctrine to justify Portuguese colonialism, "Lusotropicalism." He argued that the Portuguese were the only European colonizers to create a new civilization in the tropics, an accomplishment attributable above all to their racial tolerance. The logical conclusion was that the Lusitanian legacy would spare Portugal the anti-colonial violence found elsewhere in Africa. Freyre himself remained a staunch defender of Portuguese colonial rule.[12]

Because of Salazar's repressive regime and an enormous per capita in-vestment of resources, the Portuguese government prolonged its rule over Angola and Mozambique into the 1970s. By the time the armed struggle began in Africa, Brazil had a military government that was completely committed to the Salazar policy. Freyre, an enthusiastic adherent to the 1964 "Revolution" that installed the military, gained increased publicity for his Lusotropical theories. Meanwhile, government censorship prevented an open debate over Brazil's African policy.

As Salazar finally faded from power in the early 1970s, it was his army officers who pushed for withdrawal from Africa. The peoples of Portuguese Africa won independence, and many whites left. After those events were well underway, Brazil also experienced political change. The Geisel presidency (1974–79) brought an "opening," and the possibility for rethinking Brazil's African interests and policies.

One recent incident shows how this new relationship can call into question the Brazilian elite's image of their nation's race relations. In 1978 and 1979, Brazil's leading television network, Rede Globo, broadcast a series for children adapted from stories by Monteiro Lobato. Brazilians generally considered it a high-level effort for the children's hour. Angolan television, which is state controlled, decided to take advantage of this Portuguese-language resource by broadcasting the series in early 1979. This set no precedent, as they had shown Globo's version of Jorge Amado's *Gabriela, cravo e canela* with no apparent problems. After seven installments, however, the Angolan television abruptly cancelled the children's series. It was "racist," they charged, because Blacks were depicted only in inferior positions. Most offensive was the role of Tia Nastácia, the sixty-year-old Black cook whom the Angolans thought a caricature. Reaction in Brazil was rapid, and many questions arose. Were the Angolans justified? How should Blacks be depicted? Had Lobato's characterization been faithfully rendered in the televised script? What is the true meaning of Tia Nastácia's role in the household?[13] Brazil is undoubtedly in for more such surprises in its cultural relations with Africa. It is not the world Freyre had led the Brazilian elite to expect.

These fundamental changes in Brazil's external points of reference in race relations — the U.S. and Lusophone Africa — did not produce an immediate rethinking of race relations in Brazil. That began only in the late 1970s. As Michael Mitchell's contribution to this volume offers a detailed analysis of the reasons for this, I will restrict my comments to a few major points.

First, the Brazilian elite tenaciously defended their image of Brazil as a racial democracy. They did it in a number of ways. One was to attack as "un-Brazilian" anyone who raised serious questions about race relations in Brazil. Such a tactic was common among politicians, cultural luminaries, and media controllers. The usual argument was, "the only racial 'problems' in Brazil result from the agitation of those who claim there are problems." An interesting case is the reaction to a small "Black is beautiful" movement, primarily in Rio de Janeiro. In August 1976, the prominent Rio daily *Jornal do Brasil* ran a feature story of "Black Rio," with photographs of young Black men wearing Afro hairstyles and platform shoes. This publicity ignited an angry reaction from readers who denounced the movement and its coverage by the press. Critics implied that reporting on such "un-Brazilian" groups was itself divisive and unpatriotic. As for the movement, it was branded by many whites as a foreign import, illustrating little more than the "cultural alienation" into which Brazilian Blacks could slip.[14]

Such vigilance by the elite cannot suffice to explain the lack of debate. There was a second factor, government repression. After 1965, and especially after 1968, successive military governments closely controlled the media and all public events. They justified repression as necessary to meet the threat of "subversion," which in the early 1970s did include a guerrilla movement. But the military branded as "subversive" not only kidnappers with guns, but also social scientists with ideas. That was bound to include academics who had raised questions about Brazil's "racial democracy."

One of the most dramatic cases in point was the purge of the faculty at the University of São Paulo in 1969. Prominent among those social scientists involuntarily retired were Florestan Fernandes and his colleagues Fernando Henrique Cardoso and Octavio Ianni. Given their well-known, although differing, ideological and political views, it was not surprising that they should be targets for a military concerned with "national security." Can it be coincidental, however, that they were also among the handful of Brazil's researchers into race relations? And that, by their research, writing, and teaching, they had raised troubling questions about the realities of Brazilian race relations?[15] The military government frequently intervened to suppress news that contradicted the official image of racial harmony. Under full-scale censorship from 1969 until gradual liberalization began in 1975, television and radio were closely watched. Vigilance was especially intense on the popular television soap operas (telenovelas), as well as on samba songs. More often than once, television scripts rejected by the censors touched the subject of race relations.[16]

A similar preoccupation appeared in the censorship of the print media. In 1973 a new journal of opinion, Argumento, appeared on the newsstands of São Paulo. It was quickly confiscated by the authorities. On the cover was an African-looking boy and the title of an article comparing post-abolition race relations in Brazil and the U.S.[17] Although the police gave no explanation, many observers thought the article on race relations had, at least in part, provoked their action. Another example of such moves was the Brazilian government's 1978 decision to bar the Inter-American Foundation from further activity in Brazil. Brazilian authorities felt that this foundation, financed by U.S. government–originated funds but operating independently from other U.S. agencies, was supporting "subversive" Brazilian organizations. Among the groups receiving financing at that time were three Black organizations whose stated purpose of "consciousness raising" undoubtedly displeased Brasília.[18]

A third example of government sensitivity to the issue of race relations came in connection with a scholarly conference on Blacks in the Americas, scheduled to be held in Bogotá, Colombia, in August 1977. Countries were invited to send delegations, on the usual assumption that each government would finance their delegates' travel. Not so in Brazil. Brasília dragged its feet on the travel authorization until it was too late, and most of the Brazilian delegates missed the meeting.[19]

Another incident that occurred in the late 1960s was the most revealing of all: the decision to omit race from the census of 1970. Opponents of racial identification argued that the language of racial categories, such as *preto, negro, mulato,* and *moreno*, was applied so inconsistently that meaningful data collection would be impossible.[20] No responsible observer would dispute the fact that there is a problem, yet the Census Commission's radical solution of eliminating race altogether precluded the collection of any data by race whatsoever. Undoubtedly, many Commission members who voted for this policy genuinely believed that race could not be studied. In doing so, however, they were reflecting the elite consensus that race was not an independent variable in Brazilian society. Without data, of course, discussion would continue being reduced to the anecdotal level. That is where defenders of Brazil's racial myth have always preferred to operate, dwelling on examples of famous Brazilians whose physical features bore little relation to their station in life.

There was a third factor responsible for muting Brazilian discussion of race relations: the belief by the Left that race is insignificant. Social class is the most fundamental variable, leftists argue, both for studying society and for changing it. Advocates of this view usually dismissed race as a "false issue."[21] Since the Left has remained very strong in the university faculties that produce most Brazilian researchers, its negative attitude toward studying race relations has, ironically, helped contribute to the silence on race sought by the authoritarian government.[22]

In the late 1970s this picture began to change. Attention to race increased, in a small but perceptible fashion. Brazilians of color began to publicly question the myth of racial democracy. With the gradual political opening pursued by the government of President Ernesto Geisel (1974–1979), debate emerged into the open.

Other contributors to this symposium have described in detail the rapid growth of a Black movement that contradicts everything the predominant myth would have led us to expect. Brazil now has militant groups that may come to rival their most ambitious counterparts of the Frente Negra era in the 1930s. As Michael Mitchell clearly shows in chapter 7, the *abertura* has allowed many taboo topics to surface, with race relations high on the list. Dramatic confirmation of this change came in the decision to include race in the 1980 census. Initially, the census authorities wanted to follow the 1970 precedent of omitting race. That created a strong reaction among the staff and the public, and led to reconsideration and a reversal of the decision.[23] The less repressive atmosphere surrounding the 1980 decision facilitated the collection of data which, even if not wholly reliable, are the sine qua non for any informed discussion of race relations.

Before discussing the renewed attention to race in Brazil, it is worth noting that a more traditional area of interest has never lacked attention: Afro-Brazilian religion, folklore, and art. Interest here centered on African origins and African survivals. Most familiar are the religious cults of *candomblé* in Bahia and *umbanda* in Rio de Janeiro, both well-known tourist attractions. Included also are the "exotic" costumes and foods identified with Africa. The (adopted) patron saints of this world are Gilberto Freyre and Jorge Amado, writers who have gained much of their fame by showing the Afro-Brazilian contribution to Brazilian culture and national character. Although undoubtedly important and valuable, the study and preservation of Afro-Brazilian beliefs and customs has been politically very safe. It fits perfectly with the elite view that Brazil's historic links to Africa are now essentially quaint. For this reason, the recently founded Sociedade de Estudos da Cultura Negra no Brasil (Society for the Study of Black Culture in Brazil) represented no threat to the government or elite figures.[24] Another example was the Semanas Afro-Brasileiras held at the Museum of Modern Art in Rio de Janeiro in 1974.[25] The emphasis of such groups has allowed them to avoid the thorny questions of present-day race relationships among Brazilians.

A significant change that took place in the late 1970s was the promotion of racial consciousness among Brazilians of color. Although some leading activists were researchers, they did not use questionnaires or interview forms. They felt that they knew what the facts were. As people of color, they passionately believed that Brazil's claim to be a racial democracy was a fraud. They wanted Brazilians to know that their country's race relations bore no relation to the idyllic scene praised by the elite and many foreigners. This activist explosion has startled many. Is it possible that a significant "Black power" movement is arising in Brazil? To launch such a movement is certainly the hope of the organizers whose efforts are described in the chapters by Lélia Gonzalez and Michael Mitchell.

The militant tone of these activists is more aggressive than that of any group since the Frente Negra of the 1930s. They repudiate whitening — still Brazil's dominant ideology of race relations — and uphold the virtues of blackness. Most important, they want to provoke Afro-Brazilians into racial consciousness. They want to act against what they see as white exploitation — a line of protest that has been forbidden to people of color for the last forty years.

The new Black protest movements can now denounce the conditions that Brazilian scholars have long been documenting. To take one example, Thales de Azevedo, one of the doyens of Brazilian anthropology, has attacked the racial democracy myth by publishing a compilation of cases of racial discrimination as reported in the national press. Carlos Hasenbalg's important 1979 monograph used similar sources, and carried the analysis of discrimination to the most systematic level possible with the limited data then available.[26] Nelson do Valle Silva's essay (chapter 4) shows how important new economic data can be. Suddenly, we seem to be on the thréshold of a major debate about the role of race in Brazilian society.

Any debate is bounded by the terms in which it is defined. What will be the definitions for the debate on race? What are the questions to be posed? What is the subject to be studied? If it is race relations in the broadest sense, how should we proceed?

Research efforts are needed on all fronts, not least the historical. Surprising as it might seem, our understanding of the history of Brazilian race relations is extremely uneven. Despite the fame of Gilberto Freyre's writing on Brazil's patriarchal past, and much recent work on slavery by many other scholars, we know all too little about some of the most important features of Brazilian social history. One is the historical experience of free persons of color, both in the colonial era and in the nineteenth century.

In the first half of the 1800s, there was a strong mulatto movement, which even published its own newspapers. An important imperial institution, the Guarda Nacional, had become a vehicle for mulatto mobility. By the 1840s the officer corps included many mulattoes, as they were elected by the predominantly colored ranks. This channel of mobility was abruptly closed in 1850, however, when the Crown made officers appointive. The command soon turned markedly whiter.[27]

The questions are obvious: How extensive was this mulatto movement? What were its relationships to other Brazilians of color, slave and free? Why did the Crown abolish the election of officers? Did the political and social elite see a threat from the mulatto movement? How did they rationalize their actions?[28]

The early decades of the twentieth century provide similar questions. How do we explain the assertion of Black and mulatto consciousness in the 1920s and 1930s?[29] Just as they had a century earlier, Black newspapers appeared aggressively promoting the cause of the Brazilian of color. Why did they appear in the 1920s, and not immediately after final abolition in 1888? Were there unusual economic circumstances in the 1920s and 1930s? Were they comparable to those of the early nineteenth century?

This twentieth-century movement was snuffed out by the authoritarian coup of 1937. The disbanding of the Black and mulatto organizations was hardly surprising, given the fact that the Estado Nôvo government

(1937–1945) was able to repress all opposition groups. But the return of open government in 1945 did not see the movement reappear, and three decades after 1945 saw nothing comparable to the Black and mulatto movements prior to 1937, despite the persistent organizing efforts of a few individuals such as Abdias do Nascimento.[30] That did not come until the late 1970s. Why? Is there a general explanation for the militancy that erupted in the late 1970s, the 1920s to the 1930s, and the 1820s to 1830s and 1840s?

Part of the answer lies in a better understanding of the dynamics of Brazilian socioeconomic history. Most important is a deeper understanding of the role of the free person of color before slavery expired in 1888. Some of the most lasting forms of interracial social behavior must have been established in those years. The scholarly consensus has been that Brazil created a multiracial society, as contrasted to the biracial system in the United States. In his extended comparison of the U.S. and Brazil, Carl Degler suggested that the "mulatto escape hatch" was the key to the difference.[31] Yet Degler's book, the most thoughtful and exhaustive comparative analysis of race relations in Brazil and the U.S., gives virtually no hard evidence to support his thesis. The reader searches in vain for historical documentation to show that the person of mixed blood got preferential treatment. How do we know that mulattoes enjoyed mobility? What data such as census records, tax records, and court records, confirm such mobility? Degler could not provide such information because the necessary research has only recently begun. The "escape hatch" is a plausible hypothesis, but we await evidence of what actually happened.[32]

One priority area for investigation is relations between whites and persons of color in the labor force. In the United States South, for example, there was a period, roughly 1865 to 1900, when poor whites and newly freed Blacks might have made common cause against the old agrarian order. Instead, white politicians successfully got poor whites to focus on the threat of job competition from Blacks, rather than the fundamental questions of economic structure. As a result, the Jim Crow system became fixed in the South and the cause of Black progress was set back for decades to come.[33]

There are obvious perils in carrying historical comparisons too far. It might well be argued that by the time of the Emancipation Proclamation in the U.S., there was no possibility for the emergence of a multiracial society. Yet some of the explanations given for the U.S. case may suggest questions about Brazil. What were the racial attitudes of Brazilian workers? Were they manipulated by employers who used similar techniques to maximize control over the labor force? We know, for example, that racist sentiments helped divide Rio de Janeiro dock workers in the 1910s and 1920s.[34] Did this occur in other sectors? Could such patterns be seen in earlier eras? What effect did these patterns have on subsequent race relations? Such questions are implicit in virtually all our attempts to explain present-day Brazilian race relations.

No amount of subsequent research and documentation, however helpful, will answer all our questions. Just as in the study of race relations in the United States, with its avalanche of monographs, symposia, and syntheses, the questions go too deep and in the end their meaning is too elusive for us to be satisfied with the answers provided by conventional social and economic history. In Brazil also, we shall find ourselves drawn toward examining "mentalities," habits of mind, and social beliefs. What is uniquely Brazilian about Brazilian race relations? Does it have anything to do with the now oft-denigrated idea of Brazilian national character? There has been a long and rich debate over the Brazilian's alleged *cordialidade*.[35] Does that idea furnish any clues in our quest to understand how and why Brazil has created its particular form of multiracial society? What about those qualities that anthropologists, sociologists, and political scientists have explored—patrimonialism, paternalism, and clientelism? However slippery these concepts may be for the historian, we must remind ourselves that the most enduring attempt to explain the United States—that of Alexis de Tocqueville—was built around a discussion of precisely these kinds of collective traits.[36]

Our efforts to understand Brazilian race relations will necessarily carry us into the ongoing debate about the nature of Brazilian society. It will thus parallel and perhaps at times coincide with attention to the history of labor relations in Brazil, also inseparably linked to our views about the essence of Brazilian social relations.[37]

We are therefore brought to the elusive relationship between ideas and societies. Seen abstractly, they are socioeconomic structures and ideologies. When viewed historically, they embrace the many realities of human behavior and human thought. We appear to be on the verge of a new burst of inquiry into these realities, and although we may ask new questions and produce new evidence, we shall be walking familiar ground.

NOTES

1. For a firsthand description of the early years in the growth of anthropology and sociology, see Florestan Fernandes, *A sociologia no Brasil* (Petrópolis: Ed. Vozes, 1977), especially chapter 8. A useful summary of the most relevant researchers and institutions may be found in Charles Wagley, "Anthropology and Brazilian National Identity," in *Brazil: Anthropological Perspectives*, ed. Maxine L. Margolis and William E. Carter (New York: Columbia University Press, 1979), 1–18.

2. Donald Pierson, *Negroes in Brazil: A Study of Race Contact at Bahia* (Chicago: University of Chicago Press, 1942). It was reprinted with the text unchanged (Carbondale/

Edwardsville: Illinois University Press, 1967), but with a long introduction by Pierson, where he defended his original approach, which had emphasized class as perhaps more important than race in determining social position.

3. An excellent synthesis of present-day scholarly views on Brazilian race relations is John Saunders, "Class, Color and Prejudice: A Brazilian Counterpoint," in *Racial Tensions and National Identity*, ed. Ernest Q. Campbell (Nashville: Vanderbilt University Press, 1972), 141–169. Barriers to collective mobility are reviewed in Maria Isaura Pereira de Queiroz, "Coletividades negras: ascensão sócio-econômica dos negros no Brasil e em S. Paulo," *Ciência e cultura* 29(6): 647–663 (June 1977). One of the most successful efforts to place Brazil within a framework of worldwide race relations is Michael Banton, *Race Relations* (London: Tavistock Publications, 1967), 258–282. For an excellent survey, which emphasizes the lack of more recent work on race in Brazil, see Pierre-Michel Fontaine, "Research in the Political Economy of Afro-Latin America," *Latin American Research Review* 15(2):111–141 (1980).

4. Moog spoke these words before the highly prestigious Escola Superior de Guerra. (*Jornal do Brasil*, 3 August 1972.)

5. The remarks were by Senator Petronio Portella, speaking on the International Day for the Elimination of Discrimination. (*O Globo*, 6 April 1977.)

6. This also comes from Senator Petronio Portella's speech, as reported in *Correio Brasiliense*, 6 April 1977.

7. Waldo Frank, *South American Journey* (New York: Duell, Sloan and Pearce, 1943), 50–51.

8. The emergence of the "whitening" ideal is traced in Skidmore, *Black into White* (New York: Oxford University Press, 1974).

9. There is a brief discussion of the UNESCO project, along with citation of the principal sources, in Pierre-Michel Fontaine, "Research in the Political Economy of Afro-Latin America," 124; and in Skidmore, *Black into White*, 215–216.

10. It has been argued that one of the senior Brazilian researchers, Florestan Fernandes, believed from the outset that the project would "show that UNESCO was wrong, that the Negro was not equal in Brazil." The source is Fernando Henrique Cardoso, a collaborator in the project, as interviewed in Joseph A. Kahl, *Modernization, Exploitation and Dependency in Latin America* (New Brunswick: Transaction Books, 1976), 131. Looking back on the UNESCO-sponsored research after twenty-five years, Fernandes concluded that "if the study has done nothing else then, it has unmasked the myth of racial democracy in the country." See Fernandes, "The Negro in Brazilian Society: Twenty-Five Years Later," in *Brazil: Anthropological Perspectives*, 100.

11. For a discussion of possible approaches in comparing the U.S. and Brazil, see Skidmore, "Toward a Comparative Analysis of Race Relations Since Abolition in Brazil and the United States," *Journal of Latin American Studies* 4(1): 1–28 (May 1972).

12. Gilberto Freyre, *O mundo que o Português criou* (Rio de Janeiro: José Olympio, 1940), and *Aventura e rotina* (Rio de Janeiro: José Olympio, 1953).

13. Ida Lobato, "Fala, Tia Nastácia!" *Folha de São Paulo*, 17 February 1979; Mirna Pinsky, "Angola x Lobato," Folhetim of *Folha de São Paulo*, 4 March 1979.

14. The story covered four pages of the widely read "Caderno B," a prized source for publicity on the arts in Brazil. The emotions stirred up by the story can be seen in the letters published in the same paper on August 3, 1976. Ten months later "Black Rio" had supposedly won twenty thousand followers in São Paulo, an alarming development in the eyes of some samba composers. See *Folha de São Paulo*, 11 June 1977.

15. Details on the purges at USP, including a number of contemporary documents, may be found in *O Livro negro da USP: O controle ideológico na universidade* (São Paulo: Ed. Brasiliense, 1979).

16. For a general account of censorship, see Peter T. Johnson, "Academic Press Censorship under Military and Civilian Regimes: The Argentine and Brazilian Cases, 1964–1975," *Luso-Brazilian Review*, vol. 15, no. 1 (Summer 1978), 3–25. Details on censorship of TV programming are given in a long dispatch on race relations in Brazil by *New York Times* correspondent David Vidal in the June 5, 1978 issue.

17. *Argumento*, Ano 1, No. 1 (October 1973). The article was my "O Negro no Brasil e nos Estados Unidos," a translation, without footnotes, of Skidmore "Toward a Comparative Analysis of Race Relations."

18. One of the grants was for an Instituto de Pesquisa das Culturas Negras (Institute for Research of the Black Cultures) "to assist Brazilian black communities to appreciate their own history, to achieve more effective participation in development, and a more just distribution of wealth," *Journal of the Inter-American Foundation* (Summer 1977), p. 17.

19. Letter to the editor from Sebastião Rodrigues Alves in *Visão*, 28 November 1977; *Versus* (October 1977), p. 34.

20. A brief discussion of the controversy may be found in Skidmore, *Black into White*, 218. It should be noted that race was included in the 1976 PNAD of the IBGE.

21. A scholar who has offered one of the more subtle approaches emphasizing class is Octávio Ianni. See, for example, his *Escravidão e racismo* (São Paulo: Editora Hucitec, 1978).

22. For a stinging attack on the Brazilian Left because it played into the hands of the "reactionaries" by refusing to see that race is not reducible to class in Brazil, see Abdias do Nascimento, "O Negro e o Brasil na década dos 80," *Singular & Plural*, February 1979, 28–29.

23. My sources are staff members in the IBGE (Instituto Brasileiro de Geografia e Estatística), who were firsthand observers of these events.

24. SECNEB was founded in 1974. Its publication is *Sárépegbé*, whose first issue appeared dated January/March 1975. A conference on Afro-Brazilian religious syncretism, held in Bahia in 1976, was another example. Some of the papers and discussions were published in *Revista de Cultura: Vozes* 71(7), September 1977.

25. Even this group ran into difficulties when they planned a series of public seminars to discuss Black culture and Brazilian-African relations. The seminars were vetoed by the authorities, although the art exhibition came off without any problems. Details on the planning and the nature of the exhibits may be found in *Revista de Cultura: Vozes* 71(9), November 1977.

26. Thales de Azevedo, *Democracia racial: Ideologia e realidade* (Petrópolis: Editora Vozes, 1975). Carlos A. Hasenbalg, *Discriminação e desigualdades raciais no Brasil* (Rio de Janeiro: Ed. Graal, 1979).

27. The case of the Guarda Nacional is studied in Jeanne Berrance de Castro, *A milícia cidadã: A Guarda Nacional de 1831 a 1850* (São Paulo: Companhia Editora Nacional, 1977). Castro's emphasis on race is disputed in Thomas Flory, "Race and Social Control in Independent Brazil," *Journal of Latin American Studies* 9(2): 199–224 (November 1977).

28. In "Race and Social Control," his important article on race relations in the three decades after Independence in 1822, Thomas Flory argues that the elite succeeded in obscuring the racial issue in a manner that sounds very modern:

> By 1841 abiding reactionary changes in social attitudes and the structures of authority had taken place in Brazil, and the negative outcomes of the race question was one reason for the changes. Genuine race fear, by definition, could not often be mentioned aloud, while constitutional restrictions and ideology prevented racially exclusive legislation. So in informal attitudes as well as in formal regula-

tion, the race problem shaded into a social problem after 1835, and the full range of reaction was therefore directed at social categories described by behavior and class rather than by skin color.

29. There is no general history of Black and/or mulatto movements in modern Brazil, aside from the abolitionist era. That is hardly surprising, since so little research has been done on the subject. The most detailed accounts of the movements of the 1920s and 1930s are in Roger Bastide and Florestan Fernandes, *Brancos e negros em São Paulo*, 3d ed. (São Paulo: Companhia Editora Nacional, 1971), 229–268; and Roger Bastide, *Estudos afro-brasileiros* (São Paulo: Editora Perspectiva, 1973), 129–156. Signs of growing interest in this history from "official" cultural quarters could be seen in a June 1977 exhibition on "A imprensa negra em São Paulo, 1918–1965," which received national publicity, as in *Isto é*, 22 June 1977. It was organized and sponsored by the Secretaria da Cultura, Ciência e Tecnologia of the São Paulo state government.

30. In the Constituent Assembly of 1946, one senator denounced what he saw as widespread racial discrimination. His speech and subsequent efforts, largely unsuccessful, at mobilizing Black/mulatto protest are described in Rodrigues Alves, *A ecologia do grupo afro-brasileiro* (Rio de Janeiro: Ministério da Educação e Cultura, 1966). Further details on this period can be found in Abdias do Nascimento, ed., *O Negro revoltado* (Rio de Janeiro: Edições GRD, 1968).

31. Carl Degler, *Neither Black nor White: Slavery and Race Relations in Brazil and the United States* (New York: Macmillan, 1971).

32. Among the most important analyses of the fate of the free person of color until 1888 are A. J. R. Russell-Wood, "Colonial Brazil," in *Neither Slave Nor Free*, ed. David W. Cohen and Jack P. Greene (Baltimore: Johns Hopkins University Press, 1972); Herbert S. Klein, "The Colored Freedmen in Brazilian Slave Society," *Journal of Social History* 3(1): 30–52 (Fall 1969). Much valuable information on the patterns of manumission has been published in Stuart B. Schwartz, "The Manumission of Slaves in Colonial Brazil: Bahia, 1684–1745," *Hispanic American Historical Review* 54(4): 603–635 (November 1974); Luiz R. B. Mott, "Brancos, pardos, pretos e índios em Sergipe: 1825–1830," *Anais de História* 6(1974): 139–184. For evidence of occupational mobility among slaves in Rio (which has great relevance for investigating the mobility of free men of color), see Mary Karasch, "From Porterage to Proprietorship: African Occupations in Rio de Janeiro, 1808–1850," in *Race and Slavery in the Western Hemisphere: Quantitative Studies,* ed. Stanley L. Engerman and Eugene D. Genovese (Princeton: Princeton University Press, 1975). One scholar concluded his recent study of the 1822–1850 period thus: "Although the system's blurred distinctions did provide a way for a few mulattoes to rise — a mulatto escape hatch — too many historians have failed to note that the same set of conditions also placed a trapdoor under Brazilians of all colors" (Flory, "Race and Social Control," 224).

33. The classic work describing this process is C. Vann Woodward, *The Strange Career of Jim Crow*, 2d rev. ed. (New York: Oxford University Press, 1966).

34. Sheldon L. Maram, "Anarcho-syndicalism in Brazil," in *Proceedings of Pacific Coast Council on Latin American Studies* 4(1975): 101–116; Maram, "Labor and the Left in Brazil, 1890–1921, A Movement Aborted," *Hispanic American Historical Review* 57(2): 254–272 (May 1977); Maram, "Urban Labor and Social Change in the 1920's," *Luso-Brazilian Review* 16(2): 215–223 (Winter 1979).

35. The best introduction to the historic debate over the essential nature of Brazil's "social personality" is Dante Moreira Leite, *O carácter nacional brasileiro* (São Paulo: Livraria Pioneira Editôra, 1969).

36. Alexis de Tocqueville, *Democracy in America* (Garden City: Anchor-Doubleday, 1969).

37. It cannot be coincidental that the political opening brought a burst of attention to previously taboo topics — race relations and labor relations. I have discussed the latter in a comparative framework in "Workers and Soldiers: Urban Labor Movements and Elite Responses in Twentieth-Century Latin America," in *Elites, Masses, and Modernization in Latin America, 1850–1930,* ed. Virginia Bernhard (Austin: University of Texas Press, 1979).

3

RACE AND SOCIOECONOMIC INEQUALITIES IN BRAZIL

CARLOS A. HASENBALG

This chapter resumes previous analyses of racial inequalities in Brazil, using the information of the 1976 National Household Sample Research (PNAD), the most recent data on race.[1] Its main purposes are to describe the contemporary structure of racial inequalities and to assess the role of race in the intergenerational transmission of social inequalities.

A brief survey of the literature on Brazilian race relations reveals three main lines of research that have a bearing on the relationships between race, social inequalities, and social stratification. Brazil's current official position on race relations had its academic version formulated in the early 1930s by Gilberto Freyre. By stressing the positive contributions of Africans and Amerindians to Brazilian culture, he subverted the racist assumptions of contemporary social analysts such as Oliveira Vianna. At the same time, Freyre created the most formidable ideological weapon against Blacks. His emphasis on the plastic character of the Portuguese colonizers' cultural background and the widespread racial miscegenation among the Brazilian population led him to the notion of a racial democracy. The implicit corollary of this idea is the absence of racial prejudice and discrimination and, consequently, the existence of equal economic and social opportunities for whites and Blacks.[2]

Freyre's thought influenced another line of research, conducted by scholars who studied race relations in rural and urban areas of northern Brazil during the 1940s and 1950s.[3] Despite overwhelming evidence of a strong correlation between color and social status, these students, among them Charles Wagley, were so impressed by the most noticeable differences between the American and Brazilian race systems that they deemphasized racial discrimination and its effects on the social mobility of nonwhites. Some of their main conclusions are: (a) there is prejudice in

Brazil, but it is based on class rather than race; (*b*) the strong consciousness of color differences is not related to discrimination; (*c*) derogatory stereotypes and prejudice against Blacks are manifested verbally rather than behaviorally; and (*d*) such characteristics as wealth, occupation, and education are more important than race in determining patterns of interpersonal relations. In a rather inconsistent assertion, where myth, fact, and hope coexist, Wagley concludes,

> There are no serious racial barriers to social and economic advance and, as opportunities increase, larger numbers of people will rise in the social system. The great contrasts in social and economic conditions between the darker lower strata and the predominantly white upper class should disappear.
>
> There are dangers, however, along the road to this ideal. There are indications both in the present studies and in reports from the great metropolitan centres of the country that discrimination, tensions, and prejudices based on race are appearing.[4]

A third important line of research was developed in São Paulo in the 1950s and 1960s. Analyses of race relations focused on the more general process of transition from an agrarian slave society to industrial capitalism. The influential work of Florestan Fernandes focuses on the integration of Blacks into the free labor market and the emerging class society.[5] His diagnosis of the social and economic situation of Blacks in the decades immediately following Abolition links discrimination and a preference for white European workers with a deficiency explanation, where the former slaves' unpreparedness for the roles of free men and free workers is heavily stressed. Furthermore, Fernandes sees racial prejudice and discrimination as functional requirements of slave society, but as incompatible with the legal, economic, and social bases of class society. Thus, manifestations of racial prejudice and discrimination after Abolition are conceptualized as anachronistic survivals of slavery, a phenomenon of cultural lag. Relatively ambiguous evaluations of present and future race relations resulted from this approach. Despite moderately optimistic statements about the integration of Blacks into "typical class positions," this perspective fails to account for present evidence of race prejudice and discrimination and the continued social subordination of Blacks.

Thus, either the role of race in the generation of social inequalities has been denied, or prejudice reduced to a "class phenomenon" (race being only a secondary indicator of social status), or racial discrimination has been dismissed as a mere cultural hangup from the already distant past. None of the main perspectives on Brazilian race relations has seriously considered the possibility of a coexistence between racism and industrial capitalist development.

In previous works, I have offered an alternative explanation of the perpetuation of racial inequalities in Brazil, and the relationship among race, the class system, and social mobility.[6] First, the interpretation of post-Abolition race relations as a residual area of social phenomena, resulting from "archaic" patterns of inter-group relations formed during the period of slavery, were discussed on theoretical grounds. Against this line of reasoning, I argued that (*a*) race prejudice and discrimination were not maintained intact after Abolition, but acquired new meanings and functions within the new social structure, and (*b*) the racist practices of the racially dominant group, far from being a simple survival from the past, are functionally related to the material and symbolic benefits obtained by whites through the disqualification of nonwhites as competitors. In this sense, there seems to be no inherent logic of capitalist development leading to an incompatibility between racism and industrialization. In reference to the stratifying effects of racial ascription, race as a socially elaborated attribute may be conceptualized as related mainly to the subordinate aspect of the reproduction of social classes. That is, it is linked to the process of distributing individuals into the positions of the class structure and dimensions of social stratification.

As far as contemporary racial inequalities are concerned, the explanation emphasizing the legacy of slavery—anomie, social and family disorganization—and the different starting point of whites and Blacks at the moment of abolition may be put into question. The explanatory power of slavery with respect to the social position of nonwhites decreases over time; that is, the farther in time from the end of the slave system, the less one may invoke slavery as a cause of the present social subordination of nonwhites. Emphasis should instead be placed on the structural relations and unequal exchange between whites and nonwhites.

Two main factors—both of them related to the unequal structure of opportunities of upward social mobility after Abolition—may be identified as basic determinants of contemporary racial inequalities in Brazil: the unequal geographic distribution of whites and nonwhites, and the racist practices of the racially dominant group.

With regard to the first factor, a disproportionate number of Blacks and mulattoes live in the underdeveloped, agrarian Northeast of Brazil, where educational and economic opportunities are much more scarce than in the Southeast. The greatest part of the white population is concentrated in the latter region, the most economically developed in Brazil. This pattern of racial group distribution was initially determined by the slave system and later reinforced by the Southeast's official policy of promoting European immigration.

In addition to the effects of actual discriminatory behavior, a racist social organization also restrains the motivation and level of aspiration of nonwhite people. When the social mechanisms that obstruct the upward social mobility of nonwhites are considered, the discriminatory practices of whites—more subtle than overt in the case of Brazil—are abetted by the blocking effects derived from the internalization by most nonwhites of an unfavorable self-image. Thus, discriminatory practices, the avoidance of discussions of discrimination, and the symbolic violence perpetuated against nonwhites reinforce each other. These, in turn, have led Blacks and mulattoes to regulate their aspirations according to what is culturally imposed and defined as the "appropriate place" for people of color.

THE STRUCTURE OF RACIAL INEQUALITIES

The following remarks, based on the 1976 PNAD estimates, are mostly descriptive. Their purpose is to draw an updated picture of racial inequalities in Brazil through the consideration of whites and nonwhites distribution along certain demographic, social, and economic variables. The nonwhite group includes those who are categorized as Blacks (*pretos*) and mulattoes (*pardos*) in the population census and the PNAD, excluding Asians (*amarelos*). It is worth noticing here that the mulatto group occupies an intermediate position between Blacks and whites in all the dimensions considered, although its position is always closer to the Black than to the white group. Whenever possible, I will make comparisons to the situation in 1950, the year of the last population census. The data from that census can be adopted as a baseline to grasp the evolution of racial inequalities during the intervening decades.

A more detailed study of the evolution of racial inequalities should take into account the differential impact on whites and nonwhites of the economic and social policies implemented during the last thirty years. As a rough approximation it may be asserted that, due to the concentration of Blacks and mulattoes at the bottom of the social hierarchy, the eventual socioeconomic gains experienced by the urban nonwhite population during the "populist" period (1945-1964) would have been offset by a relative deterioration after 1964.

As has already been stated, one of the basic determinants of the unequal appropriation of educational and economic opportunities is related to the geographical segregation of whites and nonwhites. Table 1 shows the modifications in the spatial distribution of the two groups between 1940 and 1976 according to the PNAD regions. The evolution of concentration of whites and nonwhites in the Southeast is shown in table 2.

Although there are reasons to think that the 1976 PNAD overestimates the increase in the concentration of nonwhites in the Southeast, that group

TABLE 1: Geographic Distribution of the Population
According to PNAD Regions by Race, 1940–1976 (%)

Regions	1940		1950		1960		1976	
	W	NW	W	NW	W	NW	W	NW
Rio de Janeiro	9.0	8.5	9.5	8.4	10.2	7.4	10.0	10.7
São Paulo	23.4	5.9	24.5	5.2	24.8	6.9	27.5	10.7
South	19.6	3.5	21.9	4.0	24.4	4.6	26.3	9.4
Minas Gerais–Espirito Santo	17.6	19.7	15.7	18.3	15.1	16.4	13.5	14.1
Northeast	25.0	53.6	23.5	53.7	20.3	52.6	18.9	47.2
Brasília	——	——	——	——	0.2	0.2	0.7	0.9
North, Goiás, Mato Grosso	5.4	8.8	4.9	10.4	5.0	11.9	3.1	7.0

SOURCES: Population censuses of 1950, 1960, and 1976 PNAD.

TABLE 2: Concentration of the Population in the Southeast
According to Race, 1940–1976

	1940 (%)	1950 (%)	1960 (%)	1976 (%)
Nonwhites	18	18	19	31
Whites	52	56	59	64

SOURCES: Population censuses of 1950, 1960, and 1976 PNAD. The Southeast includes the states of
Rio de Janeiro, São Paulo, Paraná, Santa Catarina and Rio Grande do Sul. (Abstracted from table 1.)

would have slightly improved its geographical distribution through internal migrations to the most developed region of the country. Nonetheless,
the geographical polarization of the two racial groups is still considerable,
with almost two-thirds of the white population living in the Southeast and
a greater proportion of nonwhites concentrated in the rest of the country,
particularly the Northeast (47.2 percent) and the Minas Gerais–Espírito
Santo region (14.1 percent).

One of the effects of the geographical distribution of racial groups
among unevenly developed regions is perceptible in their rural-urban
residence, whereby 64 percent of whites and 58 percent of nonwhites are
urban residents — again with a possible overestimation of the nonwhites'
level of urbanization. Although there is no information about the area of
residence of racial groups in earlier periods, it may be suggested that a nar-
rowing of the rural-urban differential between these groups has occurred
during the last decades. One possible cause might be the deceleration of
the urbanization process of the white population which, concentrated
mostly in the urban Southeast, is approaching the saturation point. Be that

as it may, by means of internal migrations to the Southeast and rural-urban flows outside the Southeast, Blacks and mulattoes have participated in the accelerated rhythm of Brazil's urbanization.

Access to educational opportunities is another relevant dimension of racial inequality. Among other reasons, obtaining a formal education is fundamental for nonwhites as it is virtually their only passport to higher social positions.[7] Considering the rates of literacy first, table 3 shows the intergroup differences in 1950 and 1976.

Nonwhites improved their rate of literacy considerably between the two dates, thus diminishing the difference relative to whites. In 1950 the opportunities for whites to become literate were double those for nonwhites; that ratio diminished to 1.3 in 1976. Nevertheless, the proportion of illiterates among nonwhites is still twice as great as that of whites. Considering the urban-rural dimension, in 1976 the educational disadvantages of nonwhites were greater in rural areas. Among the urban population, the literacy rates were 85 percent for whites and 72 percent for nonwhites, whereas the proportions for the rural population were 64.5 percent and 41.7 percent respectively.

If racial differences in the opportunities of becoming literate still persist, although in decline, the degree of inequality or exclusion experienced by Blacks and mulattoes increases swiftly when higher educational levels are considered. Table 4 shows the 1976 distribution of whites and non-whites in the educational hierarchy. The data attest to sharp inequalities of educational attainment. Compared to whites, the most notorious facts are (a) the high proportion (46 percent) of nonwhites with no instruction or less than one year of school; (b) the significantly smaller percentage of nonwhites who completed between five and eight years of school; and (c) the relatively small proportion of Blacks and mulattoes who achieved nine or more years of school. Thus, whites have a 1.55 greater chance of completing between five and eight years of school and a 3.15 times greater chance of completing nine or more years of school. The majority of the group with nine or more years of school, only 3.5 percent of which is nonwhite, consists of those entering senior high school and a smaller group of those with college education. This indicates that Blacks and mulattoes have been virtually excluded from the boom of university enrollment that has occurred in Brazil during the last fifteen years.

The participation of the two racial groups in the labor force, with respect to sectors of economic activity, is the next dimension of racial inequalities to be examined (see table 5 for the data under discussion). The first notable fact is the disproportionate concentration of nonwhites in agriculture, the construction industry, and services (mostly personal), the sectors that absorb most of the unskilled and underpaid workers. In 1976,

TABLE 3: Rates of Literacy of Persons of Five Years and Older
According to Race, 1950 and 1976

	1950	1976
Whites	52.7	78.4
Nonwhites	25.7	59.8

SOURCES: 1950 census and 1976 PNAD.

TABLE 4: Years Education of Persons of Five Years
and Older by Race, 1976

Years of Education	Race	
	Whites (%) (N = 52,238,247)	Nonwhites (%) (N = 36,368,143)
No instruction to less than one year	26.7	46.0
One to four years	43.5	38.3
Five to eight years	18.7	12.1
Nine years and more	11.0	3.5
Don't know/No answer	0.1	0.1

SOURCE: 1976 PNAD.

TABLE 5: Sectors of Economic Activity by Race, 1976

Activity	Race	
	Whites (%) (N = 22,713,756)	Nonwhites (%) (N = 16,230,386)
Agriculture	31.8	43.8
Industry	18.2	13.3
Construction industry	5.5	7.7
Commerce	10.6	7.5
Services	14.6	16.3
Other	19.3	11.4

SOURCE: 1976 PNAD.

these three sectors employed 68 percent of the economically active non-whites and 52 percent of whites. Conversely, nonwhites were under-represented in commerce, industry, and other activities, where better-paid jobs and more skilled labor are to be found. Although the different aggregation of sectors of activity in the 1950 census and the 1976 PNAD makes the modifications in the employment structure of the two groups difficult to grasp, a few trends are discernible.

The situation of nonwhites in agricultural employment deteriorated between 1950 and 1976. In 1950, 54 percent of whites and 64 percent of nonwhites worked in this sector. The 10 percent differential of 1950 widens to 12 percent in 1976, when 44 percent of nonwhites and 32 percent of whites were employed in agriculture. Seen from another perspective, in 1950 the nonwhite population supplied 42 percent of the agricultural labor force, increasing its participation to 48 percent in 1976.

Despite being underrepresented, nonwhites maintained their relative contribution to the industrial labor force between 1950 and 1976. It should be pointed out that nonwhites have had a more extensive participation in traditional industries, located outside of São Paulo and Rio de Janeiro. In commerce, where nonwhites have been habitually discriminated against, the proportion of Blacks and mulattoes increased faster than that of whites between these years. The employment of nonwhites in this sector rose from 2.9 percent to 7.5 percent while that of whites went from 7.2 percent to 10.6 percent. However, these data should be interpreted with caution since it is very likely that, along with the increase in the number of nonwhite commerce employees, there was a greater increase in the number of Black and mulatto street peddlers.

In the service, transport, and communication sectors, the participation of the two groups increased slightly and in similar proportions, whereas in other activities (professions, banking and real estate, education and health), the employment of nonwhites, almost nonexistent in 1950, grew faster than that of whites. In broad terms, it may be concluded that the disparity in the sectoral distribution of whites and nonwhites was partially reduced, although the direction of the imbalances in the employment structure remained unchanged.

It is reasonable to expect that the inequalities between whites and nonwhites in geographical location, educational attainment, and employment structure have a strong effect on the distribution of income. This is quite clear in table 6. Among nonwhites with declared income, 53.6 percent received up to minimum wage, while only 23.2 percent of whites were in the same income bracket. At the other end of the distribution, 23.7 percent of whites and 14.5 percent of nonwhites had an income of two to five times the minimum wage and, in turn, 16.4 percent of whites and 4.2 percent of nonwhites received more than five times the minimum wage.

These data suggest that the causes of racial inequalities should not be sought exclusively in the past, as they also operate in the present. Racism, through discriminatory practices and the cultural stereotyping by whites of the roles "adequate" for Blacks and mulattoes, perpetuates an unequal structure of social opportunities for everyone.

TABLE 6: Monthly Income of Persons Aged Ten Years and Over
by Race, 1976

Minimum Wage (MW)	Whites (%) (N = 43,135,160)	Nonwhites (%) (N = 15,712,684)
Up to ½ MW	11.1	22.0
More than ½–1 × MW	21.1	31.6
More than 1–2 × MW	27.7	27.7
More than 2–5 × MW	23.7	14.5
More than 5 × MW	16.4	4.2

SOURCE: 1976 PNAD.

NOTE: The minimum wage of Cr$ 690 was roughly equivalent to U.S. $65.

THE PERPETUATION OF RACIAL INEQUALITIES

The two opposing interpretations of racial inequalities are: (*a*) that nonwhites and whites enjoy the same opportunities and the inferior social position of Blacks and mulattoes is due to the different starting points of the two groups at the time of Abolition, and (*b*) that the social subordination of Blacks and mulattoes is due not only to the different starting points but also to the persistence of unequal opportunities for upward social mobility.

In order to test these alternative propositions, this section presents some aspects of the pattern of social mobility and status attainment of whites and nonwhites, and thus determines whether or not equal social opportunities exist. This analysis consists of three stages: (*a*) examining the global pattern of intergenerational occupational mobility; (*b*) determining the influence of the fathers' social positions on the educational attainment of the respondents; and (*c*) measuring the relative improvements in occupation and income due to education achieved by the two groups. The data used in the analysis are from the 1976 PNAD and refer only to men twenty to sixty-four years of age.[8]

As a contextual reference, it should be noted that, primarily as a result of rapid urbanization and transformation of the urban occupational structure, Brazil has been and is experiencing a high rate of social mobility. Thus, in the case of the national sample under consideration, 42.9 percent of the respondents inherited their fathers' occupational status, 44.4 percent were upward mobile, and 12.7 percent were downward mobile. According to 1973 estimates, structural social mobility accounted for 56 percent of the total social mobility, the remaining 44 percent being due to exchange mobility.[9]

Since this analysis is concerned with the social mobility of two subgroups of one population and not the "openness" of the society as a whole, rather than assuming the statistical independence of fathers' and sons' status or perfect equality of opportunity, our assumption will be that there is "racial democracy" in Brazil. This means that, given the inter-generational turnover mobility matrix of the total sample, persons born in families of a given occupational status should have the same probability of reaching certain occupational destinations, irrespective of their race.

Table 7 presents the mobility matrices of the total sample and of the white and nonwhite groups. The frequencies expected under the assumption of "racial democracy" can be calculated by multiplying the row marginals of white and nonwhite sub-samples by the probabilities of the transition matrix of the total sample. In order to test the assumption of "racial democracy," a comparison between the two distributions will determine the difference between the number of observed and expected upward movements of the two racial groups.

Of the 5,909 cases of upward mobility observed in the total sample, 3,469 correspond to whites and 2,250 to nonwhites. Under the assumption of "racial democracy," the amount of upward movement by nonwhites should be 2,524 and that of whites 3,208. This means that 274, or approximately 5 percent, more of the nonwhite group should have experienced upward social movement. Without considering that the degree of status inheritance by nonwhites in the lower occupational levels is greater than expected, this evidence refutes the hypothesis of "racial democracy" and indicates that nonwhite Brazilians experience substantially limited upward social mobility.

Table 8 gives a more accurate portrayal of the flow of occupational mobility between generations. Among the sons of agricultural workers, the main destination points of the upwardly mobile are the urban manual occupations. White persons born in this group experience a small advantage over nonwhites. Not only is the whites' degree of status inheritance (45.8 percent) smaller than that of nonwhites, but also 16.3 percent of whites and only 9.6 percent of nonwhites experience long-distance social mobility, crossing the manual/non-manual line.

Interracial differences of social mobility become greater when persons born in the urban occupational strata are considered. Among people born at the lower-manual level, not only does a much greater proportion of non-whites remain at the same occupational level (48.5 percent compared to 35.8 percent of whites), but also 37.9 percent of whites and only 21 per-cent of nonwhites move up to non-manual positions. Among those whose status of origin is the higher-manual level, 40.9 percent of whites and 29.1 percent of nonwhites obtain non-manual occupations, with a greater proportion of whites experiencing long-distance mobility.

Of the persons with social origins in the non-manual social strata, it may be noted that among those born into the lower–non-manual level 63.8 per-

TABLE 7: Intergenerational Occupational Mobility of Male Respondents
Aged 20–64

Total Sample[a]					
Father's Occupation[b]	Respondent's Occupation				
	6	*5*	*4*	*3*	*2*	*1*
6	249	73	96	91	78	12
5	159	200	128	142	165	146
4	204	134	257	178	163	36
3	138	86	135	364	222	43
2	201	140	252	432	804	120
1	245	321	480	949	2,033	3,838

Whites					
Father's Occupation	Respondent's Occupation				
	6	*5*	*4*	*3*	*2*	*1*
6	206	52	72	54	45	9
5	131	149	88	90	100	85
4	156	106	185	121	105	27
3	101	64	84	221	125	14
2	146	90	165	230	379	49
1	164	208	289	553	982	1,858

Nonwhites					
Father's Occupation	Respondent's Occupation				
	6	*5*	*4*	*3*	*2*	*1*
6	36	20	23	37	31	2
5	23	45	36	46	59	57
4	45	28	62	55	55	8
3	34	22	51	137	95	29
2	53	46	79	192	411	66
1	69	99	170	355	984	1,860

SOURCE: 1976 PNAD.
[a]Includes Asians (amarelos) and people with no declaration of color.
[b]6 = professionals, managers, and big business owners; 5 = higher clerical workers and small farmers; 4 = lower clerical workers and small owners in commerce and services; 3 = workers in modern industries and unskilled workers in services; 2 = workers in traditional industries, personal and domestic services, and retail trade; 1 = manual workers in agriculture.

cent of whites and 53.4 percent of nonwhites achieve occupational levels equal to or higher than those of their fathers. In the case of higher–nonmanual origins, these proportions are 43.6 percent for whites and 25.6 percent for nonwhites. Three quarters of nonwhites born in the upper occupational level experienced social demotion, whereas that occurred among only 53 percent of whites.

TABLE 8: Mobility from Father's Occupation to Respondent's Occupation
According to Race

Father's Occupation*	Whites (%)						
	Respondent's Occupation						
	6	5	4	3	2	1	N
6	47.0	11.9	16.4	12.3	10.3	2.1	(438)
5	20.4	23.2	13.7	14.0	15.5	13.2	(643)
4	22.3	15.1	26.4	17.3	15.0	3.9	(700)
3	16.6	10.5	13.8	36.3	20.5	2.3	(609)
2	13.8	8.5	15.6	21.7	35.8	4.6	(1,059)
1	4.1	5.1	7.1	13.7	24.2	45.8	(4,054)

Father's Occupation*	Nonwhites (%)						
	Respondent's Occupation						
	6	5	4	3	2	1	N
6	24.2	13.4	15.4	24.8	20.8	1.4	(149)
5	8.7	16.9	13.5	17.3	22.2	21.4	(266)
4	17.8	11.1	24.5	21.7	21.7	3.2	(253)
3	9.2	6.0	13.9	37.2	25.8	7.9	(368)
2	6.3	5.4	9.3	22.7	48.5	7.8	(847)
1	2.0	2.8	4.8	10.0	27.8	52.6	(3,537)

SOURCE: 1976 PNAD.

*In this table: 6 = Upper (professionals, managers and big business owners); 5 = Higher non-manual (high clerical workers and small farmers); 4 = Lower non-manual (lower clerical workers and small owners in commerce and services); 3 = Higher manual (workers in modern industries and unskilled workers in services); 2 = Lower manual (workers in traditional industries, personal and domestic services and retail trade); and 6 = Manual (workers in agriculture).

Controlling for social status of origin, nonwhites have smaller chances of upward social mobility than whites. Interracial differences in the opportunities of upward mobility increase with higher social status of origin. Whites born in high social positions enjoy a greater degree of status inheritance than nonwhites, while nonwhites born in low social positions show a greater degree of status inheritance. The small group of nonwhites born in families of high social standing is much more exposed to the risks of social demotion than whites.

In order to assess interracial differences in status transmission, the way in which social background (as measured by father's occupation) conditions the educational attainment of white and nonwhite respondents will be examined next. Table 9 shows the educational levels achieved by whites and nonwhites according to their fathers' occupational status.[10]

The data show a consistent tendency of nonwhites to obtain less education than whites with the same social background. The concentration of

TABLE 9: Educational Level by Fathers' Occupational Status and Race

| Education | Whites (%) | | | |
	Upper (N = 439)	Non-Manual (N = 1,318)	Manual (N = 1,649)	Rural (N = 3,869)
College	33.5	3.4	0.8	0.1
Senior high school	13.0	5.0	2.1	0.2
Junior high school	13.4	13.0	6.7	1.0
Elementary school	29.6	44.8	41.7	24.8
Literate	8.6	24.9	32.6	31.5
Illiterate	1.8	8.9	16.1	42.4

| Education | Nonwhites (%) | | | |
	Upper (N = 151)	Non-Manual (N = 525)	Manual (N = 1,225)	Rural (N = 3,550)
College	12.4	1.2	0.3	——
Senior high school	9.0	2.8	0.8	0.1
Junior high school	18.0	9.7	5.8	0.3
Elementary school	37.2	36.2	36.4	14.0
Literate	12.4	30.2	30.0	25.6
Illiterate	11.0	19.9	26.7	60.0

SOURCE: 1976 PNAD.

nonwhites in the two lowest educational classes of illiterate and literate is substantially greater than that of whites, irrespective of their occupational level of origin.

Considering first the lowest social origin, it may be noted that, among the offspring of agricultural workers, 60 percent of nonwhites and 42.4 percent of whites are illiterate. At the other extreme of the social hierarchy, among the sons of persons in the upper occupational level, 33.5 percent of whites and 12.4 percent of nonwhites had a college education. At the same level of social origin, 60 percent of whites and 39.4 percent of nonwhites went beyond the elementary school level. Among the sons of non-manual workers those proportions are 21.4 percent for whites and 13.7 percent for nonwhites. Finally, among the sons of urban-manual workers, 51.3 percent of whites and 43.3 percent of nonwhites completed elementary school or beyond.

It is difficult to determine whether these interracial differences in educational attainment are the result of discriminatory practices both in access to schools and within them, or of factors operating outside the schools — such as family expectations or culturally imposed levels of aspiration. The fact remains that, even when we control for social background, nonwhites drop out of school earlier than whites.

Taking into account the fact that education is one of the most important determinants of occupational attainment, the next step is to determine how the educational achievements of whites and nonwhites are translated into positions in the occupational hierarchy.

The data in table 10 suggest two main conclusions. First, no matter which educational level is considered, nonwhites are concentrated disproportionally in the lower occupational levels. Although education is not the exclusive determinant of occupational attainment, the systematic character of the differences leaves little doubt about the existence of racial discrimination in the labor market. Second, the magnitude of differences in the distributions becomes greater when higher educational levels are achieved. One may consider, for instance, the percentage differences between whites and nonwhites in the two higher occupational levels: 5.4 percent of the illiterate; 9.9 percent of the literate; 13.7 percent at the elementary school level; 17.9 percent at the junior high school level; and 21.8 percent at the senior high school level, with the tendency reverting to 12.9 percent at the college level. This suggests that, up to a certain educational level, occupational discrimination increases with the educational achievement of nonwhites.

The data already analyzed indicate that the explanation for lower occupational attainment among nonwhites should take two processes into consideration. First, as previously seen, nonwhites obtain less education than whites of the same social background. This means that they enter the labor market with fewer educational qualifications. The second is that racial discrimination affects the hiring and promotion of people within the occupational structure. As a result of these processes, nonwhites are ex-

TABLE 10: Respondents' Occupation According to Educational Level and Race

| | Whites (%) | | | | | |
Occupation	Illiterate (N = 2,116)	Literate (N = 2,237)	Elementary N = (2,527)	Junior High (N = 404)	Senior High (N = 183)	College (N = 222)
Upper	2.9	8.4	15.2	35.9	45.4	54.0
Non-Manual	11.2	20.5	26.7	34.4	32.2	34.7
Manual	44.1	42.9	39.9	27.5	21.3	10.4
Rural	41.8	28.2	18.2	2.2	1.1	.9
	Nonwhites (%)					
Occupation	Illiterate (N = 2,534)	Literate (N = 1,477)	Elementary N = (1,206)	Junior High (N = 166)	Senior High (N = 43)	College (N = 29)
Upper	1.7	4.2	9.0	20.5	27.9	37.9
Non-Manual	7.0	14.8	19.2	31.9	27.9	37.9
Manual	40.3	53.4	52.8	44.0	41.9	13.8
Rural	51.0	27.6	19.0	3.6	2.3	10.4

SOURCE: 1976 PNAD.

posed to a "cycle of cumulative disadvantage" in their struggle for status attainment.

Further support for this cycle of cumulative disadvantage may be found by comparing the income returns on the education acquired by whites and nonwhites. The data in table 11 indicate a sharp income differential between whites and nonwhites within each educational level. The relative income differentials between the two groups conform to a curvilinear pattern. They go from a minimum among illiterates, where nonwhites' average income is 67.7 percent that of whites, to a maximum among people with junior high school education, where nonwhites' mean income is only 37.1 percent that of whites. Those differences decrease to 57 percent and 62.4 percent at the senior high school and college levels.

It is worth noting that the mean income of nonwhites with college education is smaller than that of whites with junior high school education. Thus, for the majority of nonwhites, the investment in additional years of education yields proportionally much smaller income improvement than that of whites. Occupational discrimination constitutes the most likely explanation for the income differential within each educational level. The fact that nonwhites cluster disproportionally in the lower occupational levels, even when controlling for education, supports this interpretation. This is also suggested by the column of standard deviation. Within each educational level, the standard deviation of whites is considerably greater than that of nonwhites. This wider dispersion of whites in the income hierarchy reflects a less homogeneous and concentrated distribution in the occupational hierarchy.

CONCLUSION

Almost nine decades after the abolition of slavery, Brazilian Blacks and mulattoes are still concentrated at the bottom of the social hierarchy. Compared to whites, the greater part of the nonwhite population lives in the

TABLE 11: Income Returns on Education by Race, 1976 (Cruzeiros)

	Whites			Nonwhites			$\overline{X}_{n}-w/\overline{X}_{w}$
	$\overline{X}$	sd	N	$\overline{X}$	sd	N	
Illiterate	1,734	5,215	2,124	1,174	2,620	2,537	0.67
Literate	2,985	8,237	2,241	1,674	1,945	1,479	0.56
Elementary	3,769	6,864	2,543	2,122	2,872	1,210	0.56
Junior High	7,790	11,461	409	2,891	3,047	167	0.37
Senior High	9,742	23,075	183	5,557	6,284	45	0.57
College	10,900	12,023	226	6,801	6,938	29	0.62

SOURCE: 1976 PNAD.

least developed regions of the country, and their access to the educational system is restricted, particularly at higher levels of instruction.

The participation of nonwhites in the economic system is repeatedly characterized by their disproportionate concentration in the sectors that absorb unskilled and underpaid labor. In turn, this results in the highly unequal participation of whites and nonwhites in income distribution and the consumption of the social product. This structure of racial inequalities is not merely a fading legacy from the distant past; it is perpetuated by the unequal social opportunities faced by whites and nonwhites in the present.

The empirical evidence indicates that nonwhites are exposed to a cycle of cumulative disadvantage in terms of intergenerational social mobility and the process of status attainment. To be born nonwhite in Brazil usually means to be born into low-status families. The chances of escaping from the disabilities inherent in a low social position are considerably smaller for nonwhites than for whites of the same background. As compared to whites, nonwhites suffer a competitive disadvantage in all phases of the process of intergenerational transmission of social inequalities.

As a result of discriminatory practices and the symbolic violence inherent in a racist culture, nonwhites have more limited educational opportunities than whites of the same social origin. In turn, the educational achievements of Blacks and mulattoes are translated into proportionally smaller occupational and income gains than those of whites. Under these circumstances, it is very unlikely that the ideal of racial equality will be achieved through individual social mobility while it continues to be limited by racial discrimination.

NOTES

1. The PNAD is conducted by the Brazilian Institute of Geography and Statistics (IBGE). The 1976 PNAD contained the most recent data on race until the publication of those in the 1980 census.
2. It is interesting to note that in the United States Blacks and other racial minorities are the acknowledged exceptions to the ideology of equal opportunity, whereas in the hierarchical and highly inegalitarian Brazilian society the ideal of equal opportunity is mostly predicated on the grounds of race.
3. Donald Pierson, *Negroes in Brazil: A Study of Race Contact at Bahia* (Chicago: The University of Chicago Press, 1942), and Charles Wagley, ed., *Race and Class in Rural Brazil* (New York: Columbia University Press, 1963). For a similar conceptualization, see also Thales de Azevedo, *As elites de côr, um estudo de ascensão social* (São Paulo: Companhia Editora Nacional, 1955).
4. Charles Wagley, "From Caste to Class in North Brazil," in *Comparative Perspectives in Race Relations*, ed. Melvin Tumin (Boston: Little , Brown & Co., 1969), 60.
5. Roger Bastide and Florestan Fernandes, *Brancos e Negros em São Paulo* (São Paulo: Companhia Editora Nacional, 1959); Florestan Fernandes, *A integração do Negro na*

sociedade de classes (São Paulo: Dominus, 1965), and *O Negro no mundo dos brancos* (São Paulo: Difusão Européia do Livro, 1972). See also Fernando Henrique Cardoso and Octavio Ianni, *Cor e mobilidade social em Florianópolis* (São Paulo: Companhia Editora Nacional, 1960) and Octavio Ianni, *Raças e classes sociais no Brasil* (Rio de Janeiro: Civilização Brasileira, 1972).

6. Carlos A. Hasenbalg, "Desigualdades raciais no Brasil," Rio de Janeiro, *DADOS* 14 (1977) and *Discriminação e desigualdades raciais no Brasil* (Rio de Janeiro: Graal, 1979).

7. Paradoxically, this is so despite the fact that occupational discrimination seems to increase together with the educational attainment of nonwhites. The growing barriers to entry into independent business activities and the decline of upward mobility through clientelist networks tend to make education the only open channel of social ascension.

8. I am indebted to Nelson do Valle Silva for making available to me all the data used in this section.

9. See Nelson do Valle Silva, "As duas faces da mobilidade," Rio de Janeiro, *DADOS* 21 (1979), 49–67. The total social mobility observed may be considered as the sum of structural mobility (mobility that reflects changes in the shape of the stratification system or the occupational structure) and exchange mobility (which does not depend on structural changes; simply, some people go up and others go down in movements that compensate each other).

10. To facilitate the presentation and interpretation of the data, the higher and lower non-manual occupational groups were added to form the non-manual level, and the higher and lower manual form the manual level.

4

UPDATING THE COST OF NOT BEING WHITE IN BRAZIL

NELSON DO VALLE SILVA

Two major hypotheses seem to characterize the literature on Brazilian race relations. The first, associated with the idea of a "mulatto escape-hatch," states that Blacks and mulattoes are expected to behave differently with respect to social mobility (Degler 1971). In particular, mulattoes are expected to attain higher educational, occupational, and economic levels. The second postulates that race plays no significant role in the process of mobility and explains the present situation of nonwhites in terms of their relatively disadvantageous initial position. [For an example of this view, see Donald Pierson, *Negroes in Brazil: A Study of Race Contact at Bahia* (Carbondale and Edwardsville, Ill.: Southern Illinois University Press, 1967)—ED.] Although the levels of attainment may differ from one racial group to another, one should expect no racial differences in the returns on the investments made.

In a previous work I debated these hypotheses in the context of a racial income differentials study based on the 1960 Brazilian Census (Silva 1978). That study used the 1.27 percent census subsample and selected the Rio de Janeiro area for analysis. The purpose of this chapter is to update and expand that analysis, using the recent 1976 National Household Survey (PNAD) and including some additional variables that were not available for 1960. It has also been expanded to include all regions covered by the 1976 PNAD.

PREVIOUS FINDINGS

In the 1978 study referred to above, several conclusions emerged from the analysis of racial income differentials. The first was that Blacks and mulattoes, contrary to an assumption frequently found in the literature, seemed to display strikingly similar profiles. This was particularly true with regard to patterns of returns obtained through experience and schooling, but similar results were also obtained with respect to other variables. An important implication is that to consider Blacks and mulattoes as composing a homogeneous "nonwhite" racial group does no violence to reality. Rather than being a mere simplification, the joint analysis of Blacks and mulattoes constitutes a sensible approach to the analysis of racial discrimination in Brazil.

A second conclusion recognized substantial differences in economic attainment between whites and nonwhites even when we control for the variables relevant to the process of income attainment. The magnitude of the income differences that can be attributed to labor-market discrimination may be considerably lower than that observed elsewhere. Nevertheless, a rather substantial proportion of these interracial differences in Brazil is caused by discriminatory practices.

In particular, it was shown that even though nonwhites experience certain advantages at the very lowest levels of attainment, these advantages are superseded by the superior rates of return to experience and schooling enjoyed by whites. The net result is that nonwhites only enjoy a relative advantage over whites at the early phase of their entry into the labor market, or at very low levels of skill, in generally poor environments such as rural areas. Whites are much more efficient in converting experience and educational investments into monetary returns while nonwhites suffer increasing disadvantages as they try to scale the social ladder. These results led me to reject the two hypotheses presented in the Brazilian sociological literature as implausible. Mulattoes do not behave differently from Blacks, nor does race play a negligible role in the process of income attainment. Rather, I found that whites enjoy a substantial advantage in the labor market over Blacks and mulattoes alike. A quantitative summary of nonwhites' disadvantages as measured by this previous study is presented in table 1.

Although discrimination generally appeared to be less important than differences in "composition and interaction" (the meaning of these components will become clear later), it still determined a large proportion of racial income differences. Thus, while 82.4 percent of the difference between the average incomes of whites and mulattoes could be attributed to differences in "composition" and "interaction," 17.6 percent could be attributed to discrimination in the labor market. The corresponding figures for Blacks were 85.4 percent and 14.6 percent respectively. These data led to the surprising result that, if anything, Blacks tend to be relatively less discriminated against than mulattoes, a contradiction of the conventional wisdom of the historical-sociological literature.

TABLE 1: Decomposition of Average Income Differentials by Color
Rio de Janeiro, Brazil 1960
(Base Color Group = White)

Component	Color		
	Mulatto (%)	Black (%)	Nonwhite (%)
Total Difference = $\bar{Y}w - \bar{Y}n$*	5,425.0 (100.0)	6,587.7 (100.0)	5,860.1 (100.0)
Discrimination	954.3 (17.6)	959.0 (14.6)	955.0 (16.3)
Composition & Interaction	4,470.7 (82.4)	5,628.7 (85.4)	4,955.1 (83.7)

SOURCE: Silva, N.V. (1980)

* $\bar{Y}w$ is the average income for whites and $\bar{Y}n$ is the average income for the corresponding nonwhite group. Thus, for instance, 6,587.7 is the white-Black monetary difference in 1960 Brazilian cruzeiros, or approximately U.S. $1,252 at the rate of Cr$ .19 to U.S. $1.00.

Another interesting aspect of table 1 is that the monetary disadvantages suffered by Blacks and mulattoes are virtually identical—about 955 cruzeiros (U.S. $181) a month. This value can be taken as representing the typical "cost of not being white" in Rio de Janeiro, Brazil, in 1960.

DATA AND METHODS

The 1976 PNAD is the basic data source for this chapter. The sample to be used here includes Black, white, and mulatto males no longer in school and aged ten to sixty-four. The PNAD covers the entire Brazilian territory, with the exception of rural areas in the northern and western regions. The total sample size is 12,351 respondents. The selected variables are the following:

   1. Color. The original survey's race classification includes white, Black, yellow (*sic*), mulatto and non-responses. Asians and non-respondents, who constitute a minute fraction of the sample, are excluded from this analysis.
   2. Income. Income was measured in terms of average monthly earnings, including not only fixed income but also variable income and an estimate of the monthly value of products and goods received as direct payment for work done.
      Table 2 presents the estimated average income for each racial group. There are clearly substantial income differences between racial groups. For example, the average income for whites is more than twice that for the Black population. There was also a relatively small but significant difference in average income between Blacks and mulattoes.
   3. Residence. This variable allows some control for spatial income differences. Two main Brazilian regions are distinguished: the

TABLE 2: Average Income by Color
Brazil (1976)

Color	N	Mean	Standard Deviation
Black	1,035	1,210.07	1,361.40
Mulatto	4,090	1,722.26	2,954.76
White	7,226	3,433.46	7,805.35
Nonwhite	5,125	1,618.86	2,717.24

SOURCE: 1976 National Household Survey (PNAD)
NOTE: Cr$ 10.67 to U.S. $1.00

developed Southeast and the rest of the country (0 = under-developed, 1 = developed).

4. Background. The respondent's place of birth is classified as rural or urban. This variable indicates an individual's farm or non-farm background (0 = farm, 1 = non-farm).

5. State or Country of Origin. As we are interested in the state or country of origin as an indicator of the respondent's skills or productivity, it suffices to group areas of origin according to levels of socioeconomic development. The same coding used for the variable "Residence" above is used here. Immigrants are grouped into the "developed" category.

6. Migration. This variable indicates the respondent's migration status. (0 = non-migrant, 1 = migrant — i.e., person born in any place other than the current place of residence).

7. Marital Status. This variable is often used as an indicator of an individual's commitment to work, in the sense that being married is supposed to affect one's productivity, hence one's income. A simple ever-married/single dichotomy is used here (0 = single, 1 = ever-married).

8. Schooling. This is used as a direct indicator of an individual's skills and productivity. It is measured here by a scale of years running from 0 (no formal schooling) to 17 years (completed college).

9. Experience. A transformation of the respondent's age is used as a proxy for length of labor market experience. More specifically, Experience = Age − (Age at Enrollment + Years of Schooling) where "age at enrollment" is taken to be a constant six years of age.

These variables, with some minor differences in definition, were the ones used in my previous analysis of the 1960 Brazilian census (Silva 1978). The present study utilizes two other variables representing "parental background":

10. Father's Occupational Status. The 1976 PNAD recorded the occupation the respondent's father had when the respondent entered the labor market. This variable was coded according to a socioeconomic status scale that I developed on the basis of the 1970 census returns (Silva 1973). It ranges from a low of 2.5 to a high of 88.8.
11. Father's Schooling. This variable is measured by years of schooling, the same scale used to measure the respondent's schooling (variable 8).

The bivariate analysis of the relationship between income and the other variables listed above indicates that an adequate and convenient specification of an earnings function based on these data could be:

$$Y = \beta_0 + \beta_1 E + \beta_2 E^2 + \sum_{i=3}^{14} \beta_i S_i + \sum_{i=15}^{19} \beta_i D_i + \beta_{20} FO + \beta_{21} FS$$

where Y and E represent, respectively, average monthly income and length of labor market experience; the S_i's are dummy variables representing different levels of schooling; the D_i's are dummy variables representing the effect of place of residence, background, and marital status variables (3 to 7 above); FO and FS are the parental background variables: father's occupation and father's schooling, respectively; and the β's are regression coefficients. With the exception of the newly introduced parental background variables, this specification is equivalent to the one used in analyzing the 1960 census data. In the analysis that follows, particular attention will be paid to racial differences in returns on investments in the more important forms of human capital, that is, in schooling and experience.

RETURNS ON EXPERIENCE

The results of the fit of our model to the data are presented in table 3. It is important to note the similarity between Blacks and mulattoes in terms of the coefficients obtained. In particular, even where we can find significant differences between the two groups, they clearly contrast with the results for whites. The coefficients for Blacks and mulattoes not only tend to be of similar magnitude, but also agree in direction and form of relationship even when they significantly differ from each other. Thus, reference to a "nonwhite," as opposed to a white, pattern seems appropriate.

The fourth column in table 3 shows the results of the fit of our earnings function for the nonwhite group, that is, for mulattoes and Blacks. The contrast with the white group is remarkable. Particularly important are the differences in the coefficients for the parental background

TABLE 3: Fit of the Earnings Functions by Color
Brazil, 1976

Variable	Color			
	White	Mulatto	Black	Nonwhite
Experience	313.08†	123.16†	73.95†	114.25†
Experience²	−4.38†	−1.83†	−1.01†	−1.68†
Schooling 1	−664.58	368.27*	220.61	362.42*
2	−669.95	128.89	138.42	127.50
3	−334.58	138.25	247.19*	163.99
4	289.10	505.09†	475.94†	511.84†
5	760.25	441.47*	236.89	408.25†
6	460.39	451.19	458.60*	452.74*
7	1,922.98†	633.03*	1,040.94†	705.41†
8	1,491.84†	1,031.53†	1,852.81†	1,116.68†
9	2,759.76†	1,473.04†	907.99†	1,430.48†
11	2,864.41†	1,577.10†	1,243.22†	1,556.96†
14	4,885.82†	3,218.40†	4,830.42†	3,401.60†
17	9,580.00†	9,054.04†	8,569.18†	9,013.05†
Background	1,000.69†	368.52†	343.46†	360.34†
Migration	1,069.39†	493.60†	197.19†	431.25†
Residence	−629.03*	514.49†	357.64†	503.88†
Origin	1,089.28†	−168.60	−174.77	−205.26
Marital Status	705.95†	212.63	209.95*	226.11*
Father's Occupation	28.88†	16.72†	11.22*	17.15†
Father's Schooling	289.31†	102.37†	128.54†	107.34†
Constant	−4,850.29	−1,510.36	−857.00	−1,418.39
R²	0.155	0.211	0.428	0.223
F	62.86†	51.79†	36.04†	69.92†

SOURCE: 1976 National Household Survey (PNAD)

NOTE: Cr$ 10.67 to U.S. $1.00

*significant at $\alpha = 05$

†significant at $\alpha = 0.1$

variables. They clearly show that nonwhites are much less "efficient" in transmitting their achieved status from generation to generation. In other words, whites obtain much greater rewards through the process of intergenerational mobility than nonwhites, given the same initial social position.

Let us now focus on the two main "human capital" variables: experience and schooling. The impact of any such factors on earnings can be found by calculating the marginal rate of return to the factor, that is, the partial derivative of the earnings function with respect to that factor. In the case of experience, the marginal rate of return is given by:

$$\frac{\partial Y}{\partial E} = \beta_1 + 2\beta_2 E$$

Turning to the data in table 3, we can see that the marginal rates of return for experience for the three racial groups are:

$$\frac{\partial Yw}{\partial E} = 313.08 - 8.76 E$$

$$\frac{\partial Ym}{\partial E} = 123.16 - 3.66 E$$

$$\frac{Yb}{\partial E} = 73.95 - 2.02 E$$

where the subscripts w, m, and b stand for white, mulatto, and Black, respectively. The marginal rate of return for experience for nonwhites is:

$$\frac{\partial Yn}{\partial E} = 114.25 - 3.36 E$$

Whites typically have much larger marginal returns for experience than nonwhites. However, since the returns are a negative function of experience and whites have a much steeper rate of decline than nonwhites, the latter can eventually have larger marginal rates of return than whites. The marginal rate of return functions are depicted in figure 1.

Clearly, whites enjoy larger marginal rates of return for experience during their first thirty-five years in the labor force, that is, up to the peak of their productive lives. After they attain this peak, a steady decline follows and the marginal rate of return for whites becomes negative. It is during this negative phase of the marginal rate of return that nonwhites start to have larger gains (more accurately, lower decreases) than whites. All groups attain their return peaks at about the same period, the steeper decline for whites determining the relative advantage for nonwhites. It should be emphasized, however, that thirty-five years represent most of the average person's active life. Thus, we can say that whites have higher relative gains for experience than nonwhites for most of their productive lives.

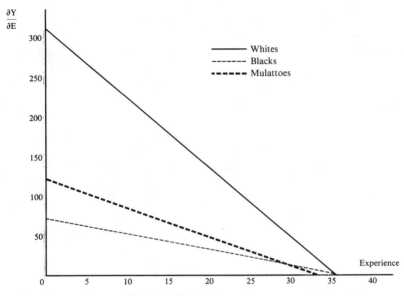

Figure 1 — Changes in the Rate of Return for Experience
by Color, Males 10–64 Years of Age, Brazil (1976)

RETURNS ON SCHOOLING

As the coefficients in table 3 imply, there are significant differences in returns on schooling favoring whites so that, even when they are at the greatest disadvantage, they are still able to enjoy absolute gains for higher levels of schooling. These observations suggest that, while whites are favored with higher marginal returns on schooling, nonwhites are subject to increasing disadvantages as they try to move up the educational ladder. On the average, whites enjoy much greater returns on schooling than non-whites, and this net difference increases with the level of schooling.

In order to evaluate the extent of these differences, consider an average individual, that is, one who displays average values for each variable in our data, except schooling. If we compute the expected earnings for such an individual at each schooling level and for each racial group, we will have calculated the average or expected returns on schooling, that is, the average income to be expected in return for a certain level of schooling. The results are reported in table 4.

The data show a similarity in the average returns for schooling obtained by Blacks and mulattoes. In fact, these results support the assertion that Blacks and mulattoes form a rather homogeneous group and thus the results presented in the last column of table 3 represent the average experience of individuals in these racial groups.

There is also a striking divergence between whites and nonwhites. Not only do whites have higher initial returns for schooling, that is, a higher average income for no formal schooling, but also the white–nonwhite divergence actually increases with schooling levels. Thus, while the average income difference for those with no schooling is Cr\$1,233 (Cr\$ = cruzeiros), the corresponding figure after nine years of schooling is Cr\$2,563.

An average marginal rate of returns for schooling can be calculated by fitting a line to the data in table 4. A visual inspection of the data suggests that an exponential function is a suitable functional form. The impact of schooling on earnings can be measured by the marginal rate of returns for schooling, the partial derivative of the average earnings functions with respect to schooling thus being:

$$\frac{\partial Y}{\partial S} = \alpha_1 \, e^{\alpha_0 + \alpha_1 S}$$

Figure 2 depicts the results of the calculation of the marginal rate of returns for schooling for the three racial groups. Again, the results for Blacks and mulattoes are similar for the first six or seven years in the

TABLE 4: Average Income Returns for Schooling by Color
Brazil, 1976

Schooling	Color			
	White	Mulatto	Black	Nonwhite
0	2,419.33	1,256.74	927.29	1,185.97
1	1,754.75	1,625.01	1,147.90	1,512.39
2	1,749.38	1,385.63	1,065.71	1,313.47
3	2,084.75	1,394.99	1,174.48	1,349.96
4	2,708.43	1,761.83	1,403.23	1,697.81
5	3,179.58	1,698.21	1,164.18	1,594.22
6	2,979.72	1,707.93	1,385.89	1,638.71
7	4,342.31	1,889.77	1,968.23	1,891.38
8	3,911.17	2,288.27	2,780.10	2,302.65
9	5,179.05	2,729.78	1,835.28	2,616.45
11	5,283.74	2,833.84	2,170.51	2,742.93
14	7,305.15	4,475.14	5,757.71	4,587.57
17	11,999.33	10,310.78	9,496.47	10,199.02

SOURCE: 1976 National Household Survey (PNAD)
NOTE: Cr\$ 10.67 to U.S. \$1.00

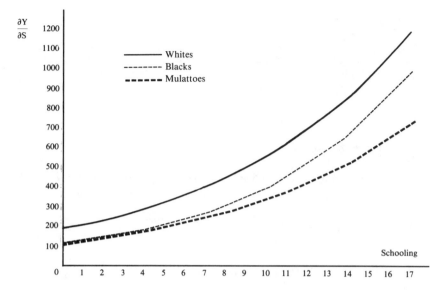

$\dfrac{\partial Y}{\partial S}$

Figure 2—Marginal Average Returns for Schooling
by Color, Males 10–64 Years of Age, Brazil (1976)

schooling process (where, incidentally, they are massively concentrated). After this point, the results for these two groups diverge, with Blacks seeming to enjoy greater rates of return than mulattoes at higher levels of schooling. In fact, the α_1 coefficient for Blacks is larger than that for mulattoes (a 12.9 percent increase per year of schooling for Blacks, 10.8 percent for mulattoes; this even compares favorably with the 10.9 percent yearly increase obtained for whites). These data clearly contradict the assumption that mulattoes have considerably more mobility than Blacks. In other words, observed differences in returns on schooling indicate that Blacks and mulattoes have similar profiles, composing a nonwhite group clearly differentiated from whites. Moreover, the only visible Black-mulatto difference, contrary to what is usually expected, actually indicates higher marginal returns for Blacks. On the other hand, the large white-nonwhite difference in marginal returns on education indicates the probable existence of discriminatory processes in the operation of the labor market.

ESTIMATING THE COST OF NOT BEING WHITE

The usual approach to the study of differences in income attainment between whites and nonwhites is to specify an earnings function:

$$Y = b_o + \sum_{i=1}^{k} b_i X_i$$

where Y is the level of income and the X's are the characteristics used to explain Y. This earnings function is estimated for the two groups:

$$Y_w = b_o{}^w + \sum_{i=1}^{k} b_i{}^w X_i{}^w$$

$$Y_n = b_o{}^n + \sum_{i=1}^{k} b_i{}^n X_i{}^n$$

where the w and n subscripts indicate the two groups. Writing $\bar{Y}$ and $\bar{X}_i$ as the averages for the Y and X_i variables respectively, we now know that:

$$\bar{Y}_w = b_o{}^w + \sum_{i=1}^{k} b_i{}^w \bar{X}_i{}^w$$

$$\bar{Y}_n = b_o{}^n + \sum_{i=1}^{k} b_i{}^n \bar{X}_i{}^n$$

Similarly, we can standardize the income variable by using one group's average $\bar{X}_i$ values and the other group's corresponding regression coefficients. Thus, we can write this procedure as:

$$f_w(N) = b_o + \sum_{i=1}^{k} b_i{}^w \bar{X}_i{}^n$$

$$f_n(W) = b_o{}^n + \sum_{i=1}^{k} b_i{}^n \bar{X}_i{}^w$$

These measures are interpretable as the expected income one group would have if it had the same returns structure (that is, regression coefficients) of the other group. Thus, $f_w(N)$ indicates the expected average income for nonwhites if they had the same earnings function as whites.

The difference in average income between the two groups can be broken down into four different components (Althauser and Wigler 1972; Iam and Thornton 1975):

$$\bar{Y}_w - \bar{Y}_n = (b_o{}^w - b_o{}^n) + \sum_{i=1}^{k} \bar{X}_i{}^n (b_i{}^w - b_i{}^n) + \sum_{i=1}^{k} b_i{}^n (\bar{X}_i{}^w - \bar{X}_i{}^n) + \sum_{i=1}^{k} (\bar{X}_i{}^w - \bar{X}_i{}^n) (b_i{}^w - b_i{}^n)$$

The first component is the difference between the two intercepts. The second component reflects the impact of differences in slopes on income differences. Both components indicate the presence of discrimination (Thurow 1967; Blinder 1973; Masters 1975). The third component is "composition differences," indicating the contribution of differences in the distribution of the explanatory variables to the income difference between the two groups. The fourth and final term, usually called the "interaction component," indicates the covariation between the differences in means and the differences in the coefficients of the two groups.

The two components reflecting labor market discrimination can be rearranged as:

$$D = (b_o^w - b_o^n) + \sum_{i=1}^{k} \bar{X}_i^n (b_i^w - b_i^n) = f_w(\bar{N}) - \bar{Y}_n$$

representing the difference between the expected income for nonwhites in the absence of discrimination in the labor market and the actual average income for this group. Likewise, the "composition" and "interaction" components can be rewritten as:

$$C = \sum_{i=1}^{k} \bar{X}_i^n (b_i^w - b_i^n) = f_n(\bar{w}) - \bar{Y}_n$$

and,

$$I = \sum_{i=1}^{k} (\bar{X}_i^w - \bar{X}_i^n)(b_i^w - b_i^n) = \bar{Y}_w + \bar{Y}_n - f_n(\bar{W}) - f_w(\bar{N})$$

so that,

$$C + I = \bar{Y}_w - f_w(\bar{N})$$

Thus, we can decompose the differences in income between our racial groups into these components, taking D as a summary measure of labor market discrimination. Applying this decomposition procedure to the data, we get the results reported on table 5. The white group is taken as a basis

TABLE 5: Decomposition of Average Income Differentials by Color
Brazil, 1976
(Base Color Group = White)

Component	Color		
	Mulatto (%)	Black (%)	Nonwhite (%)
Total Difference = $\bar{Y}w - \bar{Y}n$	1,711.20 (100%)	2,223.39 (100%)	1,814.64 (100%)
Discrimination	562.59 (32.9%)	584.04 (26.3%)	565.98 (31.2%)
Composition & Interaction	1,148.61 (67.1%)	1,639.35 (73.7%)	1,248.66 (68.8%)

SOURCE: 1976 National Household Survey (PNAD)
NOTE: Cr$ 10.67 to U.S. $1.00

of comparison, so that the decomposed income differences are obtained by comparing it with the two nonwhite groups.

Although discrimination appears to be a less important factor than "differences in composition" and "interaction," it still determines a large proportion of racial income differences. Thus, while differences in the distribution of the predictors and the interaction between these and differences in earnings functions account for a total of 67.1 percent of the white-mulatto average income difference, 32.9 percent of this difference can be attributed to discrimination in the labor market. The corresponding figures for Blacks are 73.7 percent for the "composition" and "interaction" components and the remaining 26.3 percent for the "discrimination" component. Again, we arrive at the surprising result that Blacks tend to be less discriminated against than mulattoes.

Thus, we can estimate that the monetary disadvantages suffered by Blacks and mulattoes due to labor market discrimination averaged at about 566 cruzeiros a month. This amount was the "cost of not being white" in Brazil circa 1976. [The minimum monthly wage in 1976 was Cr$ 690.—ED.]

CONCLUSIONS

Although a direct numerical comparison between the present results and those based on the 1960 census is not possible due to differences in geographical coverage and the introduction of the important parental background variables in the 1976 data, the qualitative results are essentially the same:

1. In both studies it was found that Blacks and mulattoes seem to display unexpectedly similar profiles. In this respect nonwhites clearly contrast with whites, and thus to speak of a "nonwhite" racial group does no violence to reality.

2. In both studies we found very substantial differences in economic attainment between whites and nonwhites. The average income for whites was found to be about twice that for nonwhites both in 1960 and in 1976. A significant portion of this interracial income difference can be attributed to discriminatory labor market practices. In the present study we found that this proportion can be estimated as being about one-third of the white-nonwhite average income difference.

3. These results lead us to reject the two hypotheses advanced by the Brazilian sociological literature. Mulattoes do not behave differently from Blacks, nor does race play a negligible role in the process of income attainment. In fact, it was found that Blacks and mulattoes are almost equally discriminated against and that, if anything, Blacks

tend to be relatively less discriminated against than mulattoes. This clearly contradicts the idea of a "mulatto escape-hatch" being the essence of Brazilian race relations.

Summarizing our findings, we can say that we now know the cost of not being white in the Brazilian "racial democracy": about 566 cruzeiros a month in 1976.

BIBLIOGRAPHY

Althauser, R., and M. Wigler 1972. Standardization and Component Analysis. *Sociological Methods and Research* 1: 94–135.

Blinder, A. 1973. Wage Discrimination: Reduced Form and Structural Estimates. *Journal of Human Resources* 7:436–455.

Degler, Carl N. 1971. *Neither Black nor White: Slavery and Race Relations in Brazil and the United States.* New York: Macmillan.

Iam, H. M., and A. Thornton 1945. Decomposition of Differences. *Sociological Methods and Research* 3:341–352.

Masters, S. 1975. *Black-White Income Differentials.* New York: Seminar Press.

Silva, N. V. 1973. Posição social das ocupações. Paper presented to the Seminar on Social Development Policy, Fundação Getúlio Vargas.

———— 1978. White-Nonwhite Income Differentials: Brazil–1960. Ph.D. diss., The University of Michigan.

———— 1980. O preço da côr: Diferenças raciais na distribuição da renda no Brasil. *Pesquisa e planejamento* 10:21–44 (April).

Thurow, L. 1967. The Occupational Distribution of the Returns to Educational Experience for Whites and Negroes. *Proceedings of the Social Statistics Section of the American Statistical Association.*

5

BLACKS AND THE SEARCH FOR POWER IN BRAZIL

PIERRE-MICHEL FONTAINE

The remarks that follow are somewhat tentative. One of the observations from which they spring is the apparent uncertainty or fragility of the power base of the Black politician in Brazil. There is indeed a power paradox facing the Afro-Brazilian politician. He is normally (but not always) elected by what is apparently a rather strong majority of Black voters — although this remains to be verified empirically. At the same time, he has traditionally been unable to consider himself a leader or representative of Blacks. Therefore, he has found himself in a sort of political limbo. To be sure, the increasing mobilization of Blacks has made him feel more and more pressured to decide whether he should declare himself a racial or ethnic politician, or whether he should continue to regard himself as merely a politician, and nothing more.[1] This dilemma suggests some fundamental questions, not only about Blacks in government, but about the power situation of Black people in general in Brazilian society. This is, in part, what led to this inquiry about the power situation of Blacks in Brazil.[2]

SCOPE AND LIMITATIONS OF A MODEL OF POWERLESSNESS

Several years ago, I explored the nature and implications of the Black population of Brazil's powerlessness in society (Fontaine 1975). In recent times, however, I have become increasingly unhappy with this theme. Indeed, powerlessness may not be as common or absolute as we tend to think, and perhaps if we look deep enough, we will see residues, or elements, of power that may not have been apparent on first observation.

In the 1975 study, I argued that Blacks are powerless in Brazil, and gave a series of reasons. First of all, I discussed the myth of racial democracy as an ideological manipulation of the social, racial, and political status quo. I also tried to identify a series of mechanisms of what I termed social immobility in a dynamic economy as the basis of that powerlessness. One such mechanism is educational obstruction, a problem documented in the empirical chapters by Carlos A. Hasenbalg and Nelson do Valle Silva in this volume. Also identified was socialization, which produced the world views that tended to program Blacks into powerlessness—insofar as they learned to integrate and absorb these views—through intimidation and the fostering of accommodation.

Yet another such mechanism was career obstruction, a phenomenon empirically verified by Hasenbalg and Silva. Also listed was the strategy of "blaming the victim," the tendency to call a Black person a racist if he engages in racial protest, which can be an effective way of deterring such attempts. (It is not uncommon to hear Black Brazilians spontaneously defending themselves against the charge of being racists.) Also mentioned as a factor of powerlessness was the tendency for the larger society to alternatively display hostility and indifference toward Black manifestations of racial identity or racial consciousness. Finally, I called attention to the obstructionist impact of the political system, with its strong undercurrents of authoritarianism and violence, even when, as now, it attempts once again to experiment with democracy. As such, the political system is an obstacle to the acquisition and exercise of power by Blacks, and of course by the great majority of whites as well.

As this formulation appeared to be unduly static, some more elements were advanced in an attempt to inventory political resources and liabilities, which turned out to be mostly the latter. I also cautioned that the foregoing referred primarily to São Paulo, and secondarily to Rio de Janeiro. There are indeed significant enough regional variations to suggest that one should be prudent and qualify which region one is talking about. The focus is not so much on Bahia or Pernambuco in the Northeast, or even—at least not all the time—on the state of Rio Grande do Sul in the far south, a most fascinating state indeed.

Rio Grande do Sul is an unusual region. It is the southernmost state of Brazil, and consequently has a small Black minority, inasmuch as Blacks are found in greatest concentration in the Northeast. Yet, through the 1970s and up to 1982, two of the three Blacks in the federal Chamber of Deputies were not from Bahia or Pernambuco, but from Rio Grande do Sul. In fact, one of them was a national leader of the MDB (the opposition Brazilian Democratic Movement, until the Party Reform Law of 1979 reestablished a multi-party system). This was a mulatto, Alceu Collares, who was also the head of the political institute of the MDB. In 1982 he ran unsuccessfully, but strongly, for state governor of Rio Grande do Sul. From 1979 to 1983, he was the leader in the Chamber of Deputies of

Leonel Brizola's Democratic Labor Party (PDT). Why is it that this should be the case in Rio Grande do Sul, where there are very few Blacks; where, in fact, presenting oneself as a Black candidate should be a liability? Why is it that the gaúcho state, as it is sometimes called, should have, compared to all other Brazilian states, the greatest number of prominent Black politicians at the federal level? These are questions for another study. They are only raised here to illustrate the peculiarities of Brazilian regionalism.[3] The focus of this chapter is primarily on São Paulo, and to some extent on Rio de Janeiro.

In making an inventory of Afro-Brazilian political resources and liabilities, my 1975 study also identified the unfavorable demographic situation of Blacks, due to the fact that in Brazil, "blackness" is a residual concept. As in other Latin American countries, the terms "Black" or "Negro" tend to be applied only to those who are as near as possible to the negroid phenotype, preferably showing little or no mixing at all. Blacks are thereby reduced to a relatively small number in social terms, compared to what North Americans might consider the "objective" numbers.[4] Therefore, not only are there socially many fewer Blacks than American eyes might see and Afro-Brazilian leaders might wish, but also the percentage of Blacks is officially declining. This was borne out by the census of 1980 which revealed only 6 percent Blacks. The 1970 census had shown a Black population of 11 percent. This is a liability, because Blacks therefore have less power of numbers than they would otherwise.

The 1975 paper also referred to the much-commented weakness of the Afro-Brazilians' sense of community and identity, an observation with which Michael Mitchell (n.d.) disagrees. Mitchell argues that their sense of identity and community is much stronger than is usually assumed. My paper also pointed to the weakness of the organizational dimension, the lack at the time of organizations of racial protest and the corollary weakness of leadership patterns, that is, the problem of "acephalization" of which Florestan Fernandes wrote (1972).[5] Also mentioned was the lack of salience or visibility of Blacks in Brazilian society, more precisely the fact that their condition was not then viewed as an important social issue or matter of public policy.

In retrospect, all of my comments were somewhat overstated. Perhaps it would have been better to look more closely into the interstices of life, in the nooks and crannies of power relationships. It might then have been possible to see some latent or actual power there that is invisible to a cursory examination. It should be emphasized that the purpose here is not to propose a pluralist or even a neopluralist interpretation of Brazilian society (Manley 1983). Nor am I trying to say that Black Brazilians are much better off than they claim to be.

The first task here is to emphasize the limitations of the argument of powerlessness. Foremost of these is the danger that, in diagnosing powerlessness, the analyst may become blind to the possibilities of change offered by the situation. Such an analysis might remain rather static. On the other hand, where one attempts to identify the existing elements of power, however weak, one may find that there are possibilities of action or even of change that were not previously visible. In fact, there may be certain areas of achievement to which insufficient attention has been paid. In any case, an approach based on such an absolute notion as powerlessness may not be a very effective way of finding out about societies. Therefore, it behooves us to think in terms of the minimal plausibility of total powerlessness and of the possibility, however limited, of power for Blacks in Brazilian society. Before looking at three dimensions of the question of power, let us examine where this power may be located.

One of the reasons why power for Blacks in Brazil is not readily visible is that one is simply looking at the relationship between Blacks and whites, and in that dimension all the power belongs to the latter. That would seem to be consistent with the definition given by Parenti, who argued tht if you are dealing with a group that is dominant and a group that is subordinate, you cannot really refer to both groups having power (1977). He was thus criticizing Richard Merelman who presented a scheme in which relationships of power are identified in terms of power on both sides (1968). I am inclined to agree with Merelman, however, and to suggest that there are differential degrees of power among all involved. It is indeed appropriate to think that, in relationships involving A, B, and C, there can be differential levels of power rather than a monopoly of power on one side and the absence of it on the others. This would seem to be a rather unrealistic way of looking at social reality.

Furthermore, it may be that, whatever power is possessed by Blacks, given their low social status, their low economic strength, and their low level of salience in Brazilian society, is likely to be located at the community level. That is to say, it will be found in power relationships among Blacks themselves rather than between Blacks and whites, even though situations of power of Blacks over whites also exist.[6] Let us then look at some possible dimensions of power.

INTERSTITIAL POWER

First, we will explore the "interstices of power," that is to say the cracks, the nooks, crannies, and small pockets in which power can be found. Consider, for example, the *favelas*, the squatter settlements where the majority of the urban Blacks live. Although they are by no means ghettos in the ethnic or racial sense for, like all lower- to middle-class areas in Brazil, they are racially integrated, they do constitute a useful locus for the examination of power relations involving Blacks. The works of anthropologists Leeds and Leeds (1970), Perlman (1976), and Valladares (1978) indicate that there is a considerable area of power relationships in the favela that many observers tend to ignore because they think of it as a place where people are completely powerless or marginal.

This is not to say that political scientists are altogether unmindful of the reality of this power. It was analyzed in the work of Frank Bonilla as far back as 1961 (1970). On the one hand, Bonilla made the mistake, as everyone did at the time, of thinking of the *favelados* as being rural. There was a theory of urban rurality, in the sense of rural people living in the urban environment. This theory was attacked later by people who questioned the "myth of rurality" (Leeds and Leeds 1970). On the other hand, even though Bonilla conceptualized the favelados as rural people in urban contexts, and although he saw the favelas as a burden on the larger society — a view which Perlman (1976) criticized in her more recent study — he was able to see, through his empirical work, the reality of the political power within the favela. He found that, "From one point of view the *favela* can even be optimistically viewed as an integrating element — as a sort of staging area in which the recently arrived rural migrant is initiated into the mysteries of city life, learns new forms of solidarity, acquires new social and political skills" (Bonilla 1970, 75).

He went on to say, "the problem of the favela is not primarily one of social disorganization within the confines of the favela itself, but rather one of the relationship between the favela and the rest of the society. The favelado himself feels that he is part of a fairly cohesive solidarity group." This is significant, as it refutes a very prevalent myth that the favelados are living in a state of personal and social disorganization.[7] One of the ways in which this solidarity group is effective is by forming organizations for the purpose of manipulating the political and administrative environment in which they find themselves. Not only does each favela have its own association of favelados for this purpose, but these associations are themselves aggregated in large federations, such as the Federation of Associations of Favela Dwellers of the State of Rio de Janeiro (FAFERJ).

The term "favelado" is, of course, not an adequate substitute for "Black," simply because while the great majority of the inhabitants of the favelas are usually Black, this is not necessarily the case in every single favela. The figures that Bonilla gives for the period, probably derived from the 1950 census, indicate that the proportion of Blacks in the favelas was 38 percent at the time and that of mixed bloods was 39 percent. It is reasonable to assume that probably 90 percent of these mixed bloods were people who would be considered Black in the U.S., and that in fact a good 10 percent or 15 percent of the whites (who are 33 percent of the favelados), would also be considered Blacks. Brazilian figures give a total of 77 percent Black and mixed bloods, which probably would mean 80 to 85 percent Black by North American standards. Perlman, on the basis of field work conducted in 1968 to 1969, put the population of Rio's favelas at 20 percent Black and 30 percent mulatto (1976, 59). At the same time, she calculated the Black and mulatto presence in the favela elite sample at 12 percent and 24 percent respectively. These figures clearly indicate that the racial inequalities of the larger social order are reproduced within the favelas. Nonetheless, the degree of Black and mulatto presence in the favela elite is infinitely greater than in the society at large, thus evidencing a far greater level of racial equality. Because of the inordinate Black presence in the favela, we are using the favela as being more or less synonymous with the habitat of Black people in squatter settlement conditions, although not all Blacks live in the favelas.[8]

Some works on squatter settlements discuss the various organizations that emerge in the favelas and the way such organizations are used to manipulate the outside social system (Leeds and Leeds 1979). This they do, for example, at election time by exchanging promises of votes for promises to pave streets, put up street lights, install running water, provide jobs, and the like. At these particular moments, these people exercise a certain amount of power, the power to withhold their votes unless they are promised something in return. But one might argue that what is exercised here is not power but merely influence. Besides, this alone does not denote much more than a passive, or at best a very moderately active political orientation. However, Leeds and Leeds go farther and point to a higher level of activism and participation in the favela, stating, "A great many favela residents are not only interested in, but value actual participation in political matters." They go on to say, "Along with the professional politicians and administrators of the Brazilian polity, the favela residents are the most subtle and conniving politicians we have ever met anywhere, far and away more politically minded in all senses than the American population as a whole and quite incomparable to any equivalent category of people in it, that is to say, in the United States" (Leeds and Leeds 1970, 255).

The case may be slightly overstated here, but the central argument is the existence of detectable amounts of interstitial or residual power, temporary perhaps, furtive or ephemeral, but not less real in those sectors of Brazilian society. One could go further and show how, after the dissolution of the traditional political parties by the bureaucratic-authoritarian regime in the late 1960s, the process of political dialectic between politicians and the favelas turned into a dialectic between bureaucrats and the favelas, in which the same game of mutual manipulation continued. One of the forms this "game" (*jogo*) has taken is what has been characterized as "system distortion" (Valladares 1978). This refers to the ability of the favelados to defeat the most persistent policies of the government by reorienting their implementation through their own initiative or inertia.

More importantly, there have been instances in which the organizing ability of the favelados produced quite remarkable results. Salmen has noted two very significant sets of situations (1969). One includes cases in which mobilization by the favelados prevented them, at least temporarily, from being removed from their neighborhoods to housing projects built by the government in areas where they did not wish to go. The other set refers to cases in which, when a particular governor left office, projects that he had started in the favelas were abandoned. As a result, one favela was in complete disarray because it had become completely dependent on the government, whereas in another favela with a high level of organization, the people were able to negotiate the reestablishment of some of the terminated programs, as well as the initiation of new ones. Again, these processes involve power, however minimal or circumscribed. The goal here is not simply the forestalling of undesirable government action, but the successful negotiation of desirable ones. Favelados have even been found to develop their own legal systems, albeit framed by and subordinate to the larger legal system (Santos 1977).

RESIDUAL POWER

At a second level, we can identify "residual power," that which derives, as already implied, from the mutuality characteristic of patron-client relationships. Patronage involves a face-to-face mutual relationship, albeit unequal and obviously exploitative, between an apparently powerless client and an apparently all-powerful patron. These relationships are pervasive in Latin American society in general and in Brazil in particular, especially in relationships between Blacks and whites. Whatever power can be used by the subordinate element in the relationship, that residual power is worthy of being taken into consideration.

One example of this is a Black person who is *cabo eleitoral* and who will try to gather votes for a white candidate who wants to carry the Black vote. By virtue of his position, the cabo eleitoral may be able to make promises in return for the votes. He is in a position of leadership in relation to other Blacks, a position that he might not otherwise have been able to occupy. Not only can he exercise this power toward his fellow Blacks, but he can also have some elements of power in relation to his boss, the white candidate, who depends on him for votes. There is mutuality in this unequal relationship of patronage, which generates what one might call residual power.[9]

It also happens that this cabo eleitoral, or any other subordinate person in a patronage relationship, is able to establish a subsidiary patronage system, in which some of this residual power is used to his own benefit. Furthermore, some Blacks have attempted to develop their own political patronage systems, their own systems of power. Of direct interest in this respect is Adalberto Camargo, the former Black congressman from the state of São Paulo, who is both a politician and a businessman, and president of the Afro-Brazilian Chamber of Commerce (which is not so much a chamber of commerce of Black people in Brazil as it is an organization to promote trade and investment between Africa and Brazil). This embryonic system of full patronage, not just subpatronage, not of someone who was the cabo eleitoral to somebody else, but someone who claimed to be his own master and a leader of others, steadily declined in the late 1970s and was shattered by the results of the 5 November 1982 elections. Camargo and all of the candidates associated with him lost, following their desertion of the opposition to join the newly formed government Social Democrat Party in 1979.

A different kind of patronage system is discussed by Fernandes in relation to Black faith healer and miracle worker João de Camargo of Sorocaba, a town in the interior of the state of São Paulo (1972, 217–238). João de Camargo came to exercise a great deal of influence around the church which he established there and which resulted in considerable expansion of the city, through the construction of satellite houses, schools, hotels, and other establishments.[10]

INCREMENTAL POWER

The third dimension of power for Black Brazilians is that which is incremental. It may have been true that, in the period between Abolition in 1888 and the early 1930s when the Brazilian Negro Front (Frente Negra Brasileira) began, Blacks lived a life of personal and social disorganization, as Fernandes (1969, 1972) and others have said. Nevertheless, it may be useful to postulate that, from the 1920s onwards, there has been an incremental process of power, at least for some Blacks. Even if it has not been the case principally in relation to whites, it must have occurred in relation to other Blacks, for the FNB could have emerged only as a result of increasing social differentiation and, therefore, of increasing power relationships within the Black milieu. One should therefore look into the relationship between power and socioeconomic mobility and ask whether, as

Blacks become more socioeconomically mobile, they do not ipso facto increase their power potential both in relation to members of the dominant group and in reference to members of their own.

The same question arises with respect to internal migration of Blacks from the Northeast to the South. Does this not affect their power? Finally, it is also useful to inquire the extent to which the *abertura democrática* contains at least the seeds of increased power for Blacks in Brazilian society (see chapter 7).

LOCI OF POWER

Thus far I have suggested, if not demonstrated, that the condition of Blacks in Brazil must be analyzed in terms of power rather than helplessness. What would be the signposts of that power? What would be its mechanisms, sources, and instruments; its loci? Perhaps it should be sought primarily at the community level. If this be so, then what would be the specific entities in which that power is to be found? Two sets of entities may be identified: one that is specialized, or racial-ethnic in character, and another that is general, or society-wide.

SPECIALIZED ETHNIC LOCI OF POTENTIAL POWER

An example of specialized, racial-ethnic entities would be the social clubs, such as the Renaissance Club in Rio or the Aristocrat Club in São Paulo. They are loci and instruments of community power. Their presidents are men of substance who can do favors for people, and do so in a a variety of ways. One of them customarily organizes the equivalent of a potlatch on New Year's Day. It is a display of his wealth in the form of a dinner for a large gathering of people, including lawyers, politicians, at times a congressman, and a variety of others.

Of course, there is another side to it, an expression of the weakness of the organizational structure. During his long tenure, a recent president of one of the clubs had to carry the organization almost single-handedly by financing many of its activities out of his own pocket, not finding within the community the amount of financial support that he would have liked.

Be that as it may, the Aristocrat Club is a source from which community power is extracted and used. It is for this reason that Paulo Salim Maluf, the eventual candidate of the governing Social Democratic Party (PDS) in the 1984 indirect presidential election, paid visits to the club during 1983. There are other associations of all kinds that are characterized for the most part by their ephemeral nature, their inability to fulfill their objectives due to the poverty of their members (Moura 1981). One reason, according to the conventional wisdom, is that the people who have resources tend to stand aloof from such organizations. There are some doubts about this, but it is true that many resources fail to become available to these organizations. The same problem is thought to exist to a lesser extent in the United States and to restrict the independence of some Black organizations there due to their reliance on non-Black sources of funds.

As examples of other specialized ethnic entities, perhaps the most interesting groups are the *irmandades*. One such entity, the Irmandade de Nossa Senhora do Rosário dos Homens Pretos (Brotherhood of Our Lady of the Rosary of the Black Men) has been in existence since the eighteenth century. Irmandades constitute some of the oldest organizations in existence in the Americas. They own or support churches, maintain burial funds, and perform a variety of mutual support tasks. The directors of these groups are, of course, people of substance, but because of their religious orientation in an increasingly secular world and the development of a public welfare organization, among other factors, the irmandades are currently in a state of decline, according to a study by Roberto Camara Benjamin (n.d.) of the Federal Rural University of Pernambuco. The irmandades were also identified as vehicles of status and influence in Azevedo's study of the elites of color in Bahia (1953). One should look into these brotherhoods as loci or instruments of community power.

Another set of important specialized ethnic entities consists of the Afro-Brazilian religious temples of *candomblé*. Their political potential is especially visible at election time, when politicians visit the *terreiros* in search of votes from the faithful. Thus the priest or priestess of a particular terreiro is a potential powerbroker, inasmuch as he or she is a person who controls, or at least leads, a number of people in religion — a dimension that is very significant in the society. This might legitimately be considered a source of power, due to these religious leaders' ability to give or withhold votes. Quite apart from this clearly political strength, candomblé represents more subtle, less tangible forms of power, those of cultural survival, of alternative belief systems, of being separate, and of artistic expression.

GENERAL LOCI OF POTENTIAL POWER

Other sources of power are the more general, society-wide entities, such as sports clubs, business organizations like the Afro-Brazilian Chamber of Commerce, and, of course, the *escolas de samba*, although most have been commercialized and presented as folklore for the benefit of the dominant sectors of society. However, a few samba schools, such as the Escola de Samba Quilombo in Rio de Janeiro, are regarded as authentic instruments of collective self-affirmation and cultural integrity for Blacks.

If one looks at religion from the point of view of society as a whole, then one can consider the *umbanda* temples, which are no longer Afro-Brazilian, in the sense that they have been incorporated into the larger society. Some have erroneously interpreted this phenomenon as signaling an upgrading of the status of Blacks and at least of their culture in Brazilian society. Of greater importance is the dialectic of the evolution of these religions from the ethno-racial to the national realm.

There is such a dialectic, in the sense that umbanda seems to have ceased to be a primarily Afro-Brazilian religion and become primarily Brazilian. It is a syncretic religion unlike candomblé, which is said to be authentically Afro-Brazilian (Ortiz 1978; Brown 1974). There is a relationship of power here at the religious level that is probably very significant and which political scientists need to investigate. In this dialectic of faith and power, the thesis is candomblé and the antithesis umbanda. A new synthesis is being achieved as the more authentic Afro-Brazilian *umbandistas* react to the increased whitening of the religion by developing the Quimbanda, "an attempt by Blacks to regain the religious leadership partially taken away from them" and through which they "symbolically attack a discriminatory society" (Moura 1981, 165).

The Catholic church is another possible focus and instrument of mobilization and power for Black people in Brazil. The Church's increasing efforts to reach Blacks, among other "minorities," is reflected in its various *pastorais*, including the "*pastoral* of the Blacks." An incident in Rio de Janeiro in September 1979 illustrates the dilemma facing the Church. It took place at a round table on the racial question, organized by the satirical weekly *O Pasquim* at the Brazilian Press Association Building. A very popular Black Catholic priest shared the podium with other leaders. The incident exemplifies the kind of traumatic transformation that the Catholic church has been undergoing: the pressures of its crisis of legitimacy; its belated, sometimes frantic, attempt to meet Black people on their own terms, to change and make up for a reputation for having condoned the oppression of Blacks. When the priest spoke, he declared that he was a representative not only of the Catholic church, but also of candomblé, a very remarkable statement coming from a Catholic priest, Black or otherwise.

Not unexpectedly this startling attempt at ecumenism was rejected as paternalistic and the priest was immediately rebuked by several members of the audience. His act was symptomatic of the Church's realization of its own lack of responsiveness to the Black population in the past. The outspoken Black archbishop of Paraiba, Dom José Maria Pires (1981) referred to this period as the "sorry past" of the Church, in a lecture given a few years ago at the Institute for Research on Black Cultures (IPCN) in

Rio de Janeiro. The archbishop has since reportedly shed his nickname of Dom Pelé for the more authentic one of Dom Zumbi, after Zumbi of Palmares, the seventeenth-century hero of the Black movement (*Informativo CEAO*, 4).

TOWARD A THEORY OF POWER FOR THE DISPOSSESSED

When added together, all of these elements can be seen as components of a theory of power for the dispossessed, a theory of "minority" power in an authoritarian and inegalitarian polity and society. The existing models for the study of Blacks in Brazilian political life might be divided into two groups. The first consists of those models which focus on the apparent powerlessness and paralysis of Black Brazilians and whose principal task is to find out why Blacks are powerless and immobile. One can place Lamounier (1968), Souza (1971), Hasenbalg (1979), and Fernandes (1969, 1972) in this particular group. Mitchell (n.d.), however, gives a clear indication of another model, one which at least implies power among Blacks, insofar as they have a racial identity and tend to act out that identity, that is, to stake out their claims to a place in the power relationship. Mitchell does this primarily in relation to the wider society and in terms of electoral politics. In fact, this phenomenon of power should be examined not only in relation to whites, but also in terms of the Blacks' interactions among themselves, and not just in the electoral realm. What political scientists call political behavior is what Mitchell has concerned himself with (n.d.), but one must also look into the domain of the spiritual, and examine what has been called "spiritual resistance" (Ianni 1978).

Ianni is in a middle position, in the sense that he accepts the possibility that there may be certain elements of power there (1978). For example, he talks about the power dimension in Afro-Brazilian religions, although he is ambivalent about that. On the one hand, there probably are some power structures there, but on the other hand, he contends, it has not been proven that the Afro-Brazilian religions present a counter-ideology or counter-structure, as some have suggested. Perhaps one should consider here the argument of Ziegler, who, in a larger context, discusses some of the issues dealt with here under the rubric of "African Power" (1971). Ziegler analyzes Haitian *vodun*, Brazilian candomblé, the concept of African time, and the African sense of history, that enigmatic structure which governs the millennial future of the Black people. He also includes the African liberation movements of the time, as well as the movements of spiritual resistance. All of this he places in a perspective of African-style power, which he sees as being pervasive, not only in Africa, but throughout the African Diaspora.

One can find in all of this the materials for a theory of power. That would include, for instance, the role of Afro-Brazilian religions as power structures, considering not only the relationship between religion and politics at the conceptual level, but also the fact that, inasmuch as the Afro-Brazilian religions constitute non-conformist and unorthodox structures, they are in a position of conflict and/or confrontation with the dominant culture and society. This is so even though they can be and have often been corrupted. The power potential of Afro-Brazilian religions manifests itself, among other ways, in the frequent inclusion of attendance by or visits to the principal *ialorixás* of Bahia in important public functions and ceremonies in that city, including audiences by the president of the Republic or the governor of the State. It was part of the process of abertura under way in the 1980s. As the Brazilian state pursued the reestablishment of contact with what Brazilian social scientists call "civil society," it sought to take on a populistic image, reinforced by the folksy, simple, and direct style of President João Figueiredo. The obverse side of this is, of course, cooptation and control; the possibility of Afro-Brazilian religions being used for purposes of social control. Nevertheless, the potential is also there for them to operate as centers of spiritual resistance. There are at least two views in this respect. One is that of Santos (1977) and Moura (1980), who would see these religions as centers of spiritual resistance contraposed to the existing order. On the other hand, Ianni argues that this has not been proven, although it may be the case (1978).

It bears reiteration that another element of a theory of power for the dispossessed in Brazil is that of organization, as manifested in the Black brotherhoods, clubs, and associations, and the structures of leadership within them. How do they contribute to the allocation of values in society? What do people derive from membership? And what do they have to give up for being members? What are the benefits of membership and the penalties of not being members?

Also important are the elements of political subpatronage and patronage discussed earlier. Embryonic Black patronage provides latent opportunities in a system of concealed prejudice and unsystematic discrimination. Of course, patronage is a fundamentally conservative mechanism; it tends to be an instrument of system maintenance. Its function is to be a mechanism for distribution of residual resources among the dispossessed — which at the same time reaffirms and reinforces the unequal distribution of such resources — by generating or reproducing dependency relationships. Indeed, these elements of power are not necessarily positive forces. Nor are they necessarily conducive to the advancement of the group. They may be in need of being terminated or at least transformed, and therefore have their limitations.

Alternative roads to power exist that should be considered in a theory of the dispossessed. One of these is an essentially political, unconventional mobilization mechanism, such as the Unified Black Movement discussed by Lélia Gonzalez (chapter 8). It is unconventional in the sense that it is not based on the patronage system and is not under the wing of a dominant-group politician, although it seeks to have alliances, dialogues, and rapport with both Black and white politicians. Not only that, it wants to push politicians in a certain direction, to ask them to give certain benefits to Black people in exchange for their votes. This is, then, a very unconventional and unorthodox road to power in the Brazilian context, and it is not for particular individuals, but for the group as a whole.

Such alternative avenues to power have to face the obstacle of inertia, that is to say, the weight of both the seemingly low orientation of Blacks toward racial mobilization and of the extant patronage systems. The future of the Black movement in Brazil and the political future of Brazilian Blacks in general is going to depend very much on the way in which that power relationship is resolved; on whether these systems of patronage and subpatronage will be swept aside in favor of alternative roads to power, or whether they will succeed in blocking them. Now that full civilian government has returned with the election of the late Tancredo Neves to the Presidency of Brazil by the Electoral College on 15 March 1985, this question is a most crucial one.

NOTES

1. The debacle suffered by Black candidates in the states of Rio de Janeiro and São Paulo (only two elected out of about sixty candidates in São Paulo) in the November 1982 elections would seem to suggest the option of remaining a mere politician. This is not so clear, however. While it is possible to repeat with several disgruntled politicians that "negro não vota em negro" (Blacks don't vote for Blacks), there are enough alternative explanations for this massive electoral failure to justify caution in reaching a conclusion on the subject.

2. The 1982 electoral disaster provoked a great deal of soul searching among Black candidates and within the Black Movement itself. Some have dug to the very root of the problem and have even argued with a good measure of persuasiveness that, historically, electoral politics has always weakened and even decimated the Black Movement (Ferreira and Pereira, 1983).

3. It is remarkable that the third Black federal deputy in the 1970s and until early 1983, Adalberto Camargo, was from São Paulo, another southern state, which is identified more with sizable populations of Italians and Japanese, though substantial numbers of Blacks have moved to that industrial center over the last century in search of economic opportunities. Equally challenging is the fact that the only elected Afro-Brazilian senator, the mulatto Nelson Carneiro, is from Rio de Janeiro, yet another southern state which in the past several decades has been the recipient of millions of southward-migrating

Blacks who have gone to crowd its *favelas*. Even the two Afro-Brazilian substitute senators (*suplentes*) who served briefly in 1980 and 1981 were not from the predominantly Black Northeast. One was Valdão Varjão (1980) from Mato Grosso in the Center West. The other was the mulattress Senator Laélia Contreiras Agra de Alcantara (PMDP) from Acre in the Far West. One of the only two Blacks in the Federal Congress following the 1982 elections, Abdias do Nascimento (PDT-RJ), has pointed out the incongruity that the state of Bahia, with a majority Black population, does not have even one Black state legislator. (See "Deputado volta a criticar Jorge Amado," *O estado de São Paulo*, 23 November 1983, and Gilson Rebello, "Jorge Amado, racismo em xeque," *O estado de São Paulo*, 27 November 1983.) The state of Bahia, however, has not been completely devoid of Black municipal politicians, including Edvaldo Britto, former mayor of the capital, Salvador, and considered by some to be a possible state governor. As for the neighboring northeastern state of Sergipe, its current governor, João Alves Filho, is Black.

4. In an article that has since become a classic, Oracy Nogueira (1955) offered a cogent distinction between Brazil and its assimilationist model characterized by prejudice based on physical appearance (*preconceito de marca*) and the United States and its segregationist model based on consanguinity (*preconceito racial de origem*). More recently, Pereira (1982, 1293) has noted how contemporary Black ideology attempts to invert the demographic trends by "ideologically and politically 'constructing' more Blacks" (my translation).

5. Subsequent research on my part has not only verified the validity of Mitchell's (n.d.) position on racial identity but also the existence of a far larger and more complex universe of Black organizations than most had suspected (Fontaine 1981, n.d.).

6. As late as 1979, Taylor (1979, 1405) complained that, in the U.S., "social science research has been notably ethnocentric in its treatment of black ethnicity. The emphasis has been largely on the etiquette of intergroup relations and on the attitudes and behaviour of whites toward blacks, with little attention given to black-black relationships."

7. The same fallacy of the alleged personal and social disorganization of Blacks in American urban ghettos was exposed by research conducted in the late 1960s and the 1970s by, among others, Suttles (1968), Stack (1974), and Gutman (1976).

8. As Perlman (1976, 58) states, "The third who are black represent nearly *all* of Rio's blacks; favela whites, on the other hand, are but a fraction of all whites living in the city."

9. Of course, for this process to operate smoothly and effectively, the white officeholders must to a minimal extent deliver on their promises. They do not always, however, as many São Paulo Black politicians and movement leaders discovered to their bitter disappointment following the 1982 general elections. When as late as the second quarter of 1983 the victorious opposition party of the Brazilian Democratic Movement had failed to deliver the high state government posts promised to the Black leadership in return for their support, a furious debate followed on the treacherousness of white political parties and politicians (Ferreira and Pereira 1983; "Entidade negra peemedebista critica Montoro," *Folha de São Paulo*, 7 March 1983; Paulo Valle, "Presença no governo não exclui o racismo," *ibid.*, 8 May 1983; "Montoro e Brizola estiveram no centro das discussões," *ibid.*). This state of affairs led Ferreira and Pereira (1983) to reject traditional electoral politics in favor of strengthening the Black movement as an independent social force with the participation of the majority of Blacks. The usefulness of electoral politics to Blacks is not dependent on absolute numbers. Gerber (1976) has shown that Ohio Blacks had more political power — which resulted in favorable state civil rights legislation — between 1860 and 1910, when they constituted only 3 percent of the state population, than in the subsequent period when their numbers grew. The explanation was in the small margins of victory in the Reconstruction period between Republicans

and Democrats and the resulting stiff competition for the Black vote. Nationwide, however, even during the Reconstruction period, the white pursuit of the Black vote was naturally aimed at strengthening the parties or white sectional interests within them (Grossman 1976).

10. This urbanizing imperative has been identified by Queiroz as a common characteristic of rural messiahs in Brazil who, in her judgment, "were gripped by what might be termed a 'fear of living alone' which made them want to live in the city [and] was shared by the rest of the population." One must, however, question Queiroz's subsequent assertion that "Afro-Brazilian cults . . . are of no interest at all to the majority of Brazilians [and] only subsist in 'pockets' in a few areas where agriculture for export markets has grown up." She was excessively critical of Roger Bastide's concept of religious duality and of the limited scope of his studies on the religious phenomenon in Brazil (Queiroz 1977, 308).

BIBLIOGRAPHY

Azevedo, Thales de 1953. *Les élites de couleur dans une ville brésilienne.* Paris: UNESCO.

Blalock, Hubert M. 1967. *A Theory of Minority Group Relations.* New York: Wiley.

Benjamin, Roberto Camara n.d. *Festa do Rosário de Pombal.* Universidade Federal da Paraiba: Editora Universitária.

Bojunga, Claudio 1978. O Brasileiro negro, 90 anos depois. *Encontros com a civilização brasileira* 1 (July): 175-204.

Bonilla, Frank 1970. "Rio's Favelas: The Rural Slum within the City." In *Peasants in Cities: Readings in the Anthropology of Urbanization,* edited by William Mangin, 72-79. Boston: Houghton Mifflin.

Brown, Diana B. 1974. Umbanda: Politics of an Urban Religious Movement. Ph.D. diss., Columbia University.

Dzidzienyo, Anani 1971. *The Position of Blacks in Brazilian Society.* London: Minority Rights Group.

Fernandes, Florestan 1969. *The Negro in Brazilian Society.* New York: Columbia University Press.

———— 1972. *O Negro no mundo dos brancos.* São Paulo: Difusão Europeia do Livro.

———— 1977. *Circuito fechado.* São Paulo: HUCITEC.

Ferreira, Yedo, and Amauri Mendes Pereira 1983. *O Movimento Negro e as eleições.* Rio de Janeiro: Pamphlet No. 1, SINBA, Instituto de Pesquisas das Culturas Negras (IPCN).

Fontaine, Pierre-Michel 1975. The Dynamics of Black Powerlessness in Brazil: The Case of São Paulo. Washington, D.C.: African Heritage Studies Association. Mimeo.

———— 1981. "Transnational Relations and Racial Mobilization: Emerging Black Movements in Brazil." In *Ethnic Identities in a Transnational World,* edited by John F. Stack, Jr., 141-162. Westport, Conn.: Greenwood Press.

———— n.d. *Race and Class in an Authoritarian Social Order: The Black Condition in Brazil.* Forthcoming.

Freyre, Gilberto 1956. A escravidão, a monarquia e o Brasil moderno. *Revista brasileira de estudos políticos* 1 (December 1956): 39-48.

———— 1963. Ethnic Democracy: The Brazilian Example. *Americas* 13 (December): 1-6.

———— 1966. *The Racial Factor in Contemporary Politics.* Sussex, England: University of Sussex.

Gerber, David A. 1976. *Black Ohio and the Color Line 1860-1915.* Urbana, Ill.: University of Illinois Press.

72   Pierre-Michel Fontaine

Grossman, Lawrence 1976. *The Democratic Party and the Negro: Northern and National Politics, 1868-92.* Urbana: University of Illinois Press.

Gutman, Herbert 1976. *The Black Family in Slavery and Freedom: 1750-1925.* New York: Pantheon.

Hasenbalg, Carlos A. 1979. *Discriminação e desigualdades raciais no Brasil.* Preface by F. H. Cardoso; translated by Patrick Burglin. Rio de Janeiro: Edições Graal Ltda.

Ianni, Octávio 1978. *Escravidão e racismo.* São Paulo: Editora HUCITEC.

Informativo CEAO 1983 Centro de Estudos Afro-Orientais, Federal University of Bahia, Salvador, Bahia 5(9).

Lamounier, Bolivar 1968. Raça e classe na política brasileira. *Cadernos Brasileiros* 8(3): 34-50 (May-June).

Leeds, Anthony, and Elizabeth Leeds 1970. "Brazil and the Myth of Urban Rurality." In *City and Country in the Third World: Issues in the Modernization of Latin America,* edited by Arthur J. Field, 229-285. Cambridge: Schenkman.

Manley, John 1983. Neopluralism: A Class Analysis of Pluralism I and Pluralism II. *The American Political Science Review* 77(2): 368-383 (June).

Merelman, Richard M. 1968. On the Neo-Elitist Critique of Community Power. *The American Political Science Review* 62(2): 451-460 (June).

Mitchell, Michael n.d. *Racial Consciousness and the Political Attitudes and Behavior of Blacks in São Paulo, Brazil.* Forthcoming.

Moura, Clovis 1980. "Organizações negras." In *São Paulo: O povo em movimento,* edited by Paul Singer and Vinicius Caldeira Brant, 143-175. Petrópolis: Editora Vozes.

Nogueira, Oracy 1955. Preconceito de marca e preconceito racial de origem. *Anais do XXXI Congresso Internacional de Americanistas* 1:409-434. São Paulo: Ed. Anhembi.

Ortiz, Renato 1978. *A morte branca do feiticeiro negro.* Petrópolis: Editora Vozes.

———— 1982. Os negros e os partidos. *Folha de São Paulo* (June 13): 10-11.

Parenti, Michael 1977. *Power and the Powerless.* New York: St. Martin's Press.

Pereira, João Baptista Borges 1982. Aspectos do comportamento político do negro em São Paulo. *Ciencia e cultura* 34(10): 1286-1294 (October).

Perlman, Janice 1976. *The Myth of Marginality.* Berkeley: University of California Press.

Pires, Dom José Maria 1981. *A vez do negro na Igreja.* Rio de Janeiro: COOMCIMPRA.

Queiroz, Maria Isaura Pereira de 1977. Messiahs, Miracle Workers and Catholic Duality in Brazil. *International Social Science Journal* 29(2): 308ff.

Salmen, Lawrence F. 1969. A Perspective on the Resettlement of Squatters in Brazil. *América Latina* (January-March): 73-95.

Santos, Boaventura de Souza 1977. The Law of the Oppressed: The Construction and Reproduction of Legality in Pasargada. *Law and Society Review* 12(1): 5-126 (Fall).

Santos, Juana Elbein dos 1975. *Os Nagos e a morte,* 2d ed. Petrópolis: Editora Vozes.

Souza, Amaury de 1971. Raça e política no Brasil urbano. *Revista de administração de empresas* 2(4): 61-70 (December).

Stack, Carol 1974. *All Our Kin: Strategies for Survival in a Black Community.* New York: Harper & Row.

Suttles, Gerald 1968. *The Social Order of the Slum.* Chicago: University of Chicago Press.

Taylor, Ronald L. 1979. Black Ethnicity and the Persistence of Ethnogenesis. *American Journal of Sociology* 84(6): 1401-1423 (May).

Valladares, Lícia do Prado 1978. *Passa-se uma casa,* 2d ed. Rio de Janeiro: Zahar Editores.

Varjão, Sen. Valdon 1980. *Negro sim, escravo não.* Brasília.

Ziegler, Jean 1971. *Le pouvoir africain.* Paris: Editions du Seuil.

6

BROWN INTO BLACK: CHANGING RACIAL ATTITUDES OF AFRO-BRAZILIAN UNIVERSITY STUDENTS

J. MICHAEL TURNER

The historical context this chapter covers is the period from 1971 to 1978. It is a study based upon observations, interviews, and other research activities conducted in Brazil. Particular emphasis will be given to the years from 1976 to 1978.[1] It appears that during those three years significant transformations occurred in the perceptions of racial group identity on the part of Afro-Brazilian students at the major universities throughout Brazil. In 1971, the very few Afro-Brazilian students enrolled in universities tended to identify with white cultural norms and sought to disengage from Black culture, as represented by religion or music. They perceived these cultural manifestations and direct identification with African culture to be lower class and therefore undesirable.[2]

The majority of these students, when asked about race relations within Brazil at the beginning of the 1970s, concurred with Brazilian public opinion that there was a general absence of racial prejudice in the country. When acts of discrimination were admitted, the explanation supported by the students was that these occurrences were based upon class perceptions rather than upon racial identification. The person being discriminated against was perceived as being of the lower classes, not Afro-Brazilian; this class explanation was a precept dearly held by both students and nonstudents. Repeated questioning by foreign researchers would almost inevitably elicit the response that discrimination was based upon class.[3]

Changes within national society and within the Afro-Brazilian community had substantially modified university student opinion as to race and class by 1976. The popular "Black Rio" movement, which began in the slums of Rio's Zona Norte, had made inroads into the Afro-Brazilian student population.[4] As the cultural and quasi-political movement spread from Rio to other major Brazilian urban centers, the influence of the "soul" identification also spread within their Afro-Brazilian university student populations.[5] Students at the University of Brasília would meet to talk about "Afro" culture and its relationship to their group at an elite university in a manner which was replicated by students at Porto Alegre's Federal University of Rio Grande do Sul. There was a transformation of attitude among Afro-Brazilian students, which for a foreign researcher away from Brazil between 1971 and 1976 (with a brief visit to Bahia in 1974) was both surprising and initially somewhat bewildering.[6]

The period from 1976 to 1979 witnessed the growth of more Afro-Brazilian student organizations and cultural groups connected with institutions of higher learning, with such activities as study weeks of Afro-Brazilian culture in Joinville, Santa Catarina, as well as at the Fluminense Federal University in Niterói, Guanabara Bay, across from Rio de Janeiro.[7] The impetus for this student activity came from within the universities, which were experiencing various kinds of political unrest on the campuses between 1976 and 1978, as well as from larger concerns and tensions within the national society itself.[8] Increased numbers of Afro-Brazilians at the nation's colleges and universities also served to increase this organizational activity, although not all of them were interested or willing to take part in discussions of Négritude or the implications of the Foreign Ministry's well-publicized African foreign policy for the nation's Black community.[9] Those who were committed to such discussions were never large in number, but they were vocal, reasonably well organized, and able to obtain access to a mimeograph machine.

What tended to distinguish the student groups of 1976 to 1978 from those of the previous period, were their frequent attempts to articulate the problems of disadvantaged Afro-Brazilians while avoiding a polemic that would overstep the boundaries set by government, be it at a national, state, municipal, or university level.[10] Conferences and seminars, study weeks, and encounters inevitably centered upon themes of Afro-Brazilian culture and historical contributions to the formation of the national society. Discussion at such gatherings usually took place during the period reserved for questions and answers. From the accepted themes and topics, participants could then move on to issues or problems of more immediate concern to the group, within the more general and innocuous context of a discussion of culture. There was an acute sense of what was permissible and what would be problematic.[11]

The students viewed their own concerns as identical to those of poor Blacks and declared that their access to a university education, often at great family financial sacrifice, had to be employed to improve conditions for the larger community. The manner in which this was to be done remained vague, but the philosophy and ideological standards of the groups were clear. This represented a change from earlier in the decade when it was thought, if not publicly stated, by some of the students that the university education process should serve to "whiten" the individual, bringing that person within the collective mentality of Brazilian society and making him or her less Afro-Brazilian and therefore more socially acceptable.[12] By 1977, that attitude seemed no longer prevalent among Afro-Brazilian students I encountered in Brasília, Rio, São Paulo, and Porto Alegre. The following sections demonstrate the evolution of this racial consciousness.

SALVADOR DA BAHIA (EARLY 1970s)

There was a general impression among the population under study in the early 1970s that the fact of having obtained an education, or enrollment in a professional course or foreign language study, could provide access to desired social mobility. When social mobility did not occur as anticipated, understandable feelings of resentment and confusion resulted as to the causes of this "failure." The following example will serve as an illustration of this.

"Antonio," an Afro-Brazilian from Bahia, was twenty-two years of age in 1971, married, with one child. He had completed secondary school but did not have enough money to pay for a pre–college-entrance examination cram course, which he needed to take if he were to be a successful candidate for admission to the Federal University of Bahia. Antonio was able to pay for English courses at a language institute, demonstrated an aptitude for languages, and took pride in his ability to speak a foreign language. In 1971 he was working for a North American oil drilling company prospecting for oil off the Bahian coast. While Antonio found the work to be difficult, dirty, and demanding long hours, he felt that working with non–Portuguese-speaking Americans served to improve his English language skills.

During the same period he attempted to pass a series of written and oral examinations for clerical positions. The positions all required a spoken and written knowledge of English. He was never successful in any of the examinations. If he passed the written section, he was rejected in the oral follow-up.[13] Each rejection resulted in increased frustration and a determination to take a more advanced English course. As his language studies did not yield him a better job, Antonio finally concluded that, for him, remaining in Brazil was useless, because as a Black, he would never be able to obtain a position commensurate with the skills he had acquired.

A second example illustrates the complexity of the problem of acceptance for educated Afro-Brazilians:

"José," a very well-trained Afro-Brazilian lawyer and legal scholar, attempted to pass a set of examinations to be appointed to the Law Faculty of the University of Bahia in 1970 with all proper academic credentials and the required thesis. In a competition organized within the University, the candidate received the highest scores on the written examination and defense of his thesis, but was failed in the oral examination. José repeated his unsuccessful attempt for four years until 1974, when the competitive oral examinations were opened for attendance by the general public. José invited friends, legal associates, and colleagues to attend his examination. He again received the highest scores on all of the written examinations and, as the public had been invited to attend, he also passed the oral.

In both examples there was an implicit, though unproven understanding that racism was the determining factor in the difficulties Antonio and José faced in achieving their desired professional goals. There was also a reluctance on the part of both individuals to accept prejudice as an attitude and discriminatory behavior as facts of Brazilian national life (Dzidzienyo 1971). After each failure to obtain a clerical position, Antonio would initially blame himself, or the fact that he had married and assumed family responsibilities too quickly, which prevented him from devoting sufficient time to studying, resulting in his failure to qualify for the position. He also blamed himself for not having sufficient funds to pay for the cram course which would have meant admission to the university and a supposed open door to later professional achievement. The experience of José suggests that admission to the university and a brilliant academic career were not necessarily guarantees of professional success for Afro-Brazilians and that the oft-proclaimed theory of "whitening" or social mobility through education and intellectual endeavor was simply not functioning.[14]

The prevalence of the ideology of racial democracy among Blacks as well as whites was confusing and frustrating for the foreign researcher interested in understanding the Brazilian racial mosaic at the beginning of the 1970s. There appeared to be an emotional necessity to believe in the racial democracy and "whitening" theories, as the ideas had been so propagated within the country that to speak against them seemed at times to be speaking against Brazil, a subversive act. In the early 1970s, the era of the Medici government, to be deemed subversive was dangerous and possibly fatal.[15] The foreign researcher would point to example after example of seemingly blatant discrimination or attitudes indicative of racial prejudice, only to be told by Afro-Brazilians that one had not understood the reality or social context of the situation, or all of the mitigating factors and circumstances. Discussion concerning race relations in Brazil often became difficult for the foreign researcher and Brazilian colleagues as levels of frustration rose. In the early 1970s there was a general, although not total, public commitment to the racial democracy theory in Bahia.[16]

RIO DE JANEIRO (EARLY 1970s)

The situation in Rio presented certain differences. Some of the students there did publicly question the racial democracy theory and its implicit assimilationist assumptions. As a muted critique of the theory, they used the concept of Négritude. This cultural awareness and consciousness was linked to an interest in and an emotional commitment to Africa. In the early 1970s the African embassies of Senegal, Ghana, Nigeria, and Ivory Coast were still located in Rio, providing possibilities for social interaction with African diplomats and cultural materials concerning Africa. Négritude, when expanded from the Senghor-Césaire-Diop model, was a popular concept among many students, as it sought to reevaluate, in their own terms, traditional African cultures and manifestations of these cultures within the Diaspora.[17] The relationship of culture to political activity described by the three francophone authors and activists also interested the Afro-Brazilian students, as the evident, if not explicit, relationship was sufficiently viable to offer conditions for discussion during the repressive political regime of 1971. Culture was and continues to be a reasonably safe umbrella under which varied topics may be discussed, including the themes of politics and economics.[18]

Race relations in the United States, as perceived by Afro-Brazilian students at the beginning of the 1970s, posed serious problems as they saw only the violence and the imprisonment of Black protestors and did not want to have such scenes repeated in their own country. In Brazil, the seeming absence of overt racial violence was a point of pride, and comparisons were quick to be made between the two countries, underlining the intractability of the racial situation in the United States. For a North American researcher the Brazilian image of race relations in the United States often seemed to be ten years behind the actual events occurring. In 1971 the situation as perceived by Brazilians was more of the era of 1963 to 1964, with bus burnings and church bombings and massive civil disobedience, instead of the actual selective police actions against Black Panthers and other so-called radical groups.[19]

Black American researchers arriving in Brazil were sometimes treated as survivors of a war, while comments on the part of some Afro-Brazilian students indicated an unwillingness ever to visit the United States because of fear of violence. There was also a certain nationalistic pride that the U.S. was experiencing such obvious difficulties in resolving the problems of being a multiracial society, whereas in Brazil the more subtle interactions seemed not to result in civil disobedience (foolhardy under an authoritarian regime), or in group violence. However, the question remained whether the apparently subtle system of discrimination, which in certain geographic areas was decidedly less subtle (namely, southern Brazil), would be easier to counteract than the more overt North American brand of prejudice.[20] By the mid-1970s, aspects of the Brazilian and North American situations would bear more and more resemblance to one another, and the responses of Afro-Brazilians to their own condition would become more overt and decisive.[21]

AFRO-BRAZILIAN STUDENT MOVEMENTS IN THE MID-1970s

By the middle of the decade, images and symbols had come to represent cultural and political identifications for Afro-Brazilian students. In 1971, the "Afro" hairstyles were considered to be unattractive and demeaning by many Afro-Brazilians. By 1976, Afros as worn in Brazil (hennaed red and of large circumference) were more noticeable than they had been in the United States, where by the mid-1970s the style had become less popular and less of a political and cultural statement.[22] African clothing, such as dashikis and headties, were fashionable among Afro-Brazilian students, and there was and continues to be much serious discussion concerning the desirability of using the word *preto* in substitution for *negro*.[23] "Black Rio" had arrived.

While a full discussion of the Black Rio, or Soul-Brazil, movement is not within the purview of this chapter, the immediate effects of this cultural and quasi-political movement were felt within the Black university community with the growth of a consciousness of blackness and of the worth and value inherent in that Black (but as yet undefined) identity. The movement, which was never really organized as such, but so perceived by the national media, began among the lower-class Black urban youth in Rio de Janeiro but quickly spread to all of the country's major urban centers, so that it was possible to talk about a "Black Porto Alegre," as well as a "Black Salvador," or a "Soul-Brasília." The Blacks-only dances, the soul handshakes, and ostensible adherence to music that was either from the United States or derived its origins from U.S. soul music, had an impact on many young Afro-Brazilians, who staged soul parties and gatherings throughout the country.

White Brazilian reaction was quick and, not surprisingly, extremely hostile to this expression of Afro-Brazilian proto-cultural nationalism. Publications such as the *Jornal do Brasil* (Rio) ran articles, signed by writers such as Gilberto Freyre, condemning Black Rio as an imposition of North American cultural values and racist separatist tendencies on what had been a "calm and happy" Black Brazilian populace.[24] Coming at the time of Brazilian irritation with perceived North American meddling in the area of human rights violations in Brazil and attempted interference in the transfer of West German nuclear technology there, the Soul-Brazil movement was classified as another form of interventionism.[25]

Black Rio was attacked not only in the press but also in the more popular broadcast media. The weekly television variety program "Fantástico" launched several attacks on and critical assessments of the movement. The tone of the critique was interesting, as the United States was castigated for imposing yet another set of cultural values upon Brazilians, while Afro-Brazilians were criticized for abandoning the samba and other authentic Afro-Brazilian cultural forms to embrace foreign "soul."[26] White Brazilians could not understand this "betrayal" of the national culture and made it clear that they would not easily tolerate manifestations of Afro-Brazilian cultural nationalism expressed in soul handshakes, or dances and parties with a philosophy of admission for Blacks only. There was a sense of bewilderment that Afro-Brazilians seemed to be abandoning the one possession historically left to them in Brazil, their culture. During the carnaval parades of 1977, when groups of young Afro-Brazilians abandoned samba dancing and formed lines to present a dance called the "California strut," there was a feeling of consternation among the watching crowds in Bahia and Rio de Janeiro.[27] Afro-Brazilian self-expression and definition had changed with Black Rio, and despite its nebulous ideology and political stance, this lower-class–urban youth phenomenon marked a departure from the past. It would also affect relations with Afro-Brazilians who had not directly participated in the movement.

Afro-Brazilian university students watched the national "backlash" to the Black Rio movement closely, and they understood that society prescribed precise limits for expressions of cultural nationalism beyond which it was not prepared to tolerate such activities. The students reinforced their efforts to work within the existing limits to raise the level of awareness concerning problems confronting Afro-Brazilians. They were concerned that the regular and popular manifestations fo their culture, as expressed in the religious ceremonies of *candomblé* and *macumba*, or in music and dance as represented by the carnaval parades and samba schools were daily being appropriated by the dominant Euro-Brazilian society.

The acceptance and co-optation of their culture—one has only to remember photographs published in the national media of the Governor of Bahia and novelist Jorge Amado posing with their *mãe-de-santo*, all affirming their commitment to Black culture[28]—did not result in the acceptance of Afro-Brazilians in other parts of Brazilian society (Dzidzienyo

1978). For them, despite the fashionable fascination with their culture, socioeconomic status remained marginal in relation to the rest of society. It was from within this state of general deprivation that they saw their traditional culture being wrested from their control. At the same time, national attention was focused on several incidents of blatant racial discrimination directed against middle-class Afro-Brazilians.

These racial incidents occurred in the interior of Rio Grande do Sul, Rio de Janeiro, and Salvador, and served as an indication that, when obtained by Black Brazilians, the cherished middle-class or professional status did not serve as an impregnable defense against racism (Hasenbalg 1979, 271–281). It was always necessary to remember that before the university degree or title, and in the eyes of the general society, the individual was first Black and then a middle-class professional. As the incidents were not concentrated in a single geographical region, Afro-Brazilian students understood that discrimination could happen anywhere in the country and that there was no automatic immunity to the consequences of blackness (Oliveira, Porcaro, and Araújo 1980).

It was during this period that students at many of the nation's universities began organizing study weeks, conferences, and symposia on Afro-Brazilian history and culture. The meetings usually coincided with the date of the death of Zumbi, the leader of the independent state of Palmares, who was said to have been killed on 20 November 1695 (dos Santos 1981). The date has become a symbol of awareness and Black consciousness for many who do not recognize the "national" Black Brazilian Day, 13 May, which commemorates the date of the abolition of slavery in 1888.[29] The November study weeks occurred in São Paulo, Minas Gerais, Ceará, Rio Grande do Sul, and Rio de Janeiro, indicating the national commitment of students to raising these issues and concerns. An example of the evolution of such a program at the Fluminense Federal University in Niterói (Rio de Janeiro) serves to indicate the problematic nature of the student group's program genesis and possible future development.

Afro-Brazilian students at Fluminense organized their first study week in 1974. As a result of that initial series of meetings, they asked the university for at least one course dealing with either Afro-Brazilian history or culture. Their request was granted by the Anthropology Department, which then fashioned an essentially culturalist course that concentrated on religious and cultural contributions to national society. The course did not concern itself with more contemporary issues and the condition of the Afro-Brazilian, nor did it attempt to analyze or even provide a basic chronology of the historical contributions of Blacks to Brazilian society. While it was offered for several semesters beginning in 1974, it had become only a listing in the course catalogue by 1977, as the Anthropology Department could not find an instructor for it. During the semesters the Afro-

Brazilian course had been offered, its program content, outline, and reference bibliography were never modified or updated by the professors teaching it. As of the final semester of 1979, it continued to lack a professor. While there are courses on Brazilian slavery, no offerings specifically dealing with Afro-Brazilians, or indeed Africa, are available or presently contemplated at Fluminense.

The Fluminense student group known as the André Rebouças Study Group (named after the nineteenth-century Afro-Brazilian abolitionist leader and intellectual), was able to institutionalize its annual November study-week and have the event officially registered with the Federal Ministry of Education in Brasília.[30] It has not been as successful in achieving its desired goals within its own university. Student requests for the recruitment of minority faculty have been countered by the University's claim that finding qualified Afro-Brazilian professors with at least an M.A. degree, if not a doctorate, has proved to be impossible. Courses on Afro-Brazilian or African history also remain impossible to offer, as the University maintains that there is an absence of qualified professors. Attempts by the students to present as candidates Afro-Brazilians with publications and experience in community affairs as well as in Afro-Brazilian Studies (but lacking advanced university degrees), have not been successful, as Fluminense has maintained that hiring instructors without an advanced degree would be detrimental to the institution.

During the 1977 symposium, the subject of minority staff recruitment was discussed with the rector of the University, and University officials were reminded that in other departments (Communications being cited as an example), instructors had been hired without advanced degrees and made excellent contributions to the institution. Nevertheless, as of the first semester of 1981, the University still refused to consider minority candidates without advanced degrees (but with relevant life-experience) for instructorships.

For the André Rebouças Group, the inability to follow through upon student and general community interest generated by the annual week-long symposium and to present either continuing courses or public lectures or cultural events, has led to a certain atrophy of the annual event. The danger has developed of a certain ritualization of the annual seminar and the concomitant loss of the primal energy or force that was present in its earlier stages and which led to demands for innovation in courses and staffing from the student organizers.[31] It will be necessary to create other forums to recapture this energy. All of this remains difficult, however, if students lack professors to encourage, assist, and advise them on programs and organizational goals and problems. The very small number of Afro-Brazilian faculty throughout Brazilian universities remains a serious problem, not only for students needing role models as well as instructors, but more generally for the eventual introduction of Afro-Brazilian Studies courses and curricula within Brazil's higher education system.[32]

Some of the problems encountered by the André Rebouças Group have also been experienced elsewhere, particularly in the matter of course offerings in Afro-Brazilian or African Studies. The Federal University of Bahia and its Center of Afro-Oriental Studies, despite a long and often distinguished institutional history supporting research on Afro-Brazilian religions, and linguistic and cultural manifestations, lacked a professor for course offerings on African history for more than four years. Only in 1981 was African history again offered in Bahia at the Federal University. African history, with the exception of a "Post-Independence Political History" course offered at the Candido Mendes University's Center of Afro-Asian Studies in Rio, is rarely taught at Brazilian universities, despite its occasional listing in catalogues, as in Salvador and at the University of Brasília. The Center of African Studies at the University of São Paulo does offer courses on Africa, listed and taught within the Social Science Department of the University. However, a general survey course on the history of the African continent was not available as of the first semester of 1981. Members of the Faculty Search Committee of the History Department at Brasília argue that they have been attempting to recruit a professor of African history for more than two years, but have not been able to find a person with a doctorate degree to fill the teaching position created during the time that this author was a faculty member in that department.[33]

Research that is directly related to Afro-Brazilian Studies and coordinated among a group of interested scholars often remains outside of the universities. These study groups, such as the Rebouças Group at Fluminense, or researchers at the São Paulo state university of São Carlos, might have some institutional ties. Or, as is the case of SECNEB, they are private institutes, with independent and limited funding capacities and resources.[34] There is another distinction to be made between such unofficial research institutes and groups that attempt to relate a concern for and interest in Afro-Brazilian culture with projects for social and community action. Activist organizations such as Quilombo, Rio's alternative samba school, the Afro-Brazilian Research Dance Company Olorum Baba Mim, the IPCN, Porto Alegre's Instituto Senghor, or the Palmares organization, have succeeded in publishing newsletters, newspapers, and occasional papers on Afro-Brazilian culture and contemporary issues and problems confronting that community. In all cases, these institutes and groups are producing materials on Afro-Brazil with minimal resources. The scholarship and content of these materials are often quite good. Nevertheless, the impact of the production, and its immediate audience, are usually limited to the small group of the already-committed, that is, those who understand the importance of Afro-Brazilian Studies and its cultural and potentially important political implications.[35]

The next step is to devise a method or strategy for successfully moving Afro-Brazilian Studies from its present institutionally marginal position to one more interrelated with Brazilian social science. Those concerned with Afro-Brazilian Studies as a discipline must ask themselves what are the short- and long-range objectives for a program of research, training, and application. As it is probable that in Brazil there will be even greater difficulty in establishing the legitimacy of Afro-Brazilian Studies than was the case in the United States, it becomes of critical importance that those committed to the concept define and understand their aims and objectives as fully as possible. The Brazilian social science community, when not openly hostile to the idea of Afro-Brazilian Studies (criticizing it either from a leftist perspective for failing to give credence to a class analysis of social change, or from the right for being demagogic and potentially racist), still tends to ignore such research, relegating it to folkloric studies.[36]

Students are presently attempting to develop a program devoted to the study of Afro-Brazilians, and assessing the potential of such a program or discipline for analyzing and improving conditions for poor, non-white, Brazilians. In meetings with student groups throughout Brazil, I have listened to discussions concerned with applying the knowledge and information being acquired at the universities to the solution of problems within the community. The students understood that critical analysis, without suggestions for change, could give little of direct benefit to a poor and disenfranchised people. Both student and non-student members of the Rio IPCN group and members of the Unified Black Movement have attempted to start social action projects in urban areas of the city aimed at addressing some of the grievances of the *favelados*. In one neighborhood a cooperative movement is contemplated to utilize the sewing skills of residents to make and then market inexpensive garments for sale inside the community and possible sale and distribution in areas outside of the favela. Another project, directed at women in a poor neighborhood, seeks to apprise them of their basic legal rights within the larger society while providing a basic literacy program to help them master rudimentary language skills.[37] While neither project is publicized as being for Afro-Brazilians only, and both seek to improve the situation of those living in socially and economically deprived conditions, the choice of favela communities ensures that the vast majority of persons involved in the programs will be nonwhite.

The students participating in social action programs in Rio, as well as their colleagues in other Brazilian cities, are attempting to avoid what they believe to have been tactical errors made by Afro-Brazilian intellectual groups and movements in the past. They feel that too often these intellectuals and professionals have sought to speak for but not to lead a popular movement whose members they never understood. Due to elitism, the students contend, the intellectuals led and represented no one but themselves. The failure to surmount class and socioeconomic differences among Afro-Brazilians prevented these movements from ever becoming truly popular and mass-oriented, despite the rhetoric employed.

Current strategies seek to eliminate these barriers, demonstrating the commonality of the Afro-Brazilian experience. Various symposia and conferences have discussed possible interclass participation in the solution of problems in various program areas deemed critical by the community as a whole.[38] The disproportionate number of young Afro-Brazilian males in the nation's prisons, often incarcerated for minor infractions, or even for failure to possess identity or working papers, is rightly perceived to be a serious problem for the entire community. It has been suggested that Afro-Brazilian lawyers could study the judicial system and its treatment of Afro-Brazilians, as well as providing direct counseling assistance to Black prisoners. Health services for poor urban and rural Blacks remain inadequate, as is the case for all poor Brazilians. It should be possible for Afro-Brazilian physicians and health professionals to create a program that provides services to a group of urban favelados, or to a rural community in need of a basic health service–delivery program. Afro-Brazilian educators could study the school-leaving patterns of Black students, which have resulted in the virtual disappearance of Blacks in the nation's secondary schools and institutions of higher learning, while they are statistically well represented in the primary school population.[39]

The student groups understood the tenuous, fragile nature and condition of the Afro-Brazilian middle and professional class. They realized that the professional and socioeconomic gains of this minority could easily be swept away by the current adverse economic conditions now threatening the small gains achieved by all of Brazil's middle class during the 1970s. That an alliance must be formed between all classes and groups of Blacks was clearly understood by the students, who sought to raise the level of awareness of that small professional and middle class concerning the nature of discrimination and its myriad effects on all Blacks regardless of socioeconomic status. The students recognized the need for Afro-Brazilian professionals first to identify as Blacks and then as professionals, if the middle class is ever to relate to the majority of Brazilian Blacks and their problems of socioeconomic and political marginalization.

Africa has again come to be of interest to students, less for cultural reasons than for its current geopolitical and economic importance to Brazil. The diplomatic and commercial rapprochement towards Africa initiated by the Brazilian Foreign Ministry in the 1970s has brought Africa to the attention of the Brazilian news media. It has also indirectly, and it is hoped positively, started to focus more international interest and attention on Brazilian race relations.[40] As an ideological component of Brazil's declared foreign policy has been the country's alleged racial democracy, Africans and other peoples of African descent are investigating the historic and present condition of Afro-Brazilians and the prospects for their future leadership and development within Brazilian society. The commercial and cultural exchange programs which Brazil has developed with African countries have produced an immediate increase of Africans visiting Brazil and studying in Brazilian universities (Dzidzienyo and Turner 1981, 201–218).[41] An easy and genuine affinity has been noticeable on Brazilian university campuses between the newly arrived African students and their Afro-Brazilian colleagues. Those Africans arriving from recently independent lusophone countries are asked endless questions by Brazilian students, who see in the declared policies of the new countries an expressed commitment to social justice and the rectification of past inequities that Afro-Brazilians seek for their own society. African social and political models and approaches to education and culture all represent possible future models for Afro-Brazilians, who follow events in Lusophone Africa with interest.

For many Brazilians, white as well as Black, Lusophone Africa remains an — as yet — successful revolutionary dream in the process of self-realization. In a manner not unlike the idealism of the first generation of North American Peace Corps volunteers in the early 1960s, Brazilian university students are eagerly attempting to obtain teaching and technical assistance positions in Guinea-Bissau and Cabo Verde (Cape Verde), with the hope of later being accepted for posts in Mozambique or Angola. The diplomatic and commercial attention being paid to Lusophone Africa by the Brazilian government has been closely watched by the students, who seek to participate actively in an example of total social transformation which they believe has been frustrated in their own country. Whether the Brazilian students are any more prepared to understand and work with African realities than their North American counterparts of an earlier generation remains open to question. It can be argued that arriving in Africa with an already formed ideal of correct social revolution can easily lead to as much disillusionment as carrying preconceived concepts of cultural nationalism to that continent. Many of the intellectual and psychic discontinuities suffered by Afro-Americans in Africa await Afro-Brazilians, although ideology may initially mask some of the cultural differences.

In Brazil, despite the popular interest in Afro-Brazilian religion and culture, general knowledge concerning Africa — African history and

African cultures—is very limited. The popular image of Africa in Brazil stems, as it has in the United States, from the Hollywood films of Tarzan and the witless African "natives." Brazilians need to have accurate visual images of Luanda and Maputo, as North Americans needed to have images of Nairobi and Lagos, to begin to understand the continent and its peoples in African terms. This process of public information concerning Africa, not particularly advanced in the United States, is only just beginning in Brazil.[42] Obviously the university community should have access to African information resources, as its knowledge and comprehension of international relations will directly determine Brazil's future foreign policy.

Entering the decade of the 1980s, Afro-Brazilian university students appear to have a firm sense of their own identity, which is increasingly defined through a cultural affirmation of blackness, with less clear links to the socioeconomic and political consequences of such an identity. This cultural identification should not be confused with the rhetorical cultural nationalism that paralyzed certain Black North American groups and movements in the 1960s and 1970s. As Afro-Brazilian culture in its religious, musical, and plastic art forms seems to be daily more and more co-opted by the Eurocentric Brazilian society, the reaffirmation by Afro-Brazilians of their culture becomes increasingly important and political. As this cultural awareness is discussed and debated within a larger socioeconomic and political context (made more interesting by expected democratizing of the national political system), strategies for improving conditions for Afro-Brazilians will become more defined.

The students and professionals under study are increasingly taking an interest in and joining cultural groups devoted to the rediscovery and preservation of traditional cultural forms.[43] These groups not only represent a rich cultural heritage for the student members, but also present opportunities for them to interact with nonacademic persons and to begin building the necessary bridges between Afro-Brazilians in different socioeconomic groups. In Rio, the alternative samba school Quilombo, the research dance troupe Olorum Baba Mim, and Bahia's Ilé Allé, a carnaval afoxé group using African historical themes, all have Afro-Brazilian members from diverse socioeconomic backgrounds. These groups, while emphasizing the interpretation of authentic cultural forms, communicate to their members and adherents the essentially political relationship which culture can have with society as a whole. They have restored dignity to the expression of Afro-Brazilian music, dance, and religion, while making a political and social statement about Afro-Brazilians and their position within society.

Recent history has demonstrated the political nature of Afro-Brazilian culture. In 1978 the government publicly expressed its displeasure with a planned cultural festival whose goal was to promote encounters between

Afro-Brazilian and Black North American artists and intellectuals. The former were explicitly advised not to participate in the meetings (the August Festival was scheduled for Salvador and Rio), and to avoid contact with "demagogic and possibly racist" Black North American tourists.[44] Despite these warnings issued by Brasília, Afro-Brazilians did participate informally, at some risk to themselves. The theme of the 1978 Festival was cultural manifestations of the African Diaspora in Brazil and the United States.

In 1979, the Afro-Brazilian Porto Alegre newspaper *Tição* was indicted by the Federal Censorship Bureau for publishing so-called subversive materials denouncing racial prejudice and discriminatory behavior in southern Brazil. Although the federal case was later discontinued ("archived" is the legal expression used in Brazil), the editors of the newspaper, including several university students, were investigated by the police. The potential risks to these individuals' professional, as well as personal, lives should not be minimized. It has been an act of courage for all Afro-Brazilians and their supporters to challenge the national ideology of racial democracy and begin creating conditions for an honest public discussion of Brazilian race relations.

FROM BROWN TO BLACK

While national political changes have created a climate that is generally more favorable for such critical discussions, the most important transformations and changes have come from within the Afro-Brazilian community itself. A developing sense of identity and awareness, along with the refusal to acquiesce to a national myth that is historically injurious to their community, have contributed to these changes among all groups of Afro-Brazilians. Black Rio began among lower-class urban youths, while the Porto Alegre newspaper and the "non-Festival" in Bahia involved intellectuals and professionals, thus demonstrating a diversity of class involvement and forms of participation.[45]

Afro-Brazilian university students have come to understand that the first ethnicity-based definition that society imposes most often serves as a final identification, despite proclaimed ideologies and popular myths. That is, the identification of being Black, even when one is termed brown or *moreno*, eventually comes to serve as the label used by society, far more noticeable than a medical degree, an advanced university diploma, or a highly paid government post. Using a middle-class, or professional, status as insulation from racism is never completely successful, as there always comes a point at which the society refuses to look beyond that epidermal exterior. For Afro-Brazilians that is the point when brown again becomes Black.

NOTES

1. This essay is a preliminary study and discussion of Afro-Brazilian university students. As such, it is necessarily based upon documented sources and interviews conducted intermittently during a period of almost nine years of visits to, and residence in, Brazil. During the period emphasized here (1976-1978), I was professor of African history at the University of Brasília.

2. Attitudes of Afro-Brazilian students and professionals formed a part of the study by Anani Dzidzienyo (1971). For data referent to the mid-1970s especially useful are the studies of Carlos A. Hasenbalg (1979), Anexo I (pp. 261-269), and Apendice (pp. 271-281), and Pierre-Michel Fontaine, "Research in the Political Economy of Afro-Latin America," *Latin American Research Review* 15(2): 111-141 (Summer 1980).

3. Exhaustive discussions of the relative weight of the variables class and ethnicity are to be found in the "classic" studies of the São Paulo School of Sociology, that is, Florestan Fernandes' *O negro no mundo dos brancos* (São Paulo: Difusão Européia do Livro, 1971); Octavio Ianni, *As metamorfoses do escravo* (São Paulo: Difusão Européia do Livro, 1962); and with the third variable of sex in the recent research of Lélia Gonzalez, "Qual é o lugar da mulher negra enquanto força de trabalho" (1978), a paper presented at the International Symposium on Women in the Labor Force in Latin America; "Racismo e sexismo na cultura brasileira" (1980), a paper presented at the Fourth Meeting of the National Association of Post-Graduate Studies and Research in the Social Sciences (ANPOCS); Oliveira, Porcaro, and Araújo (1980), and Gonzalez, Costa, and de Oliveira, "Mulher negra: Uma proposta de articulação entre raça, sexo e classe" (1981), a research project supported by the Ford Foundation social science competition award.

4. The Northern Zone is the poorer section of Rio de Janeiro. By contrast, the Southern Zone (Zona Sul) is characterized by such wealthy *bairros* as Ipanema Leblon, Lagoa, and the newer Barra da Tijuca, even though it includes several *favelas* easily seen on the *morros* that dominate the Zone. Indeed, in 1974 the plush districts of Lagoa and Barra da Tijuca boasted no fewer than seventeen and eight favelas respectively. — ED.

5. See Carlos Benedito Rodrigues da Silva, "Black Soul: Aglutinação espontânea ou identidade etnica, uma contribuição ao estudo das manifestaçoes culturais no meio negro," Fourth Meeting of ANPOCS, October 1980.

6. The at times subtle, but important, distinctions between perceptions of North American and South American Blacks on Brazilian race relations can be seen in the written exchange between Professors Henry Jackson and Abdias do Nascimento in the pages of *Encore* during 1980.

7. From 1976 to 1978 I served as official translator at the Ghana Embassy in Brasília. The Embassy received constant requests from Afro-Brazilian cultural groups located throughout the country for African diplomats to attend local symposia and provide information about Africa. All African embassies in Brasília received such requests and invitations, and attempted, with limited financial resources, to respond appropriately to, and encourage contact with, these cultural groups. One somewhat problematic relationship involved the Senghor Foundation, a transnational organization with headquarters in Dakar, devoted to the cultural and sociopolitical concept of Négritude, the philosophy of Sénégal's first president, Léopold Sédar Senghor. While the relationship between the Brazilian chapter of the Foundation, located in Rio, and the Senegalese Embassy was always "semi-official," the Brazilian Foreign Ministry was not happy with what, to them, appeared to be Senegalese encouragement of African cultural nationalism among Afro-Brazilians. But this was never really the intention of the Senegalese Embassy.

8. Some reference should be made to the general policy of *abertura* or *distensão*, a gradual liberalization or return to democratic political systems which came to typify official statements of the Geisel presidency after 1977. Among other social consequences within Brazil, it has permitted various so-called progressive groups, among them Afro-Brazilian activist organizations, to begin to more publicly articulate grievances and prescriptions for changing the country's social problems.

9. The Afro-Asian Studies Center at Rio's Candido Mendes University organized the First International Symposium on Brazil-Africa Relations (August 4–7, 1981), with the participation of the Brazilian Foreign Ministry, African ambassadors resident in Brasília, African, Latin American, North American, and European scholars, representatives from international organizations, and members of Afro-Brazilian cultural and social activist organizations. The Symposium attempted to critically analyze the development of a Brazilian-African foreign policy and determine the outlines of the African response to this initiative, both diplomatic and commercial.

10. Particularly interesting in this regard is the situation of student activists enrolled at the University of Brasília, the majority of whom are civil servants in Federal government ministries and agencies. It was not uncommon to encounter students participating in student assemblies and picket lines on campus during the morning, and during the afternoon, soberly and formally attired for their jobs in the Senate or Ministry of Justice.

11. Permissible limits of expression of discontent served as one of the discussion topics during the preparation of the 1977 Annual Week of Debate and Discussion organized by the André Rebouças Study Group of Afro-Brazilian students at the Fluminense Federal University in Niterói, Rio de Janeiro.

12. The theoretical underpinnings of the whitening concept are examined in Thomas E. Skidmore, *Black into White: Race and Nationality in Brazilian Thought* (New York: Oxford University Press, 1974); the still debatable concept of the "mulatto escape hatch" is discussed extensively in Carl Degler, *Neither Black nor White: Slavery and Race Relations in Brazil and the United States* (New York: Macmillan, 1971).

13. The case studies of "Antonio" and "José" (below) are the results of interviews conducted during two visits to Salvador, Bahia, from January to June 1971, and in February 1980. While both the persons and their histories are real, the names are fictional. For elite positions within Brazilian society the seemingly "rigidly" competitive and impartial entrance examination is often divided into several sections. While a candidate may be successful in written portions of the test, the so-called psycho-technical oral interview has often been used to eliminate candidates who have passed the preliminary written examinations.

14. See Degler, *Neither Black nor White*, which examines the thesis of the "third" racial group's social and racial mobility in Brazil. Degler posits the theory that the mulatto group, with its greater access to education, was able to improve its social status, "whitening" itself socially to become more acceptable to the Brazilian Euroculture, thus creating a safety-valve within the system of Brazilian race relations and an intermediate category between those classified as Black and those labeled white. The popularly held belief was that through education, professional status, and accumulation of personal wealth, a Black or mulatto could be perceived as less Black, more socially acceptable (for a significant challenge to this idea, see chapter 4). Research conducted by this author in Salvador and by Dzidzienyo would indicate that for the dominant society the mulatto was held in the same regard as those classified as *negro* or Black.

15. The Candido Mendes Afro-Asian Studies Center and the Bahian Society for the Study of Black Culture in Brazil presented the Semanas Afro-Brasileiras, a weekly series of cultural and scholarly presentations on Afro-Brazilian art, music, dance, religion, and history at Rio's Museum of Modern Art in 1974. While the cultural manifestations and

art exhibition encountered no difficulties with the authorities, the lecture series was cancelled by the Museum upon orders from government officials in Brasília. The various cultural presentations were attended by more than six thousand persons, attesting to a popular interest in representations of Afro-Brazilian culture.

16. See Anani Dzidzienyo (1978) for a discussion of "frozen africanity" in Bahia, a popularly held belief that Bahia's African quality does not change or evolve over time. The reverence for African cultural retentions in Salvador and the affective relations between whites and nonwhites served to retard mobilization efforts of Black groups in Salvador, as Bahia was always represented as the classic example of the Brazilian racial democracy. The recent emergence of the Bahian chapter of the Unified Black Movement (MNU) and the reemergence of the *afoxés* (circa 1978) are indications that Bahia is more pluralist than has been popularly believed.

17. Of particular interest to students in the mid-1970s were Léopold Sédar Senghor, *Les fondements de l'Africanité ou Négritude et Arabité* (Paris: Présence Africaine, 1967); the journal *Présence Africaine*; Aimé Césaire, *Cahiers d'un retour au pays natal* (Paris, 1947); and the writings of Cheikh Anta Diop, such as *The African Origin of Civilization* (Westport: Lawrence Hill, 1974).

18. There are, however, some limitations to the umbrella of culture, such as the fact that the Institute for Afro-Brazilian Studies and Research at the Pontifical Catholic University in São Paulo, formed in 1980 under the direction of its founder Abdias do Nascimento, has been unable to obtain the approval of the Brazilian Foreign Ministry for the 1982 International Congress of African Cultures in the Americas, an event which, if approved by the federal government, would become eligible for funding from the Organization of American States and UNESCO. Also, the difficulties encountered by the organizers of the 1974 Afro-Brazilian Exhibition at the Rio Modern Art Museum serve as indications of the limits of Afro-Brazilian cultural expression. [However, a 12 May 1985 article in the *Jornal do Brasil*, "Movimento negro ja conta 400 entidades e cresce no Brasil," indicates a growing social, cultural, and political awareness on the part of Brazilian Blacks. Afro-Brazilian scholars and social activists interviewed in the article openly criticized the perceived police violence directed towards Afro-Brazilian youths, the failure of the myth of Brazilian racial democracy when compared to the socioeconomic realities of daily life for the majority of Brazilian Blacks, and the difficulties encountered by the Afro-Brazilian movement in transforming a cultural movement into a program of social welfare and community action to deal with the problems of severely disadvantaged and poor Afro-Brazilians. — AU.]

19. The 1981 Symposium on African-Brazilian relations included references to U.S. race relations, including a historical indictment presented by historian José Honório Rodrigues that contrasted North American racial violence with the contemporary Brazilian racial democracy. Rodrigues did admit that the absence of Afro-Brazilians in positions of importance and the presence of Black North Americans in such positions in the U.S. could indicate that the Brazilian system might also be deleterious for Blacks.

20. Interviews conducted in Porto Alegre, Rio Grande do Sul, in July 1978 with Afro-Brazilian teachers of English elicited several personal histories concerning the experience of being Afro-Brazilian in the states of Rio Grande, Paraná, and Santa Catarina. Two teachers from the interior of Rio Grande described growing up in small towns in which residential segregation existed — white and nonwhite neighborhoods. As told by the respondents, Afro-Brazilians did not enter white neighborhoods after sunset, as there existed the possibility of physical confrontation. Many of the teachers also discussed the difficulty of being the only nonwhite faculty person in a school and attendant problems with students and the administration in being accepted as a professional. However, several of them also stated that they preferred the more open and honest expression of racial

sentiment in southern Brazil, as contrasted with the masking of attitudes, nationally, towards Afro-Brazilians. They believed that it might prove easier to change attitudes and behavior that were more overt than those where no one admitted the existence of a problem.

21. As described by Hasenbalg (1979), there is increasing evidence, documented in the Brazilian media, that middle-class and professional Afro-Brazilians are encountering instances of discrimination based upon color that would tend to belie the popular belief that education and money "whiten" a person, making the individual less susceptible to discrimination.

22. There is a considerable body of writing concerning race relations and symbolic manifestations seen comparatively, as in H. Hoetink, *Caribbean Race Relations: A Study of Two Variants* (London: Oxford University Press, 1967) and specifically, A. Meier and E. Rudwick, *The Making of Black America* (New York: Atheneum, 1971). In Brazil, the symbology of "Afro" or "Black" also proved important in initially physically defining a style or manner that could later serve as hallmarks for a movement. As of 1981, the symbology continues to be employed, seen to represent in a hairstyle or use of an African garment the expression of cultural pride in being Black.

23. The usage of preto and negro and subsequent contemporary translations of these words into English have suffered some modification in recent years. Many Afro-Brazilians now advise translating negro as meaning Black in the U.S. context. Preto, often employed by North American researchers who believe it corresponds to Black as understood in the U.S., is still rarely used in Brazil publicly to designate Afro-Brazilians and continues to have a popularly conceived pejorative meaning.

24. While the *Jornal do Brasil* published several critical articles on Black Rio during 1976 and 1977, occasional references to the movement still appear in critics' reviews of musical performers, such as the *Jornal do Brasil's* review of a record by Dona Ivone Lara, August 15, 1980. Traditional performers are often lauded for being true representatives or authentic purveyors of Brazilian soul.

25. The coincidence of the Black Rio phenomenon and Brazilian displeasure at various aspects of U.S. foreign policy led to accusations that the movement was North-American-inspired, but it does not fully explain the violence of the reaction.

26. An important difference between Brazil and the U.S. that should be discussed briefly is the position and impact of Black culture within each of the societies. While much has been written about the historical and contemporary importance of Black cultural manifestations in the U.S., among the general non-Black public in the U.S. there is little specific knowledge about that culture and history. This is not true for Brazil, in which Afro-Brazilian culture is not only obvious but also known and exercised by non-Afro Brazilians, the most obvious example being religious manifestations such as candomblé, macumba, and umbanda. The attempted appropriation by Afro-Brazilians of a cultural manifestation seen by them as being solely for Blacks would naturally cause consternation on the part of society, not perceiving that co-optation of a group's culture can be as damaging as ignoring it.

27. In Salvador, the reemergence of the once-forbidden afoxés, apart from stimulating an interest in African history and cultures, also represents an incipient interest in bridging recreation with social action, as the *blocos* are attempting to articulate some of the problems of the local communities in which they reside towards the future resolution of these issues. Although as yet unfocused, the potential of afoxés as a mobilizing force within Salvador presents an interesting case for study.

28. Much discussion in Salvador concerned a June 1980 public rally with political overtones, organized by Governor Antonio Carlos Magalhães in front of City Hall, which also included the participation of the reverend priestess Mãe Menininha de Gantois, who broke

years of tradition by leaving her home and terreiro upon the invitation of the governor. Still to be analyzed are the implied relationships between the political and the sacred in Bahia, which could represent a forceful combination during elections. In Rio de Janeiro the present state government is also attentive to the umbanda religious community, as political expediency again becomes an important factor.

29. The official date of May 13 has also been used as a day for counter-demonstrations, as Afro-Brazilian speakers discuss the legal implications and consequences of the 1888 Act of Abolition. In 1978 in São Paulo, the now-deceased Afro-Brazilian sociologist Eduardo de Oliveira e Oliveira organized a "museum of the street," using poster-size photographs of slavery to remind the general public of the harsh realities of that institution, officially eliminated by law ninety years before.

30. The André Rebouças Study Group in October 1978 succeeded in registering their annual week of seminars and conferences on Afro-Brazilian Affairs with the Ministry of Education and Culture in Brasília. The notification was officially published in the *Diário oficial*.

31. Problems encountered at Fluminense are symptomatic of a more generalized dilemma in that the institution, in conceding resources (which are gradually diminishing) for an annual event, does not feel compelled to accept or initiate internal changes which would benefit the Black students. As their concern is the continuation of the annual event, this becomes the focus of their mobilization activities, creating a vacuum in terms of their strategies and organization to obtain other concessions from university administrators.

32. In an October 1978 profile of the Afro-Brazilian community, *New Africa* made a reference to this author being the only Black professor at the University of Brasília, to indicate the problematic situation existing for Afro-Brazilians as regards higher education. While an increase in Black university professors can be noted as of 1981, the gains appear to be very slow.

33. Personal communication with Professor Amado Luiz Cervo, coordinator of the M.A. program in History, University of Brasília, June 1981.

34. SECNEB presents an interesting example of scientific and cultural production, employing minimal resources. Its founders, Mestre Didi dos Santos and Dr. Juana Elbein dos Santos, have been able to produce three documentary films on Afro-Brazilian religion (in co-production with Embrafilm) and a five-part television series on the Afro-Brazilians (shown on the Educational Network, TVE), production costs being minimally covered in grants received by SECNEB from the federal government. No funds were received for an adequate publicity campaign for either the films or the television series, so that there is little public awareness of their existence and availability for distribution.

35. In 1981 several small Afro-Brazilian journal and newspaper editors attempted to form a cooperative distribution network to sell publications to a potentially national audience. The Alternative Press Cooperative has encountered financial and administrative difficulties. However, it is attempting to implant a distribution service in Rio and São Paulo, and was able to mount a newsstand at the National Meeting of the SBPC in Salvador in July 1981.

36. "Folhetim," *Folha de São Paulo*, 26 July 1981; "Na SBPC, provas da discriminação," *Folha de São Paulo*, 11 July 1981. The July 1981 meeting of the SBPC was significant in that the topic of Afro-Brazilian Studies and Brazil-Africa Relations was for the first time included as a major theme for this annual meeting of Brazil's intellectual elite community. The various symposia, round tables, and seminars gave a good representation of current research and research problems in the area of Afro-Brazilian Studies and garnered a fair share of coverage in the more liberal wing of the national media.

37. Community action and social action projects in Brazil (and elsewhere) are popular subjects for analysis and are receiving significant publicity and attention from national and

international organizations. The difficulty of collaborating with a community in developing projects truly responsive to the needs of its members (and not imposing values and systems upon it), represents a challenge not only for Afro-Brazilians, but all progressive groups within the society interested in constructive and positive social change. In part because of its recent political history but also because of a series of cultural and longer-range historical factors, Brazil lacks a long tradition of grass-roots organizations upon which to build coherent policies and strategies of community organization. Middle-class and liberal professionals, while understanding the theories and fundamentals of grass-roots organization, are not able to successfully translate ideology and theory into practice, often for financial and political reasons beyond their own control — though the efforts of the Church in this direction in recent years have been quite noteworthy.

38. In Rio de Janeiro, a group of Afro-Brazilian jurists and prison officials are considering the viability of a project to investigate the causes and effects of the high rate of arrest and detention of young Afro-Brazilians in that city's prisons. A major concern expressed by Afro-Brazilian social activist groups is the problem of police violence and summary arrest practiced against unemployed Black youths, perceived by society to be potential criminal elements.

39. The alternative samba school Quilombo is attempting to work with the children in the nearby favela of Acarí, in the Zona Norte of Rio de Janeiro. An Afro-Brazilian university professor, also a member of the samba school, has elaborated a primary school curriculum project on Afro-Brazilian culture and history which she is attempting to introduce into the community, with the collaboration of the local residents' association.

40. Panel at the Candido Mendes University's August 1981 Symposium on Africa-Brazil devoted to the historical and contemporary impact of Africa's influence upon Brazil.

41. At the time I was a professor at the Universidade de Brasília (1977–1978), there were sixteen African students enrolled in both the graduate and undergraduate divisions of the University, the majority from Cape Verde and Guinea-Bissau. At that time the Universidade de São Paulo had more than forty-five Nigerian students. In 1980 there were approximately one hundred Nigerian students enrolled at the University (information provided by Anani Dzidzienyo, who visited USP in April 1981).

42. Joseph Lelyveldt, *Newsweek* correspondent in Johannesburg, also serves as correspondent for the *Jornal do Brasil*, thereby being the only journalist in Africa writing for a Brazilian newspaper.

43. The emphasis on the Black Rio or Soul movement has had the interesting collateral effect of encouraging some Afro-Brazilians to research conscientiously their cultural history and discover musical and dance forms that have origins in Africa; perhaps the group Vissungo best represents this tradition, as its members have recreated Afro-Brazilian instruments and discovered slave songs of the eighteenth and nineteenth centuries to present as examples of all-but-forgotten cultural history to their largely Black audiences.

44. Government opposition to the 1978 African Diaspora Festival in Bahia was made obvious in a June 1978 broadcast of the national evening news radio program "Voice of Brazil." In the broadcast the festival was characterized as being potentially divisive, and Brazilians were openly discouraged from meeting with the Afro-American tourists. The Diaspora Festival, or "non-event," as it became known among its participants, did occur on a smaller, more informal scale, with presentations by the visiting North American cultural groups and meetings between Afro-Brazilian and Afro-American scholars. The late Hoyt W. Fuller published an account of such a meeting where John Henrik Clarke and Lélia Gonzalez served as chief spokespersons, respectively, for the American and Brazilian groups ("Brazil: The Struggle for Equality Begins," *First World* 2 [2]: 17–20 [1979]).

45. The uncertain political atmosphere currently being lived by Brazil and the importance of a continuing process of abertura for the realization of any of the programs of the Afro-Brazilian groups should be noted. All progressive groups in the country are obviously dependent upon these conditions, which would permit the existence of a viable and responsible opposition movement. For Afro-Brazilians these basic democratic conditions are especially critical, as their program and platform tend to bother the traditional Left only slightly less than it does those on the Right. Together with the current political problems, Afro-Brazilian organizations have discovered difficulties in moving from an articulation of the group's condition and problems to a defined strategy of action. The dilemma, of course, is shared with many other groups within Brazil and outside of the country.

BIBLIOGRAPHY

Dzidzienyo, Anani 1971. *The Position of Blacks in Brazilian Society*. London: Minority Rights Group.

———— 1978. Activity and Inactivity in the Politics of Afro-Latin America. Paper presented at the Southeastern Conference on Latin American Studies, SECOLAS Annals IX (March).

Dzidzienyo, Anani, and J. Michael Turner 1981. "African-Brazilian Relations: A Reconsideration." In *Brazil in the International System: The Rise of a Middle Power*, edited by Wayne A. Selcher, 201–218. Boulder, Colorado: Westview Press.

Hasenbalg, Carlos A. 1979. *Discriminação e desigualdades raciais no Brasil*. Rio de Janeiro: Graal.

Oliveira, Lúcia Elena Garcia, Rosa Maria e Costa Porcaro, and Tereza Christina N. Araújo 1980. O lugar do negro na força de trabalho. Paper presented to the Fourth Meeting of ANPOCS.

Santos, Joel Rufino dos 1981. Memorial Zumbi: Brazilian Blacks Re-encounter Their History. Paper presented at the Second International Diaspora Studies Institute, Nairobi, Kenya (August).

7

BLACKS AND THE
ABERTURA DEMOCRÁTICA[1]

MICHAEL MITCHELL

A Brazilian returning from fourteen years in exile made this remark about his country's contemporary politics: "[F]oreign political scientists don't understand us because we don't appear to play politics by any established rules. . . . For example, in the strictest terms we shouldn't be gathered at this meeting of the opposition but that's exactly where we are . . . this is a strange land where our liberty hangs by a precarious thread . . . and where authoritarianism and democracy seem to exist side by side."[2]

This statement aptly expresses the feeling that most outside observers must have regarding the political trend referred to as Brazil's *abertura democrática*, or the transition to democracy. It seems to capture the sense of confusion and contradiction inherent in this recent development in Brazilian politics.

Since January 1979, a number of measures have been enacted to give Brazilians more freedom than they have enjoyed in sixteen years. Press censorship has been lifted. The great majority of political prisoners have been released and granted amnesty. Exiled political leaders, once considered enemies of the present regime, have been allowed to return without restrictions on their activities. The two-party system, created by the Castelo Branco regime to assure itself a more-or-less perpetual parliamentary majority, has been replaced by another which allows any group to form a political party (provided it meets rather stiff requirements of electoral strength) without government interference. Finally, Institutional Act Number Five, which gave juridical sanction to the institutions of repression and "internal security," has been abolished.[3]

Nevertheless, the shadow of authoritarianism continues to dwell over the Brazilian political process in the form of a constitutional amendment permitting the president (with the nominal consent of Congress) to invoke emergency powers which are perhaps harsher than those contained in the Fifth Institutional Act. Moreover, elections are still manipulated through "bionic" legislators and indirect elections for state governors. Severe chills have been created by a general who ventured out of institutional obscurity to warn the public against the imperfections of democracy. Winds of change are blowing through Brazil, but no one can be completely sure of whether they bring in their wake a new and vigorous democracy, or an ever more sophisticated style of authoritarianism retrenching itself in the guise of democratic reform.[4]

Formal concessions to democratic liberties, however, are just one aspect of the abertura democrática. The process also encompasses the reemergence of mass-based organizations which, once timid, are now openly airing grievances and challenging the legitimacy of the authoritarian regime. Workers, students, prelates, women, and Blacks have, in the past several years, staged public demonstrations expressing opposition to authoritarian rule.

Perhaps one of the more surprising protests in recent times was the demonstration organized in July 1978 by Brazilian Blacks. Some 2,000 persons rallied in front of the Teatro Municipal of São Paulo to dramatize the depth of racial discrimination in Brazilian society. Speakers came from throughout Brazil to denounce specific instances of racial discrimination and to demand greater racial equality. This protest was somewhat unusual in that it provoked many into rethinking the long-held notion that Brazil was relatively free of the kind of racial tension that would generate such a protest. Contemporary Brazilian politics is indeed difficult to understand: elites of an authoritarian system benevolently offer to surrender a large share of their powers and prerogatives; workers engage in illegal strikes which are settled through negotiations with the government that banned them; and Blacks living in a "racial democracy" protest against racial discrimination.

This chapter will concentrate on one particular facet of the strange and complex process known as abertura democrática. It will explore the ways in which Blacks fit into the abertura and what they might expect from this period of political change. Specifically, I will attempt to give evidence in support of the following hypotheses: (a) that the styles of Black political activity will be determined by the prevailing political environment; and (b) that Blacks can make an impact on the abertura democrática despite their limited organizational and financial resources.

My choice of this topic might seem rather arbitrary, perhaps even artificial. Some might argue that it is inappropriate to speak solely of racial politics in a social system where Blacks, along with other groups, make up a large proportion of the lower classes and that "Black politics" should be strictly subsumed under the heading of class analysis. Others might suggest that the abertura democrática is itself the artificial creation of an authoritarian regime and hence an inaccurate focus for any discussion of real political change. These observations are no doubt valid, but their total acceptance obscures the existence of yet another curious reality: the apparent coincidence of broad changes in Brazilian politics and the emergence of a "new consciousness" among Afro-Brazilians. Are these "macro" and "micro" changes in any way linked? Are there elements in the process of abertura democrática that bear new and as yet unexploited political opportunities for groups whose power and influence have been virtually nonexistent in Brazilian politics? It seems advantageous to examine the manner in which broad political changes, the crystallization of group consciousness, and the activation of that consciousness into political form, mutually influence each other; to see whether new forms of political organization and expression can result from such a dialectic.

To facilitate the analysis, this chapter will be divided into two parts. The first section will attempt to trace the origins and development of the abertura democrática in broad strokes. In the second, I focus on the links between the abertura democrática and Black politics. Many of the remarks made here will be, of necessity, highly speculative since the abertura is still a new, confusing, and contradictory process. This analysis may prove to be useful despite the limitations imposed by the uncertainties of Brazil's present political atmosphere.

THE ABERTURA DEMOCRÁTICA

In order to trace the origins of a democratic tradition in Brazil one might profitably begin with the struggle for independence, when the ideals of the French Revolution were extolled by publications such as the *Revérbero Constitucional*, the *Malagueta*, and the *Sentinela da Liberdade*. Other bearers of democratic tradition, among them the Pasquins of the Regency period and Ruy Barbosa, should also be mentioned. The list is not impressively long, partially due to the hostility toward democratic ideals expressed by a rural, oligarchical society. Nevertheless, there is evidence of an indigenous democratic tradition in Brazilian history.[5] Although the present abertura democrática should be considered in this historical context, there is more value—but not great satisfaction—in beginning this discussion with the 1964 *golpe de estado*.

By that year, Brazil had reached a period when several economic, social, and political factors were simultaneously producing overwhelming strains on the political system. Economic stagnation in the industrial sector was becoming endemic. The persistence of archaic social structures (particularly in the countryside), the mobilization of workers, peasants, and students demanding social reforms, together with continual electoral impasses within a factionalized party system, all served to intensify social and political cleavages in Brazilian society.[6]

Prior to the 1964 coup, two presidents had tried to implement needed reforms but failed to establish a general consensus for doing so. The first, Jânio Quadros, resigned in frustration after only eight months in office. The second, João Goulart, was deposed in March 1964.

The forces that overthrew Goulart represented a curious collection of distinct, even conflicting, groups: military officers who resented Goulart's rejection of the necessity for honor and discipline in the ranks; both officers and civilians who perceived Goulart as a threat to the fundamental social order; and still others with personal ambitions they hoped to satisfy by participating in Goulart's overthrow.[7]

Rising above these factions was Marechal Humberto Castelo Branco who, because of his capacity for leadership, was chosen as the regime's first president. Authoritarian by nature, Castelo Branco showed a commitment to correcting what were perceived as the worst abuses of the democratic era, and he promised to lay the foundation for an eventual return to a democratic political structure free of such abuses.

In Castelo Branco, Brazil once again produced a leader as complex as the political processes we are trying to unravel. How could an authoritarian military leader take a credible stance in favor of democratic ideals? The answer seems to lie in his military career. During World War II, Castelo Branco was a member of the Brazilian Expeditionary Force, which fought Italian fascism alongside the U.S. and other Western democracies. Moreover, he had been the head of the Escola Superior de Guerra, where prevailing military strategy allied Brazil with democracy and Western civilization, pitted against "anti-Christian" communism in an antagonistic international system.[8]

There were pragmatic reasons as well. In order to consolidate his political support, Castelo Branco had to contend with the great popularity still enjoyed by civilian political leaders. By leaning heavily on the concept of abertura, he was able to marshal support against both his military and civilian opposition.[9]

In the final analysis, however, the military man superseded the convinced democrat. Castelo Branco's commitment to democracy eventually gave way to pressures from a still untamed opposition. By the end of his term, he had begun to institutionalize authoritarian rule by establishing not only the indirect election of state governors, the reorganization of political parties, and the subjugation of Congress to the initiatives of the president, but also the conditions under which a state of emergency and suspension of civil liberties could be enforced. These measures were clearly designed to reduce popular participation in politics to a discreet minimum and silence any opposition to the new regime.[10]

Under the leadership of Castelo Branco's predecessors, Costa e Silva and Garastazu Médici, rapid economic development and "internal security" assumed a much higher priority than abertura. During this period (1967–1974), challenges to these regimes were handled with unprecedented severity. Workers' strikes, student demonstrations, and the Moreira Alves affair (an unusual display of legislative independence), served to intensify the authoritarian reaction. By December 1968, in response to a series of political crises, Costa e Silva outlined the extent of his dictatorial powers in the chilling Fifth Institutional Act.[11]

The Costa e Silva and Médici years were bitter ones. Individual rights were systematically violated and political participation repressed to an extraordinary degree. Torture became a routine means of intimidating and silencing the opposition. It was during this period that the regime attempted to halt the political process through appeals to national pride in economic and sports achievements. By 1974, when Médici's tenure in office ended, the authoritarian regime had become an institution.[12]

The democratic opening now under way can be viewed to some degree as a legacy of Castelo Branco. Many of his former advisers, such as General Golbery do Couto e Silva, former president Ernesto Geisel, and President João Baptista Figueiredo, became its architects.[13] When Geisel was inaugurated as the fourth military president since 1964, several factors emerged to put the issue of abertura democrática back on the political agenda. Not the least important of these was the need to resolve the problem of internal factionalism which had existed within the military since the days of Castelo Branco. The Castelo loyalists, among them Geisel himself, had considered the Costa e Silva and Médici presidencies humiliating defeats for the more politically sophisticated Castelistas. It was a simple matter for the latter to lay blame for unconscionable excesses on previous administrations, simultaneously raising the issue of democracy in order to discredit the opposition. The accession of Geisel was thus thought to be an opportunity to repudiate the "hard-liners" once and for all.[14]

Another factor which sparked interest in planning for a return to democracy was the sticky problem of legal status for civilian leaders *cassados* in 1964. If the ten-year suspensions of their rights were to be renewed, it would have to be done early in Geisel's administration. In the case of former president Juscelino Kubitschek, a popular figure whose original suspension of rights was considered unjust by many, a compelling reason would have to be given for extending it. To welcome such figures back into the political community might advance the cause of the regime and further isolate the hard-liners. The risk seemed minimal, as by 1974 virtually all armed resistance to the regime had been eliminated and with it one of the rationales for the "rule of exception."

Broader international events would also prompt a more "tolerant" attitude toward the political process. First, OPEC price increases were to have a severe impact on economic expansion. The consequent slowing of economic growth forced Geisel's government to function in a climate considerably less favorable than that enjoyed by previous administrations. Thus, by the time of Geisel's inauguration, several factors had emerged to make an abertura possible, and even advantageous. Still another external factor would emerge to influence abertura: the United States' foreign policy initiatives regarding human rights violations, which brought the issue of democratic freedom more sharply into focus for Brazilians.[15]

Geisel's initial moves in this direction seemed promising, if cautious. He named Armando Falcão as his minister of justice, signaling a potential reconciliation with those who still identified with former president Kubitschek and his Partido Social Democrático. But more encouraging still was Geisel's determination not to interfere in the congressional elections of 1974.

In short order these congressional elections became the first test of Geisel's intentions to carry out a plan of redemocratization. The election results went heavily against the government party and, for the first time, the prospect of an independent Congress had to be confronted. The results reflected a severe erosion of support for the government in the modern industrial areas, where the regime had claimed its most impressive economic successes. Furthermore, the vote tended to show that the government had virtually no support among the young, workers, and women, groups which had been historically excluded from political participation.[16]

Geisel and his advisers were quick to grasp the significance of the vote. Shortly thereafter, he announced that the process of abertura would come to an end. Nevertheless, Geisel was put on notice that he would have to confront the regime's eroding support.

During the remainder of his term, Geisel would feel still further pressures to expand political activity. These pressures, which had been building for some time and crystallized in the 1974 congressional elections, were to come mainly from businessmen, the Catholic church, students, and organized workers, who complained of the maldistribution of power and wealth and questioned the legitimacy of the authoritarian regime.

The first of these challenges developed out of the Herzog Affair, in which journalist Vladimir Herzog, after voluntarily surrendering to the authorities, was tortured and murdered in the presence of army security forces in São Paulo. Incensed by both the circumstances of his death and its attempted cover-up, public opinion exploded in outrage against the regime. When a similar incident occurred in the same army compound a few months later, Geisel was compelled to act. He responded by firing the army commander in whose jurisdiction the offenses had been committed. But the greater significance of the entire affair was that public opinion had established the limits of its tolerance. If the regime wished to maintain some semblance of legitimacy and support, it would have to end the violent intimidation of Brazilian citizens which had characterized the governments of Costa e Silva and Médici.[17]

At about the same time, the regime began to experience loss of support from its most loyal traditional ally. Brazilian businessmen began to complain that their participation in the economy was being threatened by large state enterprises (such as Petrobrás, Companhia Siderúgica Nacional, and Companhia do Vale do Rio Doce) and by multinational corporations.

At first, the debate between the business community and Geisel's regime was narrow in focus, with criticism also directed toward Geisel's efforts at redemocratization. As it grew, however, it seemed to take on a life of its own and paradoxically became linked to the cause of abertura democrática. As a result of the *estatização* controversy, Severo Gomes, considered a "liberal" in Geisel's cabinet, resigned as minister of industry and commerce.[18]

Ironically, this controversy was the legacy of Getúlio Vargas, who had recognized the political potential of state intervention in the economy decades earlier (1930–1945). Through the creation of various *institutos* to oversee the stabilization of prices and export of agricultural commodities, he was able to pacify rural oligarchical interests while he slowly drained their power. In the 1950s, Vargas used the artifice of state enterprises (specifically Petrobrás) to rally popular nationalist sentiment for his administration. He would no doubt have enjoyed the irony of a regime whose objective was to eradicate all vestiges of his populist politics from national life fervently defending the economic structures he had set in place.[19]

The Geisel regime was also beset by opposition from still another powerful sector, the Catholic church. Relations with the Church, which had not been cordial since 1964, grew increasingly tense under Geisel's government. They reached their nadir in 1976, when the bishop of Nova Iguaçu, Dom Adriano Hipólito, was kidnapped by government security forces. While in captivity, he was humiliated by being stripped naked and painted red to symbolize his supposed political inclinations. A subsequent controversy arose concerning the death of Jesuit Father João Bosco Brunier, who had been a supporter of the peasants' fight for land in the Amazon. He was found to have been murdered by local police.

Several issues divided church and state, but the most troublesome of these had to do with the Church's renewed commitment to social justice and human rights. As mentioned earlier, ordinary clergy were particularly forceful in speaking out in defense of the dispossessed, and risked their lives as a result. More prestigious religious figures, such as Helder Câmara and Paulo Evaristo Arns, also spoke out against human rights abuses both individually and in forums such as the National Conference of Brazilian Bishops (CNBB). Through organizations like the Commission of Justice and Peace, Church leaders also encouraged the laity to expose the work of the semi-official death squads, and to bring suits against the torturers of political prisoners. The work of Hélio Bicudo, Dalmo Dallari, and José Carlos Dias was especially noteworthy in this regard.

For the Church to carry its criticism of government policy to the point of questioning the legitimacy of the regime due to its human rights abuses was a strong indication that solid political support for the regime was sorely lacking in this important sector of Brazilian society.[20]

By 1977 the process of abertura had come to a critical turning point where Geisel felt compelled to reassert his "revolutionary powers" as a reminder to the opposition. At issue was a matter of secondary importance, a proposed constitutional amendment reforming the judicial system of the states. For the Brazilian Democratic Movement, the opposition party, the issue provided the first major test of congressional independence since 1968. The confrontation came when the MDB decided not to support the proposal and Geisel responded in the fashion of a stern authoritarian. He closed Congress for a period of two weeks and announced a set of decrees which came to be known as the Pacote de Abril. Among the measures were:

1. Indirect elections of one-third of the Senate by state legislatures: a process which, in effect, placed senatorial appointments in the hands of the president (those appointed have been referred to as "bionic" senators).
2. Indirect election of state governors.
3. Extension of the Lei Falcão limiting to two hours the amount of radio and television time available to *all* candidates in the 1978 elections, thus effectively eliminating the broadcast media as forums for political debate.
4. Extension of the presidential term of office from five to six years.
5. Reduction of the number of votes in Congress required for passage of constitutional amendments from two-thirds to a simple majority.
6. Legalization of divorce.

7. Enactment of the original judicial reforms which were the cause of the confrontation.

Disagreement inevitably arose regarding the motives behind the Pacote de Abril. Hugo Abreu, chief of the military household in Geisel's cabinet, attributed them to a "cynical" palace oligarchy headed by Golbery. Abreu claimed the latter was fearful of a poor showing in the forthcoming 1978 congressional elections. Walder Goes, columnist for the *Jornal do Brasil*, argued, on the other hand, that the Pacote was a skillful attempt by Geisel to steer a middle course between radical-right elements within the military, who pushed for a reimposition of the reign of terror, and the opposition whose challenges to the regime were gaining increasing respectability.[21] But whatever the motives, the net effect of the Pacote was to alter the course of redemocratization.

In order to impose his Pacote de Abril, Geisel had to expend a considerable amount of political capital, a commodity which he would be hard put to recover in the long term, despite the short-term gains envisioned. For one thing, Geisel's high-handed methods did not sit well with key supporters of the regime. Hugo Abreu eventually resigned, citing the "April Reforms" as one reason for leaving. Later, a once loyal ally, Senator José Magalhães Pinto, presented a still more serious problem by establishing a civilian presidential candidacy to oppose whomever the regime chose in the presidential succession process. Ultimately, a new democratic front was put together that placed even greater citizen pressure on the regime for redemocratization.[22]

The Pacote de Abril greatly stimulated a new round of reaction against authoritarian rule. In May 1977, confrontations reminiscent of 1968 occurred between the government and students. Initially student protests were confined to the issue of dwindling government allocations to higher education. But soon these protests blossomed into sweeping demands for (*a*) an end to military dictatorship and (*b*) unrestricted amnesty for political prisoners. And when police invaded the campuses of the Catholic University in São Paulo and the Federal University in Brasília, they discovered that the rules of political confrontation had changed substantially. Instead of quelling the protests, they were actually generating considerable support for the students' cause.[23]

Still another group was to make its entry into the political arena. Brazilian workers had been victimized consistently by government economic policies which artificially kept wages near subsistence levels. By May 1978, discontent reached dangerous proportions and for weeks striking automobile and metallurgical workers held the government at bay. Rather than crush the strike openly, Geisel decided to "negotiate" a settlement. Although in real terms the workers won few substantial economic concessions, they gained a new sense of independence and a strong, politically astute leadership in men like Luiz Ignácio da Silva ("Lula"). From then on workers were to become vigorous combatants in the arena of Brazilian politics.[24]

Perhaps the severest crisis of Geisel's government erupted over the issue of presidential succession. This dispute exposed the most serious weakness of the bureaucratic-authoritarian regime, namely the tenuousness of the agreement among the military factions that held the regime together. No other crisis brought into sharper relief the unsubstantiality of this coalition, upon which political initiatives were predicated.

The crisis involved the firing of Army Minister Sylvio Frota, who, against Geisel's wishes, was believed to be positioning himself for a presidential candidacy.[25] The circumstances surrounding the affair are complex and because of their importance probably deserve a separate, more detailed, treatment elsewhere. What follows is a summary of these events.

Even before the political elites began gearing up to vie for the presidency in 1977, Geisel had anointed his chosen successor, the chief of the SNI, João Baptista Figueiredo. His attractiveness as a candidate stemmed from the belief that, as president, he would be willing to maintain in power the Castelista faction of the military and its principal spokesman, General Golbery. But Figueiredo had several serious drawbacks as a candidate. First, he was not well-known among civilians and could claim no popular base of support. Second, he was outranked by other generals, some of whom harbored presidential ambitions of their own — like Sylvio Frota.

Geisel faced several problems regarding the succession, which dictated his eventual course of action. Public opinion was beginning to coalesce around the prospect of an independent civilian candidacy and Geisel was determined to neutralize this effort. He was equally determined to outmaneuver a possible hard-line resurgency that might jeopardize the power of the Castelistas and bury what was left of his redemocratization policy. These problems could scarcely be resolved by supporting the candidacy of a hard-liner like Frota.

There was evidence of a personality clash as well. Ever since he became army minister, Frota had been a thorn in Geisel's side. The two disagreed on army administrative policy as well as more substantive issues such as redemocratization and the recognition of both the People's Republic of China and the MPLA government of Angola. Furthermore, the strong-willed Frota seemed intent upon reversing Geisel's domestic political program. In an incident involving a journalist who was indiscreet enough to criticize the Duque de Caxias, patron of the Brazilian army, Frota actively sought the arrest and prosecution of the offender without first consulting the equally strong-willed president.

Whether Frota's dismissal was specifically due to this incident or not is unclear. What is certain is that long-standing discord existed between the two men, and the slight possibility of a Frota candidacy was probably sufficient cause for Geisel to act.

Because of the well-founded fear that Frota was capable of organizing a successful coup against him, Geisel orchestrated his dismissal with the utmost care. All members of the high command were provided with an explanation of the decision and a new army minister, General Fernando Belfort Bethlem (who shared Frota's critical opinions of redemocratization but was careful to operate within the army chain of command), was chosen before Frota learned that he was to be dismissed. When he left the government, Frota also left a demoralized hard-line military faction.

Despite Geisel's efforts to the contrary, Frota's dismissal was inevitably linked with the politics of presidential succession both in the public mind and among the political and military elites. Although it is doubtful that Frota could have acquired support outside of limited military circles, it appeared that Geisel had deliberately eliminated one presidential contender in order to advance the chances of his own protégé. Figueiredo would subsequently be obliged to prove the legitimacy of his rule as a result. His primary task in office was to establish a base of political support, particularly among civilians, and continuing his predecessor's efforts to reinstitute democracy had obvious political merits.

By the time Figueiredo assumed office in March 1979, several steps had already been taken by Geisel to ensure the continuation of the abertura process. Institutional Act Number Five, the primary instrument of repression, had been revoked (although so-called "constitutional safeguards" allowed Figueiredo to reimpose a "state of exception" virtually at his discretion), and press censorship was lifted. Clearly recognizing the damage done to him by the Frota affair, Figueiredo set out to create the public image of a man of the people by agreeing to a conditional amnesty and a reorganization of political parties.[26] Despite a momentary lapse during the campaign in which Figueiredo threatened to jail anyone who opposed redemocratization, expectations were heightened that the abertura would be extended further.

The question to be asked at this point is whether these expectations will be realized: how much further can and will the abertura be allowed to go? Because the political process depends on a precarious balance between authoritarianism and democracy, it is hard to arrive at a satisfactory conclusion. Dissidents can still be arrested and intimidated without due process,[27] and the constitutional safeguards give Figueiredo broad powers, a reminder to everyone that a state of exception can be reinstituted at any time.

Several factors help perpetuate the authoritarian-democratic predicament, one being Brazil's economic situation. A high inflation rate, estimated at 75 percent for 1979,[28] and chronic petroleum shortages will produce a continued economic slow-down and fierce competition for scarce goods. How the regime negotiates with groups that experienced relative prosperity during the boom years of the early 1970s will be crucial. Moreover, because of an extraordinarily large foreign debt (estimated at $60 billion) and the imposing presence of multinational corporations, the regime must respond to external actors whose major concern is not redemocratization—an unwieldy process at best—but a stable and predictable political environment in which business can go on as usual. Under such pressure the regime may see repressive controls as its only recourse.

A second factor has to do with the present realignment of political parties. As a consequence of the Party Reform Law, the opposition, once united in its efforts to abolish the most repressive features of the regime, has become factionalized. Natural constituencies such as labor are being courted by at least two *trabalhista* parties (those of Leonel Brizola and "Lula"), and issues once the domain of the democratic left are being usurped by parties of the center-right.[29] Perhaps the new parties will reflect the social divisions in Brazilian society more realistically than their artificially created predecessors. But if rivalries remain at present levels of intensity, the opposition faces diminishing prospects of coming to power or of altering the fundamentally authoritarian nature of the regime.

A third factor is the absence of any consensus about the definition of abertura democrática as a political concept. In the narrowest terms, abertura means a return to the "rule of law" and a minimal respect for civil liberties. In the broadest sense, however, it means creating a political order through a constituent assembly that would permit legitimacy to be conferred on any government which meets accepted standards of representation, even one which questions the premises of capitalist development. Brazilian elites have considered "the Spanish Solution" as well as "Mexicanization" as alternatives, and herein lies another grave affliction of Brazilian politics: confusion and uncertainty as to the new political model on which to build.

How long can this game of *abre-fecha* continue before tensions reach intolerable levels? Juan Linz has pointed out that since a redemocratization process means excluding old elites as well as incorporating new elements, current power holders can be expected to manipulate the redemocratization process indefinitely in order to maintain their positions of control. Furthermore, the Spanish experience suggests that an authoritarian system can withstand diverse opposition for a considerable length of time.[30] Thus, barring the unlikely occurrence of a miscalculated and protracted foreign military venture or a domestic military scandal of major proportions, the prospects of a radical solution to the abertura predicament appear to be slim.

In the final analysis, the abertura represents a distinct stage in Brazilian politics. Clearly, the naked repression of the past has come to an end, along with unified resistance to it. Nevertheless, with so many new and disparate elements added to the power equation of national politics, the abertura democrática constitutes a sort of *espaço de ninguem*, a political no-man's-land with new territories that will be vigorously contested in the months and years ahead.

BLACKS AND THE ABERTURA DEMOCRÁTICA

"The competitive social order," writes Florestan Fernandes, "emerged from a slave society and became an authentic and closed world of whites. . . . And, the structures of class society failed to eliminate, in any meaningful way, the racial structures of the previous social order. . . . This sociological dilemma is essentially a political one."[31]

Probably no other social thinker has penetrated the core of the Brazilian racial dilemma more deeply than Florestan Fernandes. In his several works he has shown that the predicament faced by Brazilian Blacks (that is, their lack of social opportunities and their victimization through racial discrimination) is fundamentally a question of the capacity of Brazil's social and political elites to preserve their power and privilege by suppressing a variety of social conflicts, while fully aware of the contradictions that give rise to these conflicts.[32] Fernandes points out that the mechanisms used to control social conflicts are formidable. Elites monopolize the instruments of coercion and ideological debate and traditionally have not hesitated to use these to suppress racial conflicts.[33]

On the other hand, Fernandes has also argued that if the racial injustices in Brazilian society are to be resolved, Blacks must force racial conflicts into the open. To expand on his argument, I would like to propose that (a) Blacks do exploit opportunities to generate racial conflicts, and (b) the current abertura democrática offers new possibilities for doing so. What follows is a discussion of the ability of Blacks to enlarge racial conflict through the mobilization of racial consciousness and racial protest. Some of the strengths and limitations of this approach to collective political action will also be reviewed.

RACIAL CONSCIOUSNESS AND RACIAL PROTEST

The abertura democrática has created a healthy climate for racial consciousness. With a number of other groups demonstrating their ability to confront an authoritarian and repressive regime, Blacks have also rediscovered the strength of collective assertiveness. In fact, one is tempted to label this recent blossoming of racial consciousness a Black renaissance comparable to that of the 1920s and '30s when the Black Brazilian press and the Frente Negra Brasileira flourished.

Some of the transformations brought on by this new consciousness are no less than astonishing. By the late 1970s, symbols of militancy which had belonged only to distant American cousins a decade ago were pervasive and commonly accepted by Afro-Brazilians. Afros and cornrow hairstyles were being worn by models appearing in the most established and fashionable Brazilian magazines; the intricate rituals of Black power greetings had been adopted by younger Afro-Brazilians; and Black university students were quoting knowledgeably from Malcolm X and Frantz Fanon. Moreover, Afro-Brazilian poetry and fiction had begun to reflect significant aspects of the racial consciousness movement.[34]

Two occurrences mark the high points in the evolution of this Black consciousness. One is the development of the cultural phenomenon known as Black-Soul and the other is the creation of the Movimento Negro Unificado Contra Discriminação Racial (MNUCDR, or MNU). As these two phenomena have been described elsewhere in this volume, I will not attempt to discuss them exhaustively.[35] Nevertheless, I will sketch a few details of these movements in order to provide some background for the discussion which follows.

The Black-Soul movement is not, properly speaking, a political expression of racial consciousness, although it does have political overtones. It embodies the changes in fashion, popular music, and dance which closely resemble changes in Black American styles during the late 1960s and early '70s. The focal point of the movement is the disco soul club frequented primarily by working-class Black youths. Like their American counterparts, the soul clubs of Rio and São Paulo offer the music of Stevie Wonder, Aretha Franklin, and others, played with a heavy beat, an extravagant presentation of colors, and the opportunity to strike postures of personal ostentation. As a frequenter of one of these clubs put it, "The dances are like a parade of vanities."[36]

The soul movement is, above all, a commerical endeavor. Its music is intended to be sold in an entertainment market for profit. In fact, some have argued that it is a Trojan horse through which multinationals (particularly Warner-Electra-Atlantic Records) can gain a stronghold into a lucrative market. The promoters of soul were ambitious enough at one point to believe that the music would have the impact on Brazilian popular culture that jazz had on American tastes a half-century ago. Although these expectations have not been fulfilled, the movement still enjoys considerable, but less ostentatious, popularity, especially among the young.

The sociological significance of the movement lies in the fact that it reflects spontaneous feelings of racial assertiveness, and even, to a large extent, overt racial hostility. On one recent occasion in São Paulo, for example, a near riot broke out over the perceived arrogance of some whites who allegedly refused to follow the informal codes of conduct in a club. Thus, the soul clubs are rarely places where the myth of Brazilian racial harmony is realized. As one initiate explained the racial antagonism, "When poor Blacks have the audacity to leave their favelas to do something besides samba, the accusation is made that they are losing their negritude, and that they ought to keep on doing the samba. This is the same as saying, 'Stay in your favela, live there, suffer there, and die there.' "[37]

One criticism that has emerged because of obvious similarities is that the soul movement is an artificial transplant of 1960s Black America. To question the authenticity of this phenomenon seems to miss the mark, however. Afro-American and Afro-Brazilian cultures were shaped by institutions in slave societies that functioned in similar ways. It should come as no surprise that, given the reality of the global dispersion of mass consumer technology, a certain degree of cross-pollination occurs.

More important still is the fact that this movement represents a genuine search for new ways to express Black distinctiveness in Brazilian society. More traditional manifestations, such as samba clubs, are being abandoned because Afro-Brazilians see them as having been corrupted by the commercial and cultural dominance of whites. Black-Soul represents one new alternative that is revitalizing Afro-Brazilian culture. Such is the case with the Escola de Samba Quilombo, which uses a traditional vehicle of Black culture—namely, carnaval—to foster reappraisals of the Black Brazilian experience. One suspects, therefore, that criticism of the Black-Soul movement stems from the bitter feelings whites experience over attempts by Blacks to free their own cultural expressions from white domination.

Whatever proves to be the final judgment on the "authenticity" of the Black-Soul movement, one thing is clear. It is a sign of racial conflicts coming to the surface. Moreover, its visibility has helped to shape the evolving political consciousness of others.

The major shortcoming of the Black-Soul movement is that it expresses feelings of racial assertiveness in diffuse ways. Florestan Fernandes, in fact, referred to this stage in the development of racial consciousness as an "innocuous inconformity."[38] The movement lacks a structure through which to channel these feelings into constructive political action.

The crystallization of this consciousness occurred in São Paulo on July 7, 1978, when the MNU launched a public demonstration against racism that attracted some 2,000 persons. Black speakers came from various parts of Brazil to condemn several of the more recent and flagrant instances of discrimination and the pervasiveness of Brazilian racism in general. The manifesto read at the demonstration clearly stated the purpose of the event:

> Today we are in these streets in a campaign of denunciation!
> We are promoting a campaign against racial discrimination, against police oppression, against unemployment and marginalization. We are in the streets to denounce the terrible living conditions of the Black community.
> Today is an historic day. A new day begins for Black people!
> We are leaving the meeting rooms, the conference rooms, and we are going to the streets. A new step has been taken in the struggle against racism.
> Let the racists take cover, for we will demand justice. Let the assassins of Black people take cover, for we shall again demand justice. . . .
> We invite the democratic sectors of society to support us in creating the necessary conditions for a true racial democracy.
> —AGAINST RACIAL DISCRIMINATION
> —AGAINST POLICE OPPRESSION
> —FOR THE GROWTH OF THE MOVEMENT
> —FOR AN AUTHENTIC RACIAL DEMOCRACY[39]

The MNU has furthered its goals in several ways. Its *centros de luta*, now renamed action groups, work to raise Black consciousness on a grass-roots level, while its leadership has attempted to establish a Black presence within the democratic Left. Moreover, the MNU has taken up the cause of the community of Cafundó, a village located near the city of Sorocaba, São Paulo, which has been involved in a bitter land dispute with a local *fazendeiro*.

Both the general ferment of the abertura and factors more directly related to the evolution of the race consciousness movement contributed to the creation of the MNU.[40] One of the events that precipitated its founding closely and sadly paralleled the Herzog affair. The incident in question involved the murder of a Black worker, Robson Silveira da Luz, while in police custody. Outrage against this injustice unmistakably called to mind the public reaction to the Herzog murder.

Another government action had its effect as well. Diplomatic recognition of the MPLA in Angola stimulated Black activism, just as the African independence movements had done for the American civil rights movement in the 1950s and '60s. The victory of a Luso-African colony after protracted fighting made the efficacy of militant political action more credible for Afro-Brazilians.

Moreover, Black university students were being exposed to the increasing militancy of the student movement in general, and the activities commemorating the ninetieth anniversary of the abolition of slavery, held on the campus of the University of São Paulo, did much to foster this kind of student interaction.

The Black-Soul movement also had its impact on the MNU. The limitations of such a movement had been apparent to many of the founders of the MNU for some time, however. They had participated in various forms of racial expression including theater, community organization, and cooperativism, and were cognizant of the limits of these approaches. In any event, the MNU was the outgrowth of several factors which saw protest activity as a logical step in the struggle to correct racial injustices.

Having thus described two important examples of the recent Black consciousness movement, I would like to raise the following questions: how do these recent manifestations fit the contours of the abertura democrática; and what possibilities does the abertura offer Blacks for effective political mobilization in the future?

I have argued that the abertura democrática is a process in which authoritarian elites are losing control over the management of social and political conflicts. The result of this is a general questioning of the nature of the present regime and a search for viable alternatives.

Can Blacks gain anything from this period of ambiguity and searching? Available evidence suggests that during periods of regime transition in Brazilian history, Afro-Brazilian race-consciousness movements do at least experience a broadening of their ideological horizons. Thomas Flory, for example, has recently called attention to the emergence of the "colored press" during the Regency period (1831–1841).[41] He points out that, besides raising the issue of racial discrimination, this press also actively took part in the intense debate regarding the legitimacy of monarchical institutions. And even though the "colored press" may have been manipulated by stronger political forces as Flory asserts, it certainly stimulated questions about the type of political order, monarchical or democratic, that would have best served free Blacks in the nineteenth century.

Similarly, the Vargas Revolution of 1930 kindled in Blacks a sense of liberation from social control by the once-dominant rural oligarchs. This spirit allowed them to contemplate what was then a novel way of participating in the political process. The Frente Negra Brasileira translated this into an independent Black political party whose purpose was to run racially conscious candidates for elective office at all levels. While the Frente Negra could not completely free itself from fascist corporatism, which the Vargas Revolution brought in its wake, some elements of the movement did break away to issue the *Manifesto in Defense of Democracy* at a time when the repressive Estado Novo was facing insurmountable attacks.[42]

This recent abertura may have the same effect as those of previous eras. With vigorous discussions now taking place about political relationships and controls under authoritarian (1964–present [1985, ED.]) as well as democratic governments (1945–1964), Blacks are coming to understand the social and political mechanisms that have frustrated their movements in the past. One small illustration of this is Eduardo Fereira de Oliveira's reply to the National Conference of Brazilian Bishops regarding their intention to create a Negro Pastoral. Oliveira, an ex-Christian Democrat and local São Paulo politician once closely associated with the populism of Jânio Quadros, expressed the fear that the Church would commit the error of extending the kind of paternalistic support to Blacks that it had in the past. On other occasions Oliveira has also suggested that Blacks guard against the reestablishment of the populism of a former era with which he was associated.[43]

In this regard, the efforts of Abdias do Nascimento to elaborate what he calls the ideology of Quilombismo can be enlightening. Quilombismo resembles the work of Cheik Anta Diop and Chancellor Williams. This approach attempts to construct a systematic explanation for the present condition of Black Brazilians and to offer a plan of political action to alter that condition. Nascimento's purpose, like that of Diop and Williams, is to recapture from white control the collective memory of an African community by emphasizing the achievements of Blacks in science, technology, and culture. In addition, Nascimento offers an explanation for the impoverishment of Blacks by attributing it to the impulses of western man and his colonization of the non-European world. In this respect Quilombismo represents an intellectual tool with which to shape the still-inarticulate but genuine feelings of many Afro-Brazilians regarding the arrogated superiority of Western civilization and the presumed inevitability of its progress.

As mentioned previously, Quilombismo also lays out the blueprint of a new social and political order, some of whose main tenets are the following:

1. The realization of an anti-racist, anti-capitalist, and anti-imperialist revolution.
2. The transformation of the relations of production by democratic and peaceful means.
3. The promotion of human happiness through economic organizations based on communication and cooperative principles.
4. The collective use of the means of production (land as well as industry) and the just distribution of their products.
5. The establishment of a system of government based on egalitarian democracy.

6. Automatic apportionment of half of all important government posts to women.

7. Establishment of employment, education, and freedom of religion as basic human rights.[44]

While the eclecticism and utopianism in this program are clearly evident, it would be an obvious injustice to criticize the program strictly on these grounds, particularly because the ideology of Quilombismo is still at an inchoate stage of development. Moreover, the apparent similarities between Quilombismo and other, more established, ideologies should not detract from its unique origins as an Afro-Brazilian ideology and hence its applicability to the particular circumstances of Afro-Brazil. In any event, the test of its durability rests with the masses of Afro-Brazilians and the degree to which they will find it convincing enough to sustain them in drawn-out and often frustrating political confrontations. If Quilombismo inspires large numbers to political action, it can also affect the future course of the abertura democrática by making racial justice one of the goals to be achieved in a new political order.

There is still another way in which the abertura provides new directions for racial protest and racial mobilization. Abertura has been described as a political no-man's-land where no combination of political forces has yet established its legitimacy or ideological hegemony. Blacks can certainly enter this vacuum with their own redefinition of racial issues for political debate. Such a move raises the stakes in the struggle by escalating the demands Blacks can make in return for their allegiance and their fundamental political identity in the Brazilian nation. Rather than demand a "second Abolition," an issue that was basic to the movements of the 1920s and '30s, Blacks can make sweeping revisions in the substance of issues around which racial conflicts are fought in the political arena.

This process has in fact already begun with the articulation of "radical" issues in the area of Brazilian race relations. An example is Abdias do Nascimento's assertion that the Black-Brazilian experience is primarily one of genocide. One solution is government repayment for the loss of life, limb, and liberty suffered during slavery. If articulated forcefully and dramatically, the issue could compel Brazilians to abandon their complacent notions about "racial democracy"; moreover, it could stimulate Blacks to rethink the extent to which their allegiance to Brazil has been taken for granted in light of the validity of their claim to compensation due for past injustices practiced by the state.[45]

Another question which Blacks have begun to articulate in this regard is whether to consider Brazil's entire inmate population as political prisoners. This issue is of immediate concern to Blacks, who comprise an inordinate proportion of the common prisoners in Brazilian jails. Again, if articulated forcefully, one scenario might have this issue provoking a radical debate over the manner in which social institutions marginalize Blacks by insidious means.[46]

The success of Afro-Brazilian protest, however, depends on more than analyzing the theoretical potential of enlarging conflicts or developing ideologies. Leadership, organization, and material resources are the more crucial components of success, the lack of which places the severest constraints on current racial-consciousness movements. Tensions have already emerged within these movements over their future direction in light of these scarcities. Some have argued that a practical course should be taken, such as the continuation of consciousness-raising efforts through cultural forms. Others insist on pursuing militant political action to guard against a recurrence of "innocuous inconformity."

Where resources are concerned, it might do well to recall the old saw that "nothing succeeds like success." That is, any victory in a new area of conflict might attract the leadership and organizational and material resources needed to sustain a political movement. It must also be kept in mind, however, that the first principle of successful protest depends on the shrewd calculation of risks to be assumed in a protest situation. The continuing drama of Brazilian race relations hinges on calculating and assuming the risks needed to "overcome" in new racial conflicts.

Because of space limitations, this discussion has only skimmed the surface of the issue at hand. Questions regarding the possibility of government initiatives in race relations, or the potential role of electoral and coalition politics have yet to be analyzed. I hope this chapter has succeeded in showing that the abertura democrática does offer political outlets for an invigorated Afro-Brazilian consciousness.

In the final analysis, Afro-Brazilians will decide the course of their political action. This writing is intended to reinforce the call to action made by the veteran Afro-Brazilian activist Abdias do Nascimento: "It may be possible to create a [Black] organization that isn't confined to research and analysis but that provides some direction to the Black Brazilian reality. We should participate on all those fronts that are fighting for redemocratization, and not remain outside of the process. That is what I see for the future. The destiny of the Black Brazilian is the same as that of the country."[47] For Afro-Brazilians, destiny remains open.

Postscript: This chapter was completed shortly after the Figueiredo government had initiated its program of political liberalization. At that early date the fate of this initiative appeared uncertain. Particularly during its early years, the direction of liberalization might have been driven off course by disgruntled elements of the authoritarian regime, which could at any moment have precipitated an unforeseen political crisis, as was the case of the Rio Center bombing incident in 1981. In this atmosphere of uncertainty, Brazilian politics continued to be calculated on the premise of overshadowing cycles of loosening and constraining of authoritarian control (abre-fecha).

After the gubernatorial elections of 1982, however, the pace of liberalization accelerated far beyond the designs of its architects. Throughout 1983 and 1984, mass mobilizations in favor of direct presidential elections and the convening of a constituent assembly thrust the process of democratization toward its conclusion. By 1985, with the inauguration of the first civilian president in more than twenty years, the possibility of a sudden closing of the political process or a return to authoritarian rule had become remote. Nevertheless, the sense of political uncertainty that had surrounded the previous regime promised to continue under the current regime. The new government would have to rise to the test of reestablishing relationships between the state and civil society along authentically democratic lines. One of these tests will occur when the new regime decides how it will handle the Black consciousness movement that emerged from the tensions of authoritarianism, the genesis of which has been described in this chapter.

NOTES

1. The research on which this essay is based was supported by the William Hallum Tuck Fund and the Latin American Studies Program of Princeton University.
2. Dr. Plínio de Arruda Sampaio, in *Anais do encontro nacional pela democracia: Paneis da crise brasileira*, vol. 3, edited by the Centro Brasil Democrático (Rio de Janeiro: Editoras Avenir, Civilização Brasileira, Paz e Terra, 1979), 77.
3. *The New York Times* has been carrying accounts of these developments sporadically. See, for example, 17 September 1979, p. 2; 13 October 1979, p. 8; 13 January 1980, Section IV, p. 3; 10 February 1980, p. 3. See also *Veja* 539 (3 January 1979) for a report on Geisel's formal revocation of Institutional Act Number Five.
4. Abertura democrática is still an issue intensely debated by Brazilians. For a sample of opinions, see Centro Brasil Democrático, *Paneis da crise brasileira*; Tão Gomes Pinto, "O jogo do abre-fecha," *Isto é* 157 (26 December 1979); Nelson Werneck Sodre, "A ditadura acabou?" *Movimento* 159 (17 July 1978); and "Receta Brasil," *Veja* 523 (13 September 1978). "Receta Brasil" contains commentaries by Raymundo Foaro, Florestan Fernandes, Francisco Weffort, Fernando Henrique Cardoso and others; Fernando Henrique Cardoso, et al., "Para onde vai o Brasil?" *Movimento* 217: 12–15 (27 August 1979). Whether democratic freedom is a truly "popular" issue has severely divided the Brazilian Communist Party recently; see *Isto é* 157: 12–14 (26 December 1979). Further commentaries can be found in "Oh Brazil," *The Economist*, 4 August 1979, 3–22 (a survey), and Robert M. Levine, "Democracy without Adjectives," *Current History* 78 (454): 49–52 + (February 1980). For more formal theoretical discussions of

redemocratization, see: Guillermo O'Donnell, "Tensions in the Bureaucratic-Authoritarian State and the Question of Democracy," in *The New Authoritarianism in Latin America*, edited by David Collier (Princeton: Princeton University Press, 1979), 285–318; Fernando Henrique Cardoso, *Autoritarismo e democratização* (Rio de Janeiro: Paz e Terra, 1975); Philippe Schmitter, "Liberation by Golpe: Retrospective Thoughts on the Demise of Authoritarian Rule in Portugal," *Armed Forces and Society* 2(1): 5–33 (Fall 1975); Nicos Poulantzas, *The Crisis of Dictatorships*, translated by David Fernbach (London: NLB, 1976); Juan Linz, *The Breakdown of Democratic Regimes: Crisis, Breakdown and Reequilibration* (Baltimore: Johns Hopkins University Press, 1978); José Eduardo Faria, *Poder e legitimidade* (São Paulo: Editora Perspectiva, 1978).

5. Nelson Werneck Sodre, *Historia da imprensa no Brasil* (Rio de Janeiro: Editora Civilização Brasileira, 1966), 53–100; Thomas Skidmore, *Politics in Brazil, 1930–1964: An Experiment in Democracy* (London: Oxford University Press, 1967), 9, 79.

6. Alfred Stepan, "Political Leadership and Regime Breakdown: Brazil," in *The Breakdown of Democratic Regimes: Latin America*, edited by Juan Linz and Alfred Stepan (Baltimore: Johns Hopkins University Press, 1978), 110–137; Alfred Stepan, *The Military in Politics: Changing Patterns in Brazil* (Princeton: Princeton University Press, 1971), chapter 7; Thomas Skidmore, *Politics in Brazil*; Ronald Schneider, *The Political System of Brazil* (New York: Columbia University Press, 1971), 21–36; Helio Jaguaribe, *Economic and Political Development: A Theoretical Approach and a Brazilian Case Study* (Cambridge: Harvard University Press, 1968), 163–174; Octavio Ianni, *O colapso do populismo no Brasil* (Rio de Janeiro: Civilização Brasileira, 1971). Jan Knippers Black, *United States Penetration of Brazil* (Philadelphia: University of Pennsylvania Press, 1977) discusses U.S. involvement in the coup of 1964.

7. See Schneider, *The Political System of Brazil*, and Stepan, *The Military in Politics*.

8. Stepan, *The Military in Politics*, 234, 243–247; Schneider, *The Political System of Brazil*, 89–90, 120–121, 131–132. See also the brief analysis of Castelo Branco's political orientation contained in *Veja* 187: 36–47 (5 April 1972).

9. George-Andre Fiecheter, *Brazil Since 1964: Modernization under a Military* Regime (New York: John Wiley and Sons, 1975), 87–88.

10. Fiecheter, 89; Schneider, chapter 5.

11. Fiecheter, 155–162; Carlos Castello Branco, *Os militares no poder: O ato 5* (Rio de Janeiro: Nova Fronteira, 1977).

12. Fernando Pedreira, *Brasil política, 1964–1975* (São Paulo: Difel, 1975), 273–290; Alfred Stepan, *The State and Society* (Princeton: Princeton University Press, 1978), 104; Fernando Henrique Cardoso, *O modelo político brasileiro* (São Paulo: Difusão Europeia do Livro, 1973); Alfred Stepan, ed., *Authoritarian Brazil* (New Haven: Yale University Press, 1973).

13. General Golbery, reputedly the principal architect of abertura, left the Figueiredo government, where he was chief of the President's civilian staff, expressing dire warnings against the authoritariansim and excessive powers of his own brainchild, the National Information Service (SNI), and its head, General Octavio de Medeiros (August 1981).

14. Hugo Abreu, *O outro lado de poder*, 3a edição (Rio de Janeiro: Nova Fronteira, 1979), 78. Abreu refers to the battles over presidential succession as world wars. The Castelistas lost the "First World War" with the election of Costa e Silva but won the "Second World War" with Geisel's election. Fernando Pedreira and Luis Perreira also suggest that Geisel's government represented return to one of the authentic goals of the 1964 movement, that is, the "perfection of democracy" which the "hardliners" under Costa e Silva and Médici had distorted through the repression of dissidents. See Fernando Pedreira, *Brasil política*, 274–278; and Luiz C. Bresser Perreira, *O colapso de uma aliança de classes*

(São Paulo: Editora Brasiliense, 1978), 157. On the conflict between "hardliners" and the Castelistas see also Schneider, *The Political System of Brazil*, 254–255, 257.

15. Perreira, *O colapso de uma aliança de classes*, 38–41; Celso Lafer, *O sistema político brasileiro* (São Paulo: Editora Perspectiva, 1975), 115–123; Walder Goes discusses the Brazilian response to U.S. human rights policies in *O Brasil do General Geisel* (Rio de Janeiro: Nova Fronteira, 1978), 163–185.

16. "O modelo nasce das urnas," *Veja* 325: 20–45 (27 November 1974); "Eleições: A redescoberta da política," *Visão* (18 November 1974), 20 + ; Bolivar Lamounier and Fernando Henrique Cardoso, eds., *Os partidos e as eleições no Brasil* (Rio de Janeiro: Paz e Terra, 1975); Alfred Stepan, *The State and Society*, 104–106.

17. Hugo Abreu, *O outro lado de poder*, 107–114; António Carlos Fon, *Tortura: Historia da repressão política no Brasil* (São Paulo: Global Editora, 1979), 68–69.

18. "Os limites da estatização," *Veja* 359 (23 July 1975); "Estatização: O debate político," *Veja* 402 (19 May 1976); "O modelo em discussão," *Veja* 425 (27 October 1976); "A saida de Severo Gomes," *Veja* 441 (16 February 1977); Peter Evans, *Dependent Development: The Alliance of Multinational, State and Local Capital in Brazil* (Princeton: Princeton University Press, 1979), 265–273; Luiz C. B. Perreira, *O colapso de uma aliança de classes*, 127–128.

19. Peter Evans, *Dependent Development*, 85–92; Thomas Skidmore, *Politics in Brazil*, 41–47.

20. "A Igreja no Brasil," *Veja*, 434 (29 December 1976); "Dom Paulo Evaristo Arns: 'A Política e uma Necessidade," *Veja* 474 (5 October 1977); Georges-Andre Fiecheter, *Brazil Since 1964*, 149–155. On the Dom Hipólito Affair, see *Movimento* 231: 12–13 (3–9 December 1979).

21. Hugo Abreu, *O outro lado do poder*, 68–71. Goes argues further that Geisel's middle course should not be interpreted as a liberal or progressive one; rather it reflected a changing locus of power within the regime from military to civilian government bureaucracies. See Walder Goes, *O Brasil de General Geisel*, 105–112; Perreira, *O colapso de uma aliança de classes*, 129.

22. "Sucessão: O candidato civil," *Veja* 466 (10 August 1977). Subsequently, former general Eular Bentes Monteiro became the civilian presidential candidate of the MDB and the strongest challenger to date to the presidential successor handpicked by the regime.

23. "A presença do estudantes," *Veja* 453 (11 May 1977); Hugo Abreu, *O outro lado do poder*, 63–68. Abreu also served as chairman of the National Security Council and was therefore the cabinet official in charge of coordinating government responses to the student protests. His self-portrait as a good soldier performing a reluctant duty is delineated in the following statement:

> Information supplied by the National Information Service suggested that the student movement could "push the government against the wall." . . . Thus, our purpose was to contain the strike movement in Brasília and to avoid larger demonstrations in other parts of the country . . . the thought of 1968 was uppermost in our minds. . . .
>
> One could ask: why didn't we have a dialogue with the students? Unfortunately, that was not part of my mission (Abreu, p. 65).

24. Labor militancy gained momentum in July 1979 when the construction workers of Belo Horizonte went on strike. This action was particularly significant because it diffused criticism that only the blue-collar aristocracy of automobile and metallurgical workers were involved in the new wave of strike activity. One of the construction workers actually lost his life in a confrontation with police during the 1979 strike. It should also be kept in mind that construction workers are among the lowest paid urban workers in Brazil.

For details on the 1978 strikes see *Veja* 508: 68–72 (31 May 1978); and *Veja* 509: 87–90 (7 June 1978). On the Belo Horizonte strike, see "A revolte dos peões," *Veja* 570: 20–25 (8 August 1979); and "Porque Minas pega fogo," *Isto é* 137: 4–11 (8 August 1979). It should also be mentioned that as early as 1977 the Brazilian labor movement, under new leadership, was beginning to make serious challenges to government economic policy. See, for example, "Redemocratização: E os operarios?" *Veja* 471 (14 September 1977). For analyses of recent labor activity see José Alvaro Moises, "Current Issues in the Labor Movement in Brazil," *Latin American Perspectives* 6(4): 51–70 (Fall 1979); and John Humphrey, "Auto Workers and the Working Class in Brazil," *Latin American Perspectives* 6(4): 71–89 (Fall 1979). Interviews with Luis Inácio da Silva (Lula) can be found in *Latin American Perspectives* 6 and Centro Brasil Democrático, *Paneis da crise brasileira* 3: 159–170. For discussion of the politics of the labor movement in general in Brazil, see Kenneth Paul Erickson, *The Brazilian Corporative State and Working Class Politics* (Berkeley: University of California Press, 1977).

25. The following account of the Frota affair is based on Hugo Abreu, *O outro lado do poder*, 87–118, and Walder Goes, *O Brasil de General Geisel*, 63–102.

26. Before he was elected, Figueiredo made the unseemly remark that he preferred the smell of horses to the smell of people. (Figueiredo is a former cavalry officer.) To correct this mistake, after his inauguration he launched a public relations campaign to create the image of a simple man who felt at ease with the "common people." He changed his dark-hued glasses, which gave him a malevolent look, for clear ones and made several well-publicized visits to the *feiras*, commenting on the high price of beans and rice as he went. However, when Figueiredo tried this ploy in the city of Florianópolis in December 1979, he was confronted by elements of the Convergência Socialista who shouted epithets about the nature of his government and, reportedly, about his parentage. Incensed, Figueiredo tried to confront his critics. Eventually, he had to be restrained by his security guards from engaging in an exchange of fisticuffs with certain members of the "*povo.*" After this incident, Figueiredo's Secretary of Social Communication declared that the "man of the people" campaign had come to an end. See also *Isto é* 154: 3–5 (5 December 1979); and *Isto é* 155:8 (12 December 1979).

27. *Isto é* 155:10 (12 December 1979).

28. By 1981, it had reached 110 percent.

29. The Partido Popular, for example, advocated such "progressive" measures as the abolition of latifúndios, redistribution of wealth, and freedom of association for workers and students. But its constituency is the generally conservative business community and the middle classes of the major cities. See *Isto é* 162: 12–13 (30 January 1980), and *Isto é* 157: 7–8 (26 December 1979). Subsequently, the situation was aggravated by Brizola's loss of the Brazilian Labor Party (PTB) to Ivete Vargas by court order and his resultant founding of a third *trabalhista* party, the Democratic Labor Party (PDT).

30. Juan Linz, "Opposition Under an Authoritarian Regime: The Case of Spain," in *Regimes and Opposition*, edited by Robert Dahl (New Haven: Yale University Press, 1973), 171–259.

31. Florestan Fernandes, "Aspectos políticos do dilema racial brasileiro," in *O negro no mundo dos brancos* (São Paulo: Difusão Europeia do Livro, 1973), 259–260.

32. Florestan Fernandes, *A integração do negro na sociedade de classes* (São Paulo: Dominus Editora, 1965); *Circuito fechado* (São Paulo: Hucitec, 1976); with Roger Bastide, *Brancos e negros em São Paulo*, 3d edition (São Paulo: Companhia Editora Nacional, 1971).

33. Suppressing racial conflict through exhortations of the ideology of racial democracy does not occur very subtly or even justly at times. A case in point is the tragic circumstance of Maria Aparecida Rosa, who was barred from a night club in the town of Juiz de Fora

in 1975 and complained loudly enough of the incident to have gotten the attention of then-President Ernesto Geisel. After Geisel learned of the fact he decreed that the offending club be closed immediately and that the perpetrators of the crime be prosecuted. Two points were instructive in this case: first was the swiftness of Geisel's action which was intended to forestall any questioning of the irony of such an incident occurring in a supposed racial democracy; and second was the cruel treatment handed out to Maria Aparecida Rosa for having caused a nation such public embarrassment. Maria Aparecida herself was ultimately accused of being a racist because she too aggressively pursued the case in her quest for justice, and she was fired from her job and forced to leave her home in Juiz de Fora for being a threat to social peace. See the *Jornal da tarde*, 13 May 1976, p. 16. On racial ideology and social control in Brazil, see Bolivar Lamounier, "Raça e classe na política brasileira," *Cadernos brasileiros* 47: 39–50 (May–June, 1968); and Thomas Skidmore, *Black into White: Race and Nationality in Brazilian Thought* (New York: Oxford University Press, 1974).

34. An example of this literature is Oswaldo de Camargo, *A descoberta do frio* (São Paulo: Edições Populares, 1979).

35. Reports of these movements have appeared in the American press. See Carol Cooper, "Black Rio: Race Consciousness Grows in Rio," *The New York Amsterdam News*, 2 December 1978; Larry Rother, "Brazil's Race Relations: In Theory and Practice," *The Washington Post*, 12 October 1978; and *Encore*, 5 March 1979.

36. *Veja* 429: 156 (24 November 1976).

37. *Ibid.* (my translation)

38. Florestan Fernandes, *Circuito Fechado*, 75–84.

39. Quoted in Abdias do Nascimento, *Mixture or Massacre?: Essays in the Genocide of a Black People* (Buffalo: Afro Diaspora Press, 1979), 213–214.

40. The following is based on Movimento Negro Unificado Contra Discriminação Racial, *Boletim informativo* 1(1) (São Paulo, n.d. xerox); Departamento de Jornalismo, Escola de Comunicação e Artes, U.S.P., Agência Universitaria de Noticias, *Boletim* 4: 41–44 (2d semester, 1979); Clovis Moura, A dificil trajetoria das organizações negras em São Paulo (São Paulo, 1979, Typescript, Commissioned by Centro Brasileiro de Analise e Planejamento [CEBRAP]), 29–33.

41. Thomas Flory, "Race and Social Control in Independent Brazil," *Journal of Latin American Studies* 9(2): 199–224 (November 1977). See also Nelson Werneck Sodre, *Historia da imprensa no Brasil* (Rio de Janeiro: Civilização Brasileira, 1966), 181.

42. See Michael Mitchell, "Racial Consciousness and the Political Attitudes and Behavior of Blacks in São Paulo, Brazil" (Ph.D. diss., Indiana University, 1977), 142–143.

43. Eduardo de Oliveira, "Pastoral do Negro Brasileiro," *Jornal da tarde*, 31 July 1979, p. 4.

44. Abdias do Nascimento, "Quilombismo: Um conceito científico emergente do processo histórico-cultural das massas afro-brasileiras," Documento No. 7 (São Paulo, 1979, Typescript); and Nascimento, "Princípios e propósitos do Quilombismo," *Folha de São Paulo*, Folhetim, 9 September 1979, p. 7.

45. The issue of genocide and reparations is discussed in Abdias do Nascimento, *O genocidio do Negro brasileiro* (Rio de Janeiro: Paz e Terra, 1978); see especially Florestan Fernandes' preface.

46. See, for example, Hamilton Bernardes Cardoso, "A vez dos presos comuns," *Isto é* 155: 42–46 (12 December 1979).

47. Abdias do Nascimento, "Nossos Negros solitários," *Veja* 512: 6 (28 June 1978).

8

THE UNIFIED BLACK MOVEMENT: A NEW STAGE IN BLACK POLITICAL MOBILIZATION

LÉLIA GONZALEZ

The purpose of this chapter is to characterize the Unified Black Movement against Racial Discrimination (MNUCDR) in the context of the Brazilian Black movements in general, and to establish its relationship with the Brazilian Negro Front (Frente Negra Brasileira, or FNB),[1] and the Negro Experimental Theater (Teatro Experimental do Negro, or TEN).[2] Although the MNU arose from both of the latter groups, the time of its emergence has imbued it with characteristics that distinguish it from its predecessors.

The process of industrialization and urbanization in Brazil took place in two stages, competitive capitalism and monopoly capitalism. The first stage ended in the mid-1950s, and the second reached its height after 1968. The sectors connected with competitive capitalism were subordinated by the hegemonic monopoly system whose tentacles extended even to the most backward regions. These events have resulted in the coexistence of two distinct labor markets that demand qualitatively distinct labor forces (Gonzalez 1979a).

This uneven development combined and integrated different eras. A great part of the surplus population became a marginal mass under the monopoly system and an industrial reserve army within the subordinate competitive sector. Precisely because the latter's capacity for absorbing manual labor is very low, a marginal mass also exists in relation to it. Clearly, conditions related to unemployment and underemployment have especially harsh effects upon that surplus population (Nun 1978).

The novelty of the MNU rests in the fact that it recognizes the problems related to the integration of the system (harmonious or conflictual relations between the parts of a system), their articulation with the problems of social integration (harmonious or conflictual relations between the actors), and the effects of that articulation on Black people. It is that recognition which distinguishes MNU from the FNB and the TEN, whose approach was concerned mainly with the problems related to racial integration. The MNU combines race and class problems as its focus of concern.

As has often happened in Brazilian history, when movements related to popular mobilization and organization appear, the dominant sectors find means to neutralize them. These means have consisted mainly of two: ideological manipulation and direct repression. Paternalism and authoritarianism, in various manifestations, constitute the essence of Brazilian society. This is especially true if we consider the period from 1930 to the present.

The military coup in 1964 tried to establish a "new order" in Brazilian society, claiming that chaos, communism, and corruption threatened that society. It was therefore necessary to substitute a new economic model for the existing one through the pacification of civil society. To guarantee the new order and the organization of the state, all political parties were disbanded and two new ones created, the National Renovation Alliance (ARENA) and the Brazilian Democratic Movement (MDB). As numerous representatives of the people were deprived of their political rights (*cassação*), Congress "assumed purely ritualistic functions within a latent process of legitimizing and consolidating the rules of the new social contract" (Lafer 1975, 73). On the other hand, there were the dismantling of the Peasant Leagues, the suppression of the urban guerrillas, imprisonment, torture, banishment, and imposed "social peace." The Institutional Acts which culminated in the famous Fifth Institutional Act (AI–5) were the instruments military power used to impose its decisions (Fontaine 1981). The basis for the "Brazilian economic miracle" had been assured. As Fontaine has pointed out,

> "The miracle" is characterized by a high rate of economic growth based on a high level of domestic investment made possible by a great concentration of wealth and the resulting capital accumulation, by a very high level of public sector investment and by massive doses of foreign loans and foreign investment. This resulted in what has been called the "Triple Alliance," joining the state, the multinationals, and local capital (1981).

By this means, the masses were completely excluded from power, having suffered a process of impoverishment; those thus affected included the great majority of the Black people in Brazil.

The years between 1964 and 1970 were characterized by the aggressive introduction of foreign capital in the country, increasing its industrial area, while at the same time denationalizing or destroying the smaller, national, enterprises (a high rate of bankruptcy occurred after 1965). It was through these small enterprises that Blacks had participated in the labor market. On the other hand, the agrarian sector was marked by a growing capitalization characterized by the disappearance of small properties and the rise of great *latifúndia* formed by powerful corporations and supported by the military government. This economic offensive resulted in high levels of unemployment in the rural areas. Due to these factors and the policy of regional differentiation of the minimum wage (which especially favored the Southeast), the only means of avoiding misery and hunger consisted in the migration to the developed regions, the urban centers. Thus began the inversion of the population ratio between the cities and the country (today approximately 60 percent of the Brazilian population lives in the urban areas, and the remainder in rural zones).

With this vast influx of cheap manual labor into the cities it was not difficult for the government to implement its project of economic development through the utilization of this manpower in the construction industry. Together with the automobile industry, the latter would pull the other sectors of the Brazilian economy into the maelstrom of multinational imperialism. The building sector was a great conduit for cheap labor, which was composed mostly of Black manpower. In this sense it is not difficult to identify the great works which characterized the period of the "Brazilian miracle," one of the most impressive examples being the Rio-Niterói Bridge over Guanabara Bay.

The concentration of industries in São Paulo created a new industrial power. Up to then the industrial centers had been Volta Redonda, Osasco, Contagem, and in the last ten years the ABC region around São Paulo with about 500,000 workers. The technological sophistication of the ABC industries requires a level of specialized skills which the great majority of Black people do not possess. As a result, upon leaving the countryside for the city, they have had to concentrate in a labor market which does not demand professional qualifications, with the consequence that Black workers were for the most part bypassed by the "benefits" of the "miracle."

The shrinking of wages in the last fifteen years led to a frightful decline in the standard of living for the great majority of workers. According to the index of 1976, the poor sector of the population received 18 percent of the national income in 1960, whereas in 1976 their share fell to 11 percent. Although in 1960 the Black population did not significantly participate in the labor market (hence its already extremely low standard of living at the time), in 1976, when its participation was higher, its share had actually declined. Therefore, greater participation in the labor market has not meant an improved standard of living for the majority of the Black population.

It was in the 1970s that new Black cultural movements began to proliferate in the Brazilian Southeast. This was the result of the liberation of Black African countries and of the Afro-American drive for civil rights, both of which events were felt in Brazil. In 1972, the Palmares Group in Pôrto Alegre, Rio Grande do Sul, launched the idea of transferring all the traditional Black celebrations from the anniversary of Abolition (May 13, 1888) to November 20, the date of the death of Zumbi, the great leader of the Black Republic of Palmares.[3] May 13 was thus abandoned as the most historically significant date for Blacks in Brazil.[4] After all, true abolition has not yet occurred. For the Brazilian Black population, the "miracle" was being revealed as an illusion. More than ever the slogan "No one can hold this country back" was felt to express a pride in development that had nothing to do with the reality of Black people.

The internal contradictions of the new economic model, together with the oil crisis, ultimately exploded the "miracle." The government of President Geisel was inaugurated under the sign of *distensão*. It was under this government that different sectors of society, students, industrial workers, and workers in general, began to contest the regime. Under the pressure of the Redemocratization Front, the "New Order" was installed by the military establishment. This was the context of the MNU's formation in the city of São Paulo.

THE CREATION OF THE MNUCDR

Two events constituted the concrete decisive factors for the creation of the MNUCDR: the torture and assassination of a Black worker, Robson Silveira da Luz, by policemen of the 44th Police District of Guaianazes on the night of April 28, 1978 ("They have deprived me of my dignity," repeated Robson as he lay dying in his bed), and the dismissal of four Black male children from the volleyball team of the Tietê Yacht Club because of their color (chronicled in the São Paulo press on 17 May 1978). A Black athlete contacted members of São Paulo Black organizations to express his anger and demand that something be done. Meetings followed to discuss what action should be taken and how. On June 18 the MNUCDR was created at the headquarters of the Center for the Study of Black Culture and Art (CECAN). The proceedings were described by journalist Hamilton Bernardes Cardoso as follows,

> Sunday a great meeting was held. A comrade from Rio, the son of a congressman, several representatives and members of associations, newspapers,

and groups. Students, "*blacks*," representatives of nobody. Artists, athletes, the daughter of a painter. A long afternoon of debates. Elsewhere, everyone was watching the soccer game between Brazil and Argentina. In the end it was decided to create a Unified Movement against Racial Discrimination. Its first act was already scheduled: the holding of a demonstration on the 7th of July on the Chá Viaduct in São Paulo. This movement should bring together all the sectors of the Black Community, independently of any ideology, against the common enemy, Racial Discrimination (1978).[5]

Contacts were established with Rio de Janeiro. A Black athlete from São Paulo happened upon a meeting of Blacks in Rio and informed them of the occurrences. It was now up to them to activate the Black organizations in Rio. A few days before, Abdias do Nascimento had arrived, returning from the United States.[6] The organizations that were contacted supported the new movement and sent messages of solidarity. In the meantime, in São Paulo, the first desertions occurred, motivated by the old fear of repression and the new fear of commitment. After all, a demonstration was something very serious, even daring. But the determination and lucidity of the other brothers and fellow activists were not weakened by such apprehensions.

July 7, 1978, became the nexus of protest and the need for political organization, which was already taking place in different states in the country. Declarations of support kept coming from these states, as well as from non-Black organizations and groups. Letters were sent by Black prisoners from the House of Detention in São Paulo, and by the Group of Afro-Brazilian Grandsons of Zumbi. Most memorable was the appearance of an old Black man who could hardly read aloud, who joined the multitude present at the demonstration in the manifesto condemning racism. Tears made it difficult for him to read. It seemed as though he might have been referring to the Brazilian Negro Front of the 1930s.

In a meeting held on July 23 in a meeting room of the Christian Charitable Association of Brazil, or ACBB, in São Paulo it was decided to add the word "Black" to the name of the movement, which became the "Unified Black Movement Against Racial Discrimination." At this interstate meeting (with delegations from the states of São Paulo and Rio de Janeiro), a six-member temporary commission was elected to prepare the basic documents of the MNUCDR: the Charter of Principles, the Action Program, and the Statutes. As the discussions continued, different tendencies appeared that ran from the most progressive to the most conservative. The former views were held by the younger generation and the latter by older people and by Blacks with a better standing within the São Paulo middle class.

A few days later, I accompanied Nascimento to Salvador in order to contact Black activists there. They immediately joined and promised to come to the National Assembly which would take place in September of that year in Rio. In August, a group of Black intellectuals from Rio and São Paulo went to Belo Horizonte, Minas Gerais, to participate in the Second Week of Afro-Brazilian Studies, organized by the Institute of History and Art of Minas Gerais. With the exception of one, they all belonged to the MNUCDR, and two among them had belonged to the temporary commission mentioned above. During that visit they obtained the adherence of a Black couple who agreed to organize the MNUCDR in Belo Horizonte. Minas Gerais also agreed to be represented at that Assembly in Rio de Janeiro.

On September 9 and 10, 1978, the first National Assembly of the MNUCDR took place at the Institute for Research on Black Cultures (IPCN) in Rio. Delegations from the states of São Paulo, Bahia, Minas Gerais, and Espírito Santo were present, as well as representatives of Rio de Janeiro. Around 300 people were there to discuss and vote on the basic documents and to determine the position of the MNU during the legislative elections to be held on November 15, 1978.

A second National Assembly was held on November 4 in Salvador. It discussed the expansion of the program of the movement and the establishment of November 20 as the National Day of Black Consciousness.

In September 1979 a national meeting took place in Belo Horizonte which undertook a critical assessment of the activities of the MNU and chose the date for the first National Congress of the movement. This congress was held on December 14 through 16, 1979, in Rio de Janeiro.

ORGANIZATIONAL FRAMEWORK AND MEANS OF ACTION OF THE MNU

The creation of basic organizational nuclei named *centros de luta* (CLs) had been proposed in the manifesto of July 7, 1978. These centers were to consist of a minimum of five persons who accepted the statutes and the program of the MNU and would promote debates, information, consciousness raising and the organization of Black people. The CLs should be set up wherever there are Blacks, such as in work areas, villages, prisons, *candomblé* and *umbanda* temples, samba schools, *afoxés*, churches, *favelas*, swamp dwellings, and shanties. Each CL is responsible for choosing the type of action to be developed among the Black people in its area. In this sense, it possesses relative autonomy.

Municipal Coordinating Committees (CMs) are constituted of the representatives of all the CLs in a municipality. The role of these bodies is purely organizational, since the power of deliberation belongs to the general assemblies, constituted of all the members of the CLs.

Above the Municipal or Regional Coordinating Committees, State Coordinating Committees were established, and finally a National Executive Commission (CEN), composed of three members from each state in Brazil. The latter is responsible, among other duties, for the elaboration of the Internal Bulletin of the MNU and the representation of the movement at national and international levels. It normally meets every three months.

The supreme policy-making body of the MNU is the National Congress, which meets once a year. It defines the political orientation of the movement, approves or modifies the statutes, and assesses the activities of the MNU during the preceding year. It has the power to dissolve the MNU by unanimous consent or by a two-thirds vote of all the members.

Practice has demonstrated that, due to regional differences, the organizing structure of the MNU has become more or less decentralized. For this reason, in some states the CLs are virtually nominal and meetings are held through the Coordinating Committees, the famous *grupão*, as some of the militants call it. In other states the CLs function autonomously, with the CMs meeting every two weeks or monthly. At the first National Congress it was proposed and accepted that the term Center of Struggle be changed to Action Group.

As for the CEN, it has met regularly at the different state headquarters and has been representing the MNU at the international level. The members of the CEN are elected by the militants of the CLs for each state, during the National Congress. The CEN also has an organizing character, although its primary function is the management of the MNU at the national and international levels.

The MNU differs radically from the FNB and the TEN in that it does not have a leader with the power to control the destiny of the organization. It is precisely in order to avoid this that the CLs and the Congress constitute the most important bodies of the movement.

The MNU defines itself as a political movement of revindication, without any distinction of race, sex, education, or political or religious belief, and without seeking profit. Its objective consists in the mobilization and organization of the Brazilian Black population in its fight for political, social, economic, and cultural emancipation, which have been blocked by racial prejudice and its practices. At the same time, the MNU also proposes to denounce the different forms of oppression and exploitation of the Brazilian people as a whole. With its program of action as a starting point, it tries to articulate the specific problems of Blacks with the general problems of the Brazilian people.

The national assemblies held in Rio de Janeiro and Salvador clearly point out this combination of goals. For instance, in an item regarding the question of racial discrimination or the racial division of labor, the issues of unemployment and underemployment, of the creation of day-care centers, or of the improvement of housing conditions in the cities and rural areas are also brought forth. While denouncing police violence against the Black population and racial discrimination in the prisons, they also attack the exploitation of prison labor, demanding the rights of organization for the prisoners and the creation of half-way houses for their effective reintegration into society. While denouncing the commercial exploitation, patronizing, and distortion of Black culture, they demand the creation of theaters in the peripheries and reject cultural colonization as a whole.[7] While protesting racial harrassment at work, they also demand better salaries, the right to unionization, and the right to strike.

The militancy of the MNU members seeks to express itself at different levels, including not only work within the communities aimed at organizing them to stand up for their rights and to attend to their most concrete necessities, but also dealing with the larger problems of society as a whole. Thus, the organization of associations of favela dwellers, the establishment of creative arts courses for children in the peripheries of the big cities, the participation in efforts such as the Movement for Amnesty and the Movement for the Defense of the Amazon, the expressed solidarity with the revindication movements of the workers, the support for prisoners' rights, and so on, all constitute forms of action for the MNU.

The movement intervened in both the first and the second congresses of the Brazilian Committee for Amnesty (1978 and 1979), and characterized the so-called common prisoner as a political prisoner:

> We constitute the majority of the Brazilian population and, therefore, the majority in the prisons, in the juvenile houses of correction, and among the beggars as well, the most oppressed of the oppressed. The reactions to this situation are diverse. The assault on private property is the most common form, and the penalties for this are more severe than for homicides. It is characteristic of this system that the greatest care should be afforded to the protection of "things" belonging to others; every one has his own, or rather the minority has its own, while the "rest" have nothing. The assault on private property, although it is a political act (it is a form of contestation), remains at the individual level. If we are to achieve a just society, it is necessary to mount a joint action involving us all. That is why, when we refer to political prisoners, who in their majority belong to the middle classes, we must consider as political prisoners as well all those considered "common" prisoners.

The MNU also intervened in the thirtieth and thirty-first sessions of the Brazilian Society for the Progress of Science (SBPC), exposing racism and racial discrimination at every level of Brazilian society. At the National

Encounter for Democracy (December 1978), a motion was presented situating Blacks and their political struggle within the general context of Brazilian society.

One must also mention the manifestos of denunciation of racism and of the police violence that victimizes Blacks, and the demonstrations in public places. One such instance was the October 1979 symbolic burial of the Afonso Arinos Law carried out in São Paulo.[8] In the same vein, on November 20, 1979, National Day of Black Consciousness, demonstrations and protest marches were held in Rio de Janeiro, São Paulo, Belo Horizonte, Salvador, and João Pessoa (Paraiba).

The campaign developed by the MNU in 1979 was primarily aimed at denouncing police violence. Its effects were felt by the larger society: the Aézio case — a repetition of the experience of Robson da Luz — was made public and aroused public opinion against the torture and assassination of poor and Black workers, objects of a systematic process of racial discrimination. It is important to point out once more that the Black Brazilian citizen is not only discriminated against by the racial division of labor and forced into the growing marginal mass, but is also deprived of his human dignity by the police, who consider him a criminal because he lacks a work passbook signed by a white boss. This is a result of the unemployment and under-employment which the majority of the Black population endures.

The First Congress of the MNU

On December 14 through 16, 1979, the first National Congress of the MNU was held in the municipality of Caxias, Rio de Janeiro, with militant representatives from the states of São Paulo, Minas Gerais, Bahia, Rio Grande do Sul, and Rio de Janeiro. This was a decisive moment for all involved, as a series of modifications and improvements was felt to be necessary, especially as regards the basic documents, strategy, and tactics to be developed.

With respect to the statutes, some modifications were achieved. The shortening of the name of the movement was discussed and adopted, and thus the Movimento Negro Unificado Contra a Discriminação Racial became the Movimento Negro Unificado. "Racial discrimination" was removed as being redundant, since the movement's main objective is obviously the struggle against racism. It was also decided that the headquarters of the MNU shall always be the meeting places of the State or Municipal Coordinating Committees, and the Centers of Struggle. The latter had their names changed to Action Groups. Actually, we had come to the realization that the previous name had a negative effect on the different

Black communities. As a result of the psychological pressures to which they had always been submitted, they felt threatened and were fearful of setting up these basic units. The old fear of police repression was responsible for such a reaction. At the same time we also desired to avoid being associated in people's minds with other, already known, organizations.

Our historical experience with those other organizations has not been the most satisfactory, for when they do not boycott us altogether, they maintain that our objectives will only be achieved with the resolution of the class struggle. This type of reductionism has characterized the Brazilian Left's conservatism vis-à-vis the racial question.

A structural analysis of Brazil's history in the post-Abolition period was undertaken at the Congress, followed by analysis of the present juncture. The Brazilian government's campaign against street violence in the major cities was characterized as a way of distracting attention from the economic crisis that the country was undergoing. By focusing on the "problem of violence," it was preparing to undertake a series of measures that would fall most repressively upon the Black population. Aside from the question of national security, the Brazilian government presents law and order as one of its main objectives. The lowering of the age threshold for criminal responsibility from eighteen to sixteen years of age, and the establishment of preventive detention clearly indicate who will be the principal victims of the system. In the newspapers, on television, and on the radio, the principal theme being presented is that of "violence."

On the other hand, the "December package" of 1979 directly affected the middle class, whose impoverishment keeps worsening.[9] The more dissatisfied the middle class feels, the more reactionary it becomes, supporting such measures as the death penalty in the belief that it will solve the "problem of violence." As a manifestation of this tendency, there have been repeated lynchings of muggers and thieves in recent times.

The inclusion of the death penalty in Brazilian criminal legislation is already accepted as normal. The smallest abandoned Black child is shown on television as a future marginal, or menace to society. In the face of all this, "More Jobs for Blacks" was the MNU's main campaign theme for 1980. By this means we intended to bring out that which the Brazilian government tries to obscure: the economic crisis and the growing unemployment rate that falls mainly on the Black population (our 1979 campaign had denounced police violence).

Another important theme discussed in the Congress was the position of the Black woman. We finally approved a resolution on what might be called "double militancy." This means that externally our priority is the struggle against racial discrimination. On this level, women are side by side with their brothers. Internally, however, women's activities will be directed towards denouncing the machismo of our comrades and deepening discussions about ourselves. If we really wish to bring about the birth of a new society, this can only happen to the extent that we ourselves become new human beings. That is to say, only if we resolve our own alienation will we be able to dialectically transform the society which we are denouncing.

As regards the new political parties, the MNU has not officially supported any of them, for the new parties have not shed their old structures, notwithstanding their "modernizing" rhetoric.[10] Rather, it has decided that, individually, the militants could enter the political groupings of their choice, but always calling attention to the racial question.

The Congress also engaged in intense ideological debates. However, although Quilombismo constitutes one of the points discussed, the commission in charge of elaborating the relevant document was not able to present its work to the assembly due to lack of time.[11] It was decided, therefore, that all the points not discussed in the assembly would be developed by the respective state organizations. The result was to be synthesized by the National Executive Commission at its next meeting. Nonetheless, by consensus, a series of criticisms of Quilombismo was expressed. Basically, it was agreed that personalism and paternalism constitute its weakest points. At the same time, the proposal of a *"quilombola* science" appeared to be devoid of any serious epistemological foundation.

The most elaborate discussions took place over modifications to the Actions they directed against the immigrants. The latter were looked upon as white foreigners who took the place of Blacks in the labor market, but that always move from the specific to the general, we attempted to base them in a more mature and more profound political perspective. The view of the international character of our struggle was greatly simplified, without ever losing sight of the need to characterize and denounce the situation of the Brazilian Black. After all, racism and racial discrimination are not exclusively characteristics of Brazilian society.

THE MNU AND ITS PREDECESSORS

Fundamental differences exist between the MNU, the FNB, and the TEN. Notwithstanding its magnificent efforts, the Brazilian Negro Front became an instrument of the Getúlio Vargas government to the extent that it reproduced its authoritarian nationalism and manipulation of the masses. Ultimately, its protest assumed moralizing characteristics because of its identification with reactionary political movements ("Integralist Action," right-wing sectors of the immigrant community). Its leadership, despite its relentless denunciation of racism and race prejudice, failed to perceive the necessity of challenging the contradictions of the system itself. The FNB did not fight for the inclusion of Blacks into the world of labor. This becomes clear when we observe, for instance, the type of denunciations they directed against the immigrants. The latter were looked upon as white foreigners who took the place of Blacks in the labor market, but were never considered as working class. In that sense, if we analyze the Decree of December 12, 1930, as well as its justification, we will realize that Getúlio himself understood this kind of criticism (addressing all the nation's workers without, of course, specifying their ethnic origins). This decree could be called the "birth certificate" of Brazilian populism, to which the Black population would become fully committed. The leaders of the FNB did not perceive the ideological manipulations utilized by the Vargas government vis-à-vis the Brazilian working class, especially within the emerging sectors of workers situated out of reach of the "subversive" discourse of the Anarcho-Syndicalists, the Socialists, and the Communists. (Anarcho-Syndicalism and Socialism were introduced to Brazil by immigrants, especially the Italians). Vargas substituted for the other ideological tendencies among these new sectors of urban workers. After the coup of 1937, he also took the place of the FNB in the eyes of the Blacks, and with greater efficacy. The labor legislation he created during the Estado Novo principally benefited the Black population. The latter maintained a kind of pact of allegiance with Vargas, especially when he created the Brazilian Labor Party (PTB). With the Estado Novo, a long period of co-optation and manipulation of the Black masses by Brazilian populism was inaugurated.

It was in this context that the Black Experimental Theater was created in the 1940s in Rio de Janeiro. As regards the mobilization of the Black population, the TEN had a far more limited character than the FNB — to the present day the FNB was the greatest Black mass movement ever achieved in Brazil. Like the FNB, the TEN did not address the integration of the system. Furthermore, when the TEN emerged in 1944, the Black population had already committed itself to Vargas.

Because they did not preoccupy themselves with the integration of Blacks into the Brazilian labor market by denouncing the contradictions of the system; because they assumed a paternalistic attitude in relation to Black people; because their leaderships were paternalistic and authoritarian; and because they failed to combine the specific with the general, these two movements failed to motivate the Black popultion as a whole and still less Brazilian society in general. In this sense, it is important to point out the strong resistance of society in relation to the racial question. As Fontaine has ably synthesized, race relations in Brazil present a triple aspect: biological miscegenation, social integration, and cultural assimilation (1979). Being politically paternalistic and authoritarian as well, Brazilian society prefers to believe that it is a "racial democracy." This is much more comfortable and tidy.

Today, the MNU faces similar difficulties, although in a different context. Seventeen years of military authoritarianism, the emergence of mass movements of opposition to the regime, the return of the exiles (who only discovered the existence of racial discrimination in Brazil while they were abroad), the liberation of the Black African nations, and the Black civil rights movement in the United States are new signposts that cannot be ignored. The internationalization of a struggle between oppressors and oppressed in which the oppressed are people of color can no longer go unnoticed by those who place themselves in the most progressive sectors of any society. For the sectors that have something new to offer and to say are exactly those connected with these oppressed, who have previously been unable to express themselves and kept in a state of infantilism maintained by the oppressor.

We of the MNU could not have engaged in our struggle without the consciousness of who we are and what we want. The FNB and the TEN are moments of our history, contradictory, flawed and full of errors; but precisely because of this, they have bequeathed us a wealth of experience. And our history continues. It is our responsibility now to carry forward the struggle initiated by our comrades of the past, who are present in all of us, in another dialectical moment. Thanks to them we now understand that the struggle of the Black people of Brazil is an aspect of a much larger struggle: the struggle of the Black people of the world. We also know that it is present and that it continues.

NOTES*

1. The Brazilian Negro Front was the first major Black movement in post-Abolition Brazil. It flourished in the 1930s; but in 1937, soon after it had transformed itself into a political party, it was abolished as a party, together with the other parties, by the Estado Novo government of Getúlio Vargas. The following year it ceased to exist altogether.
2. The Negro Experimental Theater, founded in Rio de Janeiro by Abdias do Nascimento, prospered in the late 1940s and the '50s. Its objective was to use the theater as a means to raise Blacks' consciousness.
3. Zumbi was the last leader of the *quilombo* of Palmares, the most celebrated settlement of runaway slaves, which survived as an independent polity for nearly a hundred years (1606-1696) in the seventeenth century against repeated Portuguese military assaults.
4. The anniversary of Abolition is commemorated every year by official cultural and religious activities, including masses, processions, and symposia.
5. The English word "black," pronounced "blek" and sometimes spelled "breque," is used in Brazil to designate the members of the Black-Soul Movement in Rio and São Paulo with their distinctive dresses and hair styles. The Viaduto do Chá, a heavily traveled bridge

over a major thoroughfare in downtown São Paulo near the Municipal Theatre is the principal gathering place for Black youths on Friday evenings. It is a clearinghouse of information on upcoming weekend events. There, through word of mouth and the distribution of leaflets, they exchange information on dances, parties, lectures, plays, *capoeira* demonstrations, soccer matches, and all sorts of other activities. It is an effective substitute for telephones, which most of them do not have.

6. Abdias do Nascimento (1968, 1978, 1979*b*), the most widely known Black activist from Brazil, is a co-founder of the MNUCDR and was Chairman of the Puerto Rican Studies Department at the State University of New York (SUNY) at Buffalo.

7. The "peripheries" are the outer areas of the cities where the poor live.

8. The 1951 Afonso Arinos Law against discrimination is seldom invoked in court—and usually unsuccessfully. In private conversations and public speeches, however, it is used as "evidence" that racial discrimination has been eradicated in Brazil. The Law has come under attack from the MNU, other Black activists, São Paulo Black politicians, and even some white legal experts.

9. The "December Package" is a series of measures adopted by the government in December 1979 aimed at stabilizing the economy. Regarding a 1977 "April Package" of political measures aimed at stalling the opposition and securing victory at all costs for the government party, see chapter 7. A 1981 "November Package" was enacted for the purpose of guaranteeing the victory of the government party, the so-called Democratic Socialist Party (PDS), in the November 1982 elections.

10. The post-1964 regime had abolished the traditional political parties, substituting instead a bipartite system made up of ARENA, the party of the government, and MDB, the party of the opposition. In 1979, however, in the face of MDB's increasing popularity, the government decided to fragment the opposition by reestablishing a multi-party system. The new government party became the PDS and the opposition was split into the PMDB, the PTB, the PDT, the PT, and the PP. Although the PCB and the PC do B have reemerged, they have not been legalized.

11. For an extensive exposition of the philosophy of Quilombismo, see Adbias do Nascimento, *O Quilombismo* (Petrópolis: Editora Vozes, 1980).

*Provided by the editor; a version of this chapter appears in L. Gonzalez and C. Hasenbalg, *Lugar do negro* (Rio de Janeiro: Marco Zero, 1982), pages 9–66.

BIBLIOGRAPHY

Azevedo, Thales de 1975. *Democrácia racial: Ideologia e realidade*. Petrópolis: Editora Vozes.

Bastide, Roger, and Florestan Fernandes, eds. 1953. *Relações raciais entre negros e brancos em São Paulo*. São Paulo: Companhia Editora Nacional.

——— 1959. *Brancos e negros em São Paulo*. 2d ed. São Paulo: Companhia Editora Nacional.

Bojunga, Claudio 1978. O brasileiro negro, 90 anos depois. *Encontros com a civilização brasileira* 1: 175–204 (July).

Cardoso, Fernando Henrique 1975. *Autoritarismo e democratização*. Rio de Janeiro: Paz e Terra.

Cardoso, Fernando Henrique, and Octávio Ianni 1960. *Cor e mobilidade social em Florianópolis*. São Paulo: Companhia Editora Nacional.

Cardoso, Hamilton Bernardes 1978. Afro-Latin America. *Versus* (São Paulo) 33 (July–August).

Degler, Carl N. 1971. *Neither Black Nor White: Slavery and Race Relations in Brazil and the United States*. New York: Macmillan.

Dzidzienyo, Anani 1971. *The Position of Blacks in Brazilian Society*. London: Minority Rights Group.

Fernandes, Florestan 1972. *O negro no mundo dos brancos*. São Paulo: Difusão Européia do Livro.

───── 1978. *A integração do negro na sociedade de classes*. São Paulo: Ática.

Fontaine, Pierre-Michel 1979. Models of Economic Development and System of Race Relations: The Brazilian Development Model and the Afro-Brazilian Condition. Paper presented at the Annual Meeting of the Associação Nacional de Posgraduação e Pesquisas em Ciencias Sociais, Belo Horizonte, Minas Gerais, October 17.

───── 1981. "Transnational Relations and Racial Mobilization: Emerging Black Movements in Brasil." In *Ethnic Identities in a Transnational World*, edited by John F. Stack, Jr. 141–162. Westport, Conn.: Greenwood Press.

Freyre, Gilberto 1940. *O mundo que o português criou*. Rio de Janeiro: Livraria José Olimpio Editora.

───── 1978. O Brasileiro como uma além-raça. *Folha de São Paulo* (May 1978).

Gonzalez, Lélia 1979a. Cultura, etnicidade e trabalho: Efeitos linguísticos e políticos da exploração da mulher. Paper presented at the Annual Meeting of the Latin American Studies Association, Pittsburgh, April 5–7. Mimeo.

───── 1979b. A juventude negra brasileira e a questão do desemprego. Paper presented at the Annual Meeting, African Heritage Studies Association, Pittsburgh, April 26–29. Mimeo.

───── 1979c. Racism and its Effects in Brazilian Society. Paper presented at the Women's Conference on Human Rights and Mission, Venice, Italy, June 24–30. Mimeo.

Hasenbalg, Carlos A. 1979. *Discriminação e desigualdades raciais no Brasil*. Rio de Janeiro: Graal.

Ianni, Octávio 1972. *Raças e classes sociais no Brasil*. 2d ed. Rio de Janeiro: Editora Civilização Brasileira.

───── 1978. *Escravidão e racismo*. São Paulo: Editora Hucitec.

Lafer, Celso 1975. *O sistema político brasileiro*. São Paulo: Ed. Perspectiva.

Nascimento, Abdias do 1968. *O Negro revoltado*. Rio de Janeiro: Edições GRDD.

───── 1978. *O genocídio do Negro brasileiro: Processo de um racismo mascarado*. Rio de Janeiro: Editora Paz e Terra.

───── 1979. *Mixture or Massacre? Essays in the Genocide of a Black People*. Buffalo, New York: Afrodiaspora.

Nun, V. 1978, "Superpopulação relativa, exército industrial de reserva e massa marginal." In Luiz Pereira, ed., *Populações "Marginais."* São Paulo: Duas Cidades.

Ramos, Alberto Guerreiro 1954. O problema do negro na sociologia brasileira. *Cadernos de nosso tempo* 2: 207–215.

Skidmore, Thomas 1976. *Brasil: De Getúlio a Castelo*. Rio de Janeiro: Paz e Terra.

Souza, Amaury de 1971. Raça e política no Brasil urbano. *Revista de administração de empresas* 11(4): 61–70 (December).

9

THE AFRICAN CONNECTION AND THE AFRO-BRAZILIAN CONDITION

ANANI DZIDZIENYO

> O uso de nomes africanos
> não é simples modismo.
> O livro e o filme *Roots*
> (raizes negras) mostram que
> todos que quiseram manter
> o nome de origem foram torturados
> até aceitar o nome cristão imposto
> pelo dono!
>
> Maria ou Kinda[1]

On the first day of carnaval in 1977, the ambassadors of Ghana and Nigeria, resplendent in their *kente* and *agbada* cloth, danced on Rio Branco Avenue in Rio de Janeiro in the company of the group Afoxé Filhos de Gandhi. Both ambassadors were "singing in Yoruba" and wearing the same clothes as members of the afoxé.[2] No doubt their identities confused onlookers. A newspaper columnist asked, "Who are these two personalities with complicated names?" It was also noted that they perhaps entered into the activity of celebration with much more verve and enthusiasm than had been anticipated by the officials who had invited them. Not unexpectedly in such coverage of Africana by the Brazilian press, there was some confusion of names and origins.

The participation of African ambassadors in Brazilian celebrations and activities is not new. Ambassador Henri Senghor (Senegal) had spoken at the 1971 Pontifical Catholic University seminar on Afro-Brazilian Studies in Rio.[3] General Mulamba (Zaire) had been present at the swearing-in of Edvaldo Brito as the first Black mayor of Salvador in 1978 and the ambassadors of Ghana, Nigeria, and Gabon had made a joint visit to Bahia in 1976. There have also been several visits to other Brazilian states by

African envoys through the good offices of Itamaraty (the Brazilian Foreign Ministry).

What distinguished the carnaval participation was the high visibility of the two ambassadors on the "Avenida." It was unmistakable evidence of a change in the tone of ambassadorial representation in Brazil. With only one Black Ambassador of Brazil in living memory, the arrival of African diplomats in the middle 1960s was a novelty for many Brazilians. The traditional view of Africa had to be reexamined, because treating African ambassadors in non-ambassadorial fashion would have diplomatic repercussions.

"Preto falando inglês ou francês," and representing a sovereign nation to boot, was not a "preto qualquer."[4] There was a danger that the status of the Black in question might only be discovered after an unpleasant and embarrassing incident. Therefore, the arrival of African diplomats in Brazil, whether or not through a conscious effort on their part, has had a significant impact upon the framework of traditional Brazilian race relations and the position of Afro-Brazilians therein.

Continental Africa can be said to constitute a connection between Herskovits' theory of African retentions, or survivals, and the contemporary realities of Afro-Brazilian life. The latter have not been explored and acted upon by post-colonial African governments because they have retained only the Herskovitsian view of Afro-Brazilians. Finding a satisfactory position between these two dimensions, in our view, constitutes the essence of the African connection and its relation to Afro-Brazilian social mobility.[5]

In his presidential message to the 1952 Congress, Getúlio Vargas discussed the great interest with which the government of Brazil was following political developments in the Mediterranean, the Middle East, and Africa, where nationalist movements in Morocco and Tunisia and the Egyptian government's position on a possible revision of the 1936 Anglo-Egyptian Treaty were all being observed sympathetically by his administration. The progress of the Gold Coast (now Ghana), Nigeria, and other African territories toward political autonomy was also being followed by Brazil.[6] Among the new diplomatic Brazilian missions opened was one in the Ethiopian capital, Addis Ababa.[7]

It was not until the brief 1961 administration of Jânio Quadros that Brazil's African foreign policy would experience a real, salient, leap forward. And yet, nearly a decade and a half after Quadros's dramatic rise and fall, his Foreign Minister, Afonso Arinos de Melo Franco, made the following observation, "Mas o erro fundamental de Jânio na política externa não estara no fundo, que bem planejava e concebia, mas na execução mais que dramática, teatral com que a levava a efeito por motivos de

política interna e pelo seu feitio individual de personagem e autor con-
jugados."[8] Lest the failure of the "innovative" policy be attributed exclusively to these "flaws," Afonso Arinos also criticized some divisional
heads in the Foreign Ministry with whom he had had difficulties. These
were individuals who were "accustomed" to the ill-advised African policy
of Portugal and chose to follow its lead. Being students and practitioners
of such diplomatic formalism as that of the Barão do Rio Branco, they
were unable to rise to the new imperatives of a changing world. They were
like the medieval armour displayed in European museums—impenetrable
and impressive, but hollow. "Essa gente, muitas eram amigos, criou a mais
sutil e resistente rede de seda de obstáculos a minha ação, cujo alcance não
lhes aparecia e que eu não tinha tempo de explicar."[9]

The strong Portuguese economic lobby in Rio wanted to gain a cultural
influence over Black Africa and ensure that the inevitable autonomy there
did not assume a radical character.[10] Amilcar Alencastre highlighted the
activities of that lobby in the media during the 1969 visit to Brazil of Portuguese Prime Minister Marcelo Caetano. The lobby created a one-sided,
pro-Portuguese view of the wars of liberation in Portugal's African colonies, emphasizing Portugal's relations with Brazil which were consistent
with official views of Brazil's role in the defense of frontiers of western
civilization against hostile forces in the South Atlantic, and thus siding
with Portugal's ideological position on African liberation. In Alencastre's
view this constituted a basic contradiction: Brazil could not proclaim its
anti-colonialism and support Portuguese colonialism in Africa simultaneously.[11] "Salvemos a África do Sul," (Let us save South Africa) had
been Admiral Paulo I.R. Freitas's view of the problem in Southern Africa,
because of South Africa's tactical importance for the West due to her
strategic South Atlantic position and guardianship.[12]

Constantino Ianni notes that not even the international dimensions or
repercussions of apartheid could have been expected by many Brazilians
to result in overt racially discriminatory practices in São Paulo. Nevertheless, because of the "colonialist" attitudes of the Brazilian elites in the
face of foreign practices and customs, Itamari and the National Council
of Sports excluded "colored" players from Brazilian teams visiting South
Africa because only whites could stay in hotels. According to Ianni, the
board of the São Paulo team, Palmeiras, behaved "com uma passividade
divorciada da nossa opinião pública, e do sentimento democrático já
cristalizado em lei anti racista."[13]

In the Brazilian context, the African connection is a multifaceted concept embracing official diplomatic relations between Brazil and independent African countries; the efforts of Brazilian companies to "conquer"
the African market; individual and group activities among Afro-Brazilians

interested in both historic and contemporary Africa; the way in which current developments in Africa affect Brazilians generally and Afro-Brazilians specifically; and finally, the exchanges between representatives of the Catholic church in Africa and Brazil.[14]

The discussion that follows focuses mainly on Afro-Brazilians themselves. This enables us to highlight the glaring contradictions between Brazil's renewed interest in Africa and her failure to include Afro-Brazilians in the very operation of this interest. Upon closer examination, what we have called contradictory is, in fact, totally consistent with the general absence of Blacks from the processes of decision making and policy implementation. It stands to reason that no exception would be made in the case of Brazil's official Africa policy.

The United States provides an interesting point of comparison here, particularly with reference to Afro-Americans and their symbolic importance in relations with Africa. The differences between the policies of the United States and Brazil lie in the dynamics of their race relations and the consequences for Blacks. It is not my intention to fully explore these differences here. Suffice it to say that official recognition of the Afro-American factor by the U.S. has led to the entry of Blacks at levels unimaginable in Brazil. Witness the senior appointments in the U.S. armed forces and diplomatic service.[15]

We cannot fail to recognize that between the appointment of Raymundo Souza Dantas as Ambassador to Ghana by Jânio Quadros in 1961 and the admission of Mónica Meneses de Campos as the first Black Brazilian student into the Instituto Rio Branco in 1978, there have not been many landmarks for Afro-Brazilians in the diplomatic service.[16]

On an unofficial level, however, there is growing interest manifested by Afro-Brazilians with relation to contemporary African political, economic, and social developments. It is precisely this interest that links the role of Afro-Brazilians in domestic race relations with Brazil's African policies.[17] The opportunity has thus arisen to better conceptualize the significance of Africa for people of African descent in the southern hemisphere, as compared to those in North America and the Caribbean, whose reflections on and activities in this area are better known.[18]

Manifestations of consciousness of and concern with post-colonial Africa (as distinct from historic Africa) on the part of Afro-Brazilians, aided by their own specific history; the independence of Lusophone Africa; the availability of more information, especially from the U.S.; the official interest in Africa; and the "political opening" in Brazil, all add up to a weakening of the structural, linguistic, and political isolation of Afro-Brazilians.

A writer in the *gaúcho* Afro-Brazilian publication *Tição* recently observed that Brazilians who sought information about contemporary Africa could only expect to find a distorted and sensationalist image in the media, a fact perhaps most poignantly felt by Afro-Brazilians seeking to establish or renew connections with the home of their forebears.[19] It only needs to be added that continental Africans on a similar search to renew contacts with and find information about their "descendants" on the other side would also meet with some problems. Therein lies the challenge and excitement of the connection.

The celebration of African racial, historical, religious, and cultural manifestations in Brazil has received enough attention elsewhere to permit our simply noting the fact, but under a caveat. The mere existence of these retentions does not in itself signify that they are important in Brazil's contemporary relations with Africa. Nor can it tell us anything about whether and if so, how, Afro-Brazilians feature in those relations.[20] As argued elsewhere, "africanity," or the manifestations of an African heritage, may have two distinct forms: (*a*) frozen africanity, which merely celebrates specific historical, cultural, and religious retentions; and (*b*) a dynamic variant, which links those retentions with the sociopolitical realities of contemporary Africa and Latin America. Brazil exemplifies the first paradigm, the United States the second.[21]

For the purposes of this discussion, by contemporary Africa I refer to the independent countries of Sub-Saharan Africa, with the notable exception of South Africa (although I recognize that it is of critical importance due to Brazil's involvement with the apartheid regime there, a situation that bears heavily on Brazil's relations with Black Africa). The time framework for this discussion is the period from 1961 to 1980, which is subdivided into three phases: 1961–1964, 1964–1972, and 1972–1980.

The first phase, particularly the seven months of the short-lived Jânio Quadros government in 1961, marks the formal beginning of Brazil's contemporary relations with Africa. It was then that Brazil took certain significant initiatives: articulation of the policy of *aproximação* to the Afro-Asian world, which meant deemphasizing Brazil's traditional attachment to the United States and the West; establishment of diplomatic relations with African countries; and the appointment of a Black ambassador to head the Brazilian embassy in Ghana, an unprecedented occurrence in the history of Brazil's foreign relations.[22] The Goulart government (1961–1964) to all intents and purposes followed the Quadros line, maintaining formal diplomatic relations with African countries. However, this period saw no dramatic increase in the visibility of Afro-Brazilians involved in the conduct of Brazil's relations with Africa.

The second phase, which began with the military coup d'état of March 1964, saw a return to the traditional bases of Brazilian foreign policy and an internal preoccupation with the threat of communism and subversion.[23] Brazil totally identified with Portugal on the question of Portuguese colonialism and could, therefore, justify her expulsion of Lusophone African students who were known supporters of the struggle against Portuguese colonialism in Africa.[24] Brazil was also involved in ongoing discussions about a so-called South Atlantic Pact, grouping South Africa, Portugal, Argentina, and Brazil to defend their part of the Atlantic from subversion, radicalism, and Communist influence. Indeed, their mission was to uphold the values of Western and Christian civilization.[25]

The final phase, ushered in by the 1972 tour of Africa by then Foreign Minister Barbosa, is one of renewed official interest in Africa. Specifically, Brazil now focuses her attention on "conquering" the African market, deploying carefully devised strategies for increasing her exports of tropical technology and consumer goods to Africa and her imports of such vital supplies as oil and phosphates from Africa.[26] Brazil has acted with remarkable deftness in the conduct of her diplomatic relations with Africa, specifically in her dramatic and comparatively early recognition of the MPLA; her condemnation of apartheid while maintaining links to South Africa; her formal withdrawal from discussions of the South Atlantic Pact; her repeated affirmations of historic and cultural linkages to Africa; and the growing number of African dignitaries who have made official visits to Brazil, among them President Kaunda of Zambia, the Asantehene of Ghana, and Sékou Touré of Guinea.[27]

But from the African viewpoint, what remains missing from this new period of aggressive outreach is a recognizable Afro-Brazilian involvement—particularly at official, more visible, levels.[28] Why, one may well ask, does a country that strongly affirms its cultural and historical linkages to Africa fail to include the living embodiments of those links in the conduct of her relations with Africa? Brazil, in effect, ignores the significance of the racial connection, which we shall call the "Africa Card." The Africa Card can be played by Africans themselves; by governments in the Americas (such as Cuba, Brazil, and the United States) in their political, economic, and military relations with independent African countries; and by Afro-Americans, although this has rarely occurred.[29]

The importance of the city of Salvador, or Bahia, has to be underscored as a factor in Brazilian-African relations. In the eyes of continental Africans, Bahia represents the most potent evocation of the African aspect of Brazilian life and culture.[30] But therein lies the rub, because the Africans' initial enchantment inevitably gives way to disappointment that the Black presence fails to assert itself in areas beyond what may be characterized as the folkloric. We must in fact turn to other areas — São Paulo, Rio de Janeiro, Campinas, Araraquara, Porto Alegre, Caxias do Sul, Florianópolis — for evidence of more concrete attempts to establish connections with contemporary Africa. Witness the sheer volume of activity and publications generated there.[31]

Two illustrations — one drawn from the remote, the other from the immediate past — reflect Bahia's unique role in Brazilian-African relations. The first has to do with the launching of the Frente Negra in Brazil in the 1920s. The local press denounced that organization, calling it an irrelevant export from foreign São Paulo that threatened the security of Bahia's interracial brotherhood. What this posture tells us about Bahian and Brazilian race relations is critical: in seeking to change traditional patterns which disadvantaged Blacks, the Frente Negra encountered a resistance that both extolled the status quo and condemned any move to alter it.[32]

The second, contemporary, illustration is taken from the summer 1978 visit of the Asantehene, monarch of the Ashantis of Ghana, a group well known for their wars against the British in the nineteenth century and the sophistication of their political structures. With the exception of a brief airport meeting with Edvaldo Brito, then secretary of justice, the Asantehene's party did not officially meet any Afro-Bahians in the course of its two-day stay in Bahia, a fact that was not lost on the members as they moved through the city.[33]

The Asantehene's visit to São Paulo provides a sharp contrast. Here the monarch and his party came into contact with a large number of Afro-Brazilians, including federal and state deputies, professionals, journalists, and students, principally through the efforts of Adalberto Camargo, who was the federal deputy from São Paulo, one of three Afro-Brazilians in the National Chamber of Deputies, and founder and president of the Afro-Brazilian Chamber of Commerce. Camargo's many trips to Africa have been essentially for business purposes and so fit more within the objectives of official diplomatic and commercial interests in Africa. At the same time, however, Camargo and his organization have come to serve as an important bridge between Africans and Afro-Brazilians. *Afro-Chamber*, the magazine of the Afro-Brazilian Chamber of Commerce, is published in Portuguese, English, and French, and has a circulation of 20,000 in Brazil and Africa.[34] By the very nature of its activities and interests, the chamber of commerce has not devoted much effort to analyzing the implications of Brazil's intensified activity in Africa for Afro-Brazilians beyond the sphere of trade and commercial relations. Nor has it turned its attention to the relevance of Brazilian tropical technology for Africa itself.[35]

It is in the activities and publications of recent Afro-Brazilian magazines, such as *Tição* and *Sinba*, that the ideological impact of Africa is perhaps clearest: a Rio Grande do Sul poet chose the title *Poemas afrogaúchos*; *Jornegro*, published in São Paulo, devoted sections to African names and their meanings; a player in the Gremio Football Club of Porto Alegre is called Paulo Lumumba; a *Jornegro* writer calls himself Mensah-Gamba; manifestoes exhort Afro-Brazilians never to forget their antecedents; all illustrate the increasing and welcome immediacy of Africa's importance for Afro-Brazilians.[36]

The April 1979 issue of *Sinba* noted that the remarks of António Neder, president of the Supreme Federal Tribunal, on the occasion of the United Nations Day against Racial Discrimination were insulting to the African ambassadors present. Neder's speech included a critique of Arthur de Gobineau and discussed the possible emergence of a Black Hitler, whose rise could only be thwarted if whites addicted to racist habits would no longer practice them.[37]

The Black press has also addressed the connection between Brazil's views of Afro-Brazilians and their inherent "inequality," and its consequences for Brazil's contacts with Africa. The Angolan government's rejection of a Brazilian made-for-television series, on the grounds that it perpetuated a pejorative image of Blacks, prompted the comment in *Jornegro* that "Brazil's views of Blacks will not go over in Africa." It continued, "Os países africanos tem muito a ensinar aos manipuladores das exportações culturais brasileiras. Se negro aqui protesta logo chaman racista. Não da pra fazer o mesmo com o governo de Angola. A revisão na mentalidade brasileira, que muita gente reclama, recebe força, o racismo camuflado não deu certo na Africa."[38] That the series in question was based on a novel by an important figure in Brazilian culture, Monteiro Lobato, was not enough to absolve the work from the racism that Africans perceived, *Jornegro* concluded.[39]

Among the points articulated by a group of Afro-Brazilian protesters in São Paulo in October 1979 was a denunciation of "Brazil's love affair with South Africa."[40]

Some of the more visible Afro-Brazilians involved in the official re-Africanization process have come under the scrutiny of the Black press, and the ensuing debates highlight the differences in official and unofficial views on the African connection. A recent critical essay described Olga de Alaketo, the *mãe de santo* and a not infrequent visitor in Africa, as an "objeto de consumo do poder" (figuratively, a pawn in the hands of those in power) exploited by official Brazil. The essayist cited her presence at the two major festivals of Black art and culture (Senegal in 1966 and Nigeria in 1977).[41] The essay went on to describe her meeting with President Figueiredo in Bahia, on which occasion she was invited to prepare a special dish for the president. The writer objected to the devaluation of Olga as a person and a symbol—a devaluation that was inextricably bound to the "second-class status of Afro-Brazilians."[42]

The African connection generates controversy among Blacks throughout the Americas. In the Brazilian context, the exchanges between George Alakija, a Black psychiatrist with impeccable Yoruba origins, and Abdias do Nascimento, writer, painter, and activist with equally impeccable credentials in the struggles of Black Brazilians, are particularly instructive. In his discussion of the uses and abuses of the African connection and its role in Brazil's African policies, Nascimento criticized institutions such as the Centro de Estudos Afro-Orientais in Bahia, for their lack of attention to the contemporary realities of Africa and Afro-Brazilians, a shortcoming he linked to racism in Bahia, where Blacks were largely absent from the organizations and institutions that supposedly dealt with them. He also criticized the role of Alakija at FESTAC for what he termed its irrelevance: Alakija, an official Brazilian representative at the festival, presented a paper on the state of trance in Candomblé.[43]

In his response, Alakija accused Nascimento of racism. Nascimento's paper, he went on, had been rejected at FESTAC solely on grounds of scholarship.[44] While the debate gave rise to a general discussion of Bahian racism in sections of the press, there was no open exchange between the two men. Both were present at the opening ceremonies for the exhibition of Ashanti art and culture in Salvador, but no confrontation took place.[45]

The unique role of Nascimento in Afro-Brazilian life and his importance to the African connection cannot be underestimated. He has consistently articulated the linkage between Afro-Brazilian life and the developments in continental Africa as well as other parts of the Diaspora, and he has twice been put in the position of providing a counterpoint to official interpretations of Afro-Brazil on the occasion of the two festivals of Black art and culture held in West Africa. He has taught at the University of Ife, Nigeria, participated in the Sixth Pan-African Congress held in Dar es Salaam in 1975, and has relentlessly advocated the importance of African-Brazilian links.[46]

It is perhaps fitting that his own words be recalled in a cautionary note on some of the necessary realities to be confronted: "não é só porque é africano que é bom. Nos vemos perfeitamente, dentro do nosso proprio pais, supostos irmãos afro-brasileiros, que fazem o jogo das classes opressoras. As classes que exploram os negros inteiramente até no próprio continente africano."[47]

An "African connection" impinging upon, or in any way influencing Afro-Brazilian social mobility, has not been conspicuous. In the absence of a clearly defined policy towards Brazil in which Afro-Brazilians have a role, it is highly unlikely that any African connection is at work. The conceptualization of Afro-Brazilians among Africans, both officially and unofficially, has tended to be of the "frozen" variant: a veneer of African religious, cultural, culinary, and folkloric survivals totally removed from the contemporary socio-political and economic realities of Brazil. Because of this serious lack of knowledge and active interest in contemporary Afro-Brazilian affairs, there has not emerged a national or collective Brazilian policy in post-colonial Africa. What we have called "dynamic" africanity has not characterized the current African view of Afro-Brazil.

Fascination with the historical, the cultural, and the religious aspects of Afro-Brazil is understandable, if only because it testifies to African survivals and contributions to the development of Brazilian society. It has also been the basis of Brazil's contribution to the socio-economic and political formations of some contemporary African states—Nigeria, Benin, Togo, Ghana, and Angola. However, neither of these contributions can be seen to be full explanations for the present relations between Brazil and Africa. The return of Afro-Brazilians to nineteenth- and twentieth-century Africa provides us with a fascinating reverse flow in the African diaspora, but it does not explain Brazilian-African relations today.[48]

The small group of Afro-Brazilians who, over the years, have kept themselves informed of developments on the African continent could not be said to have benefited in any significant way from socio-cultural outreach by African countries. This situation is not helped by the isolation of Brasília from the major centers of Afro-Brazilian populations—Rio de Janeiro, São Paulo, and Salvador.[49] Naturally, African diplomatic representation in Brazil is limited to Brasília, except for the presence in Rio of the Senegalese and Ivoirian consulates in the late 1970s. Nigeria is scheduled to open a consulate general in Rio. We are thus left with the situation first noted in 1970, that the center of African life in Brazil, Salvador da Bahia, has not and does not have an African cultural diplomatic presence.[50]

The case is not being argued for African relations with Brazil to be centered exclusively on culture or history. The point is meant to illustrate the contention that even in these most visible and oft-cited areas, avowed interest has not been matched by concrete action.

At a 1978 seminar in Rio, it was suggested that a good way of furthering contemporary African-Brazilian relations would be for Afro-Brazilians to visit Africa. There was a pointed response, "How are people going to pay the Cr$12,000 travel deposit?" Although that particular requirement has ceased to be operational, the fact remains that the general socio-economic position of Afro-Brazilians militates against trips to Africa. And since there are no recognizable Blacks in Brazil's diplomatic representation in Africa (or elsewhere), the official route does not appear to be very promising. For these reasons, the lack of African initiatives in Brazil becomes even more striking.

On a more positive note, the case could be made for the "symbolic" and "inspirational" contribution of the African connection to Afro-Brazilian life, such as the reactions to the Angolan government's decision on the "Sítio do Pica Pau Amarelo" show,[51] and to António Neder's Itamaraty speech expressing his fears of the rise of a "Black Hitler" in Africa. Afro-Brazilian papers are aware of such "insults" to African diplomats in Brazil, be they of the "indirect" variant as above, or of the more "direct" kind, as in the case of an African ambassador in Rio de Janiero who was ordered at gunpoint out of a taxi cab driven by a Black because the police were looking for muggers. The clear conclusion drawn on that occasion was of the general precariousness of Black life—unattenuated in this case by diplomatic status. Community of interests between Africans and Afro-Brazilians thus makes for better mutual understanding.

Inevitably, comparison with the United States must be addressed. Because of linguistic, political, and religious considerations, there has been a strong linkage between continental African affairs and Afro-American political and religious developments.[52] Not only did Kwame Nkrumah, Nnamdi Azikiwe, and other early African nationalists study in Black American colleges, but also the United States has always provided a focus of interest for contemporary Africa. Even if this interest has not always been of a uniformly positive kind, it has been undisputably active in a way that has no counterpart in contemporary Brazil. Marcus Garvey did not set foot in Africa, although his movement was widely known there. Malcolm X went to Africa, W. E. B. Du Bois died there, and a whole host of Afro-Americans, both well-known and obscure, have been to Africa and have kept up with Africa in the United States through the presence of African diplomats, students, businessmen, and others. But not even this great contact has resulted in any clear American, or specifically Afro-American, policies on the part of independent African countries, individually or collectively. Awareness of this situation might help our understanding of its Brazilian equivalent. Unlike Brazil, however, the United States has had a number of Black ambassadors and other diplomatic personnel not only in Africa but throughout the world, and the Afro-American component is officially recognized as relevant, even if not always critical or acted upon, in foreign policy. The nature of U.S. race relations, and the changes that have occurred over the last two decades or so, can account for the difference with Brazil in the matter of the African connection.

The very title of this chapter may be problematic because of the difficulty in establishing this connection in Brazil. It may have become salient only because of the reiteration of the historical, cultural, and religious linkages in official and unofficial statements, with a disproportionate amount of this reiteration emanating from the Brazilian side. At present, it continues to be what it has been since the beginning of relations between Brazil and independent African states—rather symbolic and decidedly non-material. There could be some change, dependent upon the extent to which African states will assume a portion of the initiative in defining relations with Brazil, instead of merely responding to Brazilian initiatives. More important still is the degree to which internal Brazilian race relations undergo such a change great enough to catapult Afro-Brazilians into the areas of government, politics, economics, and education, in which they have hitherto been conspicuous by their absence.

The transformation of "frozen" into "dynamic" africanity therefore becomes a multi-pronged enterprise involving Africans, Brazilians in general, and Afro-Brazilians in particular, as well as the political, social, and economic institutions through which they act and which act upon them. While prediction is not easy, it is impossible that by the end of the 1980s, African-Brazilian relations, with special reference to Afro-Brazilians, will be based on more contemporary contact: more awareness of internal political and economic dynamics and the way they influence, and are influenced by, those that are international.

If not in the foreseeable future, Africa and Brazil may eventually go beyond the rhetoric of religious, historical, cultural, and culinary linkages, important as they may be, and recognize the need for broader contact, more education on both the Brazilian and African sides—especially on the latter. This could prevent such fiascos as the meeting between members of the Nigerian Institute of International Affairs and Brazilians in São Paulo in August 1980, where the Nigerian delegation expressed surprise at the initial absence of Afro-Brazilians. When African newspapers and magazines, as well as academic publications, begin to pay serious attention to Brazil and Afro-Brazilians, Africans will be closer to approaching and understanding the Brazilian "reality."

By the same token, a more analytical approach to the study of contemporary Africa, an awareness of its political fluidity, and a keen interest in the situation of people of African descent the world over, may help Brazilians understand the nature of Africans' failure to accept claims of the relative irrelevance of the "racial" factor, or specifically of the "Blackness" element (or African connection) in multiracial societies. The African stance is primarily in view of the scarcity of people of African descent outside the marginalized sectors or those areas in which exceptionally talented Blacks have traditionally distinguished themselves in the Americas, such as the entertainment sector.

This chapter has emphasized issues which have traditionally received much less attention in the overall coverage of Brazil's relations with Africa in an attempt to indicate that they are equally important, although much less obvious than the volume of trade between Brazil and Africa. To their credit, certain Brazilian observers have been aware of these potentially problematic areas.[53] Amilcar Alencastre, for example, has noted that while Itamaraty understands that business with Africa is complicated by the South African factor, Brazil's past identification with Portuguese colonialism, and possible fallouts from the African perception of Brazil as a Black country, it is beyond Itamaraty's power to handle all these issues alone, as other sectors of the Brazilian power structure are involved in the relationship. Alencastre suggested that Brazil could better relations by changing its approach to dealing with Africa, which, in his view, is similar to Europe's dealings with Third World countries. The irony, for Alencastre, is that Europe has now recognized the importance of Africa and has sought to improve relations.[54]

At the time of this writing, the most visible Afro-Brazilian in Brazil's relations with Africa continues to be São Paulo Federal Deputy Adalberto Camargo. Abdias do Nascimento and others argue that purely formal and business approaches are too restrictive and lack the dynamism needed to involve the majority of Afro-Brazilians, whose living and working conditions exclude them from the business world, and who would be more interested in developing more participatory relationships than business allows. In their view, the dramatic developments in Brazil's trade with Africa — U.S. $1 billion, a 1200-fold increase from 1973 to 1979, in the case of Angola, going from U.S. $2.7 million in 1973 to U.S. $73 million in 1979, and with Mozambique from U.S. $2.7 million in 1973 to U.S. $8 million in 1979 — do not invalidate worries about relations with South Africa, although these had declined by 1979.[55]

A recent report in *Africa Confidential* noted that, "To strengthen political and trade links with black Africa, Brazil has been projecting itself as a leader of the Third World. As a result, it has recently been playing down its relationship with South Africa. Yet many South African firms — expecially in the mining sector — still view Brazil as a ripe area for investment."[56] Acting through Lisbon-based subsidiaries, South African firms can achieve a measure of control over the price, availability, and types of explosives manufactured, which in turn helps mining and construction subsidiaries in Brazil to operate competitively, the report went on. The fact that multinational operations involving Portuguese, South African, and British giants like ICI are dealing with Brazilian subsidiaries is a potential source of unease between Brazil and Black Africa.[57]

For the future, neither the history of the transatlantic slave trade and its consequences, the return of Afro-Brazilians to Africa and political, economic, or social roles in the nineteenth and twentieth centuries, and the preservation of African cultural institutions in Brazil, nor the one-dimensional pursuit of trade and profit, cloaked in rhetorical niceties bearing on technical cooperation among developing countries, or "South-South Dialogue" — important as they are — can take the place of a carefully thought-out policy which is mutually beneficial. The challenge points in the direction of Africa. Whether or not it will be met thoughtfully and innovatively to enhance relations in which Afro-Brazilians play an important role remains to be seen. Brazil has acted and provided ample evidence of changes in its African relations over the last decade. Thus, Africa, Brazil, Afro-Brazilians, the nature of the relationships between them, and especially the resolution of the very grave problem with the apartheid regime of South Africa promise a future which will be far from dull whatever its trajectory.

The present U.S. administration's emphasis on "international terrorism" and on those states committed to combating such terrorism, to which the apartheid regime claims membership, has contributed to a rapprochement between Pretoria and Washington. South Africa's interest in the defense of the South Atlantic has some bearing on the politics of that region and in the South Atlantic Pact, from which Brazil has publicly dissociated itself, but which continues to be of interest to African and other observers.

Thus, the colonial and post- or neo-colonial world in which African-Brazilian relations evolved in the past continues to be the venue for present and future relations. The ideological content of the South-South dialogue, technical cooperation among Third World countries, the provision of counterpoints to imperialism, and the creation of a "Third-World middle class," in the words of José Maria Nunes Pereira, do not alter the reality that the bulk of the Third World remains proletarian.[58]

We end where we began, with the African connection and the Afro-Brazilian condition, having explored the ramifications of the concept and having even questioned its validity. There can be no doubt of its significance and the urgent need to conceptualize it dynamically and innovatively for more fruitful relations between Brazil and Africa in which the Afro-Brazilian becomes more than a symbol.

At the beginning of the decade that will mark the centenary of the abolition of slavery in Brazil, the African connection promises to become ever more vigorous, surpassing expectations among both official and unofficial activists in Brazil, as well as in Africa itself. It seems unlikely that the inherent racial nexus will fade away, particularly in the African view. Therein lies the significance of the African connection for articulated Afro-Brazilian perceptions of self and their relations to Africa, as well as their role in changing Brazilian patterns of race relations.

[P]roduzem novas condições de vida no continente-mãe, tem especial significado para nós descendentes de africanos espalhados pelas Américas. Portanto, é indispensavel aproveitarmos os ensinamentos positivos da libertação africana, para que aprendamos a trabalhar melhor nas necessidades aqui e agora.

Nós e a África[59]

NOTES

1. "The use of African names is not a mere fad. The book and the movie *Roots* (black roots) show that all who wished to maintain their original names were tortured until they accepted a Christian name imposed by the master!" [editor's translation] *Tição* 2(2) (August 1978).

2. Mara Cabenero, "Embaixadores de África abrem o Carnaval na avenida," *Jornal do Brasil* (Caderno B), 19 February 1977.

3. Seminar on Afro-Brazilian Studies, 19–24 April 1971. Pontifical Catholic University, Department of Sociology; Coordinator, Professor José Nilo Tavares. Emmanuel Okin Kejuo of Cameroon and Anani Dzidzienyo were among the other Africans present.

4. "A Black speaking English or French . . . was not just any old Black." [editor's translation]

5. Special tribute must be paid here to some of the unsung heroes who have contributed to a better awareness, theoretically and practically, of the ramifications of African-Brazilian relations: José Maria Nunes Pereira and his colleagues at the Centro de Estudos Afro-Asiáticos of the Candido Mendes University in Rio for their unfailing aid to wandering or transient scholars directly or indirectly involved with Africa-Brazil; Professor Edson Nunes da Silva of Bahia, whose wisdom and help are always at the disposal of researchers; J. Michael Turner, whose "Les Brésiliens: The Impact of Former Brazilian Slaves upon Dahomey" (Ph.D. diss., Boston University, 1975) and other efforts in this field have to be returned to, as we return to Pierre Verger's *Flux et reflux*; and finally, to groups of young and old Afro-Brazilians through organizations such as the Instituto de Pesquisas das Culturas Negras in Rio and elsewhere who have sought to present an Africa in its contemporary aspects and not only as "history."

6. *Vargas, mensagem ao Congresso Nacional, apresentado pelo Presidente da República por ocasião da Abertura da Sessão Legislativa de 1952* (Rio de Janeiro: Depto. da Imprensa Nacional), 36.

7. *Ibid.*, 39.

8. "But the fundamental error in Jânio's foreign policy was not in its substance, which he planned and conceived well, but in the more than dramatic, theatrical manner in which he executed it for reasons of domestic politics and by his individual involvement as both character and author." Afonso Arinos de Melo Franco, "Portugal-Brazil-Africa," *Tempo Brasileiro* 38/39: 69 (July–December 1974). [editor's translation]

9. "These people, many of whom were friends, created the most subtle and most resistent silk cloth of obstacles to my actions whose significance escaped them and which I did not have time to explain." *Ibid.*, 71. [editor's translation]

10. *Ibid.*

11. Amilcar Alencastre, *O Brasil, a África e o futuro* (Rio de Janeiro: Grafica Editora Laemmert, 1971), 82–85, 135–136 and 165–166.

12. See Carlos Comitini, *África arde: Lutas dos povos africanos pela liberdade* (Rio de Janeiro: Editora Codecri [Pasquim], 1980. Coleção Terceiro Mundo, vol. 2.)
13. "[W]ith a passivity incompatible with our public opinion and with the democratic sentiments already crystallized in our anti-racist laws." Constantino Ianni, "Racismo, futebol e outros problemas: O Brasil envolvido pelo racismo da África do sul," in *Descolonização em marcha: Economia e relacões internacionais* (Rio de Janeiro: Editora Civilização Brasileira, 1972) 97–98. [editor's translation] This article was written in 1966. Walter, the "colored" player, was left out of the team. Ianni noted that apartheid is an affront to human civilization and contains the seeds of racial warfare.
14. Ronald Schneider, *Brazil: The Foreign Policy of a Future Great Power* (Boulder, Colorado: Westview Press, 1976). Also, "Brazil Goes Africa," *West Africa*, 30 January 1978; Marx Gruberg, "Subsaharan Africa: Potential Market, Vexing Political Challenge," *Brazil Herald*, 7 September 1977; "Descoberta da África," *Veja* 27: 28–29 (April 19). See also, "Cardeal vai a África para compreender o sincretismo religioso dos brasileiros," *Jornal do Brasil*, 3 July 1979; "Cardeal volta da África e diz que viagem teve objetivos missionários," *Jornal do Brasil*, 17 July 1979. See also interview with Padre Valentin Kiba, ex-secretary-general, Simpósio da Conferencia Episcopal Africana e de Madagascar (SCEAM) in *Afro-Chamber* (São Paulo) 3 (1979).
15. Two successive U.S. Ambassadors to the United Nations under the Carter Administration, Andrew Young and Donald McHenry, were Black. Black ambassadors have represented the U.S. in Sweden, Ghana, Tanzania, Algeria, Cameroon, Senegal, and Kenya, among others. There have been Black generals in both the army and the air force, and Black admirals in the navy within the last fifteen years.
16. Black African students had been admitted several years earlier to the Institute, Brazil's foreign service academy. — ED. Mónica Meneses de Campos gained admission to the Instituto Rio Branco amidst much fanfare in the Brazilian media in August 1978. There was slight confusion when she affirmed that she was *mulata* rather than Black. Quite remarkable was the fact of her being described as Black in the first place. Perhaps the usage "Black" in the media approximates the U.S. variant more than has hitherto been admitted. See, "Atriz necessária à política brasileira," *Jornal do Brasil*, 3 August 1978. See also "A primeira negra aprovada para estudar diplomacia prefere servir naonu," *Jornal do Brasil*, 2 August 1978; "Política externa: O preconceito do Itamarati," *Jornal de Brasília*, 3 August 1978, and "Discriminação no Itamarati, não só racial mas contra mulheres também," *Corréio Brasiliense*, 3 August 1978; and "A diplomata negra nunca sonhou com o pioneirismo," *Jornal de Brasília*, 2 August 1978.
17. George Shepard, Jr., ed., *Racial Influences on American Foreign Policy* (New York: Basic Books, 1971); Basil Ince, "The Racial Factor in International Relations of Trinidad and Tobago," *Caribbean Studies* 16 (3–4): 5–28 (October 1976–January 1977); and Thomas Skidmore, *Black Into White: Race and Nationality in Brazilian Thought* (New York: Oxford University Press, 1974).
18. W. Ofuatey-Kodjoe, "The Ideological Triangle: Reciprocal Ideological Influences Among Afro-West Indians, Afro-Americans and Africans," *Studia Africana* (An International Journal of African Studies) 1(1): 1–16 (Spring 1977).
19. *Tição* 2(2): 7 (August 1978).
20. Anani Dzidzienyo, "Afro-Brazilians, Other Afro-Latin Americans and Africanity: Frozen and Dynamic," paper presented at the Eighth Annual Meeting of African Heritage Studies Association (AHSA), Atlanta, April 1976; Rhett S. Jones and Anani Dzidzienyo, "Africanity, Structural Isolations and Black Politics in the Americas," *Studia Africana*, 32–44.
21. The relations of Brazil and the U.S.A. with Africa provide two examples of the importance of the racial factor in their international relations. See the contributions of William

Schaufele, Jr., former Under-Secretary for Africa, and Ruth Schachter Morgenthau in the special issue of *The Annals of the American Academy of Political and Social Science*, "Africa in Transition," July 1977.

22. See Wayne Selcher, *The Afro-Asian Dimension to Brazilian Foreign Policy* (Gainesville, Florida: University of Florida Press, 1974); Keith Larry Storrs, "Brazil's Independent Foreign Policy 1961–1964: Background, Trends, Linkage to Domestic Policies and Aftermath" (Ph.D. diss., Cornell University, 1972); José Honório Rodrigues, *Brazil and Africa* (Berkeley: University of California Press, 1964); Adolfo Justo Bezera de Menezes, *O Brasil e o mundo afro-asiático* (Rio de Janeiro: Edições GRD, 1960); and Samuel Yaw Boadi-Siaw, "Development of Relations Between Brazil and African States 1950–1975" (Ph.D. diss., University of California, Los Angeles, 1975).

23. See Selcher, *Afro-Asian Dimension*, and John Marcum, *The Angolan Revolution*, vol. 2, *Exile, Politics and Guerrilla Warfare, 1962–1976* (Cambridge, Mass.: M.I.T. Press, 1978); Clovis Brigagão, "Brazil's Foreign Policy: The Military Command, Itamarati Embellishes, Multinationals Gain," *International Peace Research Institute* (Oslo) 18 (1978); and Gabriel Filho, "Final de Festa," *Veja*, 18 June 1980.

24. See "Estudantes negros fazem protesto pelo tratamento que receberam da polícia," *Jornal do Brasil*, 13 September 1979.

25. See Golbery do Couto e Silva, *Geopolítica do Brasil*, (Rio de Janeiro: Editora José Olympio, 1967); "South Atlantic: Defending the Sea Lanes of the West," *Latin America Political Report*, 30 April 1976; Daniel Waksman Schnica, "Pretoria y U.S. aliados: El idilio de los conos sur," *Cuadernos del Tercer Mundo* 2(12): 52–55 (May 1977); David Fig, "Apartheid's Hands Across the Atlantic," *Guardian* (Manchester), 8 June 1979; and the interview with Brazilian Navy Minister, Admiral Maximiniano Fonseca, "Não é preciso un pacto no Atlântico Sul," *Veja*, 25 April 1979, 28–29.

26. See Jacques d'Adesky, *Analyse des échanges commerciaux Brésil-Afrique 1958–1977: problèmes et perspectives* (Rio de Janeiro: Conjunto Universitário Candido Mendes, CEAA, 1979); "Brazil . . . Just Plant and Anything Grows," in *Africa Guide* (Saffron Walden, Essex: World Information, 1979), 30–33; and Peter Eisner, "Brazil and Africa Seek Closer Ties," *Los Angeles Times*, 2 March 1980.

27. Presidents Touré of Guinea, Kaunda of Zambia, Bongo of Gabon, and ex-presidents Senghor of Senegal and Luis Cabral of Guinea (Bissau) all visited Brazil between 1977 and 1980. The Ghanaian traditional ruler, Otumfuo Nana Opoku Ware II's visit in June 1978 was perhaps the most colorful. The emphasis was on culture, history, and art. An exhibition of Ashanti art and culture which he inaugurated in Brasília was subsequently shown in Florianópolis, São Paulo, Salvador, and Rio de Janeiro. See "Rei africano vai ao planalto e entrega convite à Geisel," *Correio Brasilense*, 15 June 1978; "Presidente recebe no planalto rei africano," *O Globo*, 15 June 1978; "Maior rei tribal de Gana, em visita turística a Bahia," *Diário Oficial*, 17–18 June 1978. See "Figueiredo garante que não muda relações com a África," *Jornal do Brasil*, 11 January 1979, on the talks with Nigerian Chief of Staff, General Shehu Yau'adua; and "Brasil quer fim dos governos de minoria racial," *Jornal do Brasil*, 30 August 1979, on the welcoming of President Kaunda. See also "Sekou Toure in Brazil," *West Africa*, 3 March 1980, "Senghor in South America," *West Africa*, 14 November 1977; and on Cabral's visit, "Mão dupla: Brasil e Guiné," *Veja*, 25 June 1980.

28. The only Afro-Brazilian the Otumfuo's party met officially was Ambassador Raymundo Souza Dantas, who served in Ghana from 1961 to 1964. Dantas was the first Black Brazilian ambassador.

29. The concept "Africa Card" is borrowed from the "China Card," as used in discussions of U.S. relations with the USSR.

30. See Anani Dzidzienyo, "África, vista do Brasil," *Afro-Asia* (10–11): 79–97 (1970); "The

World of the Afro-Brazilians," *West Africa*, 5 March 1973, 301.

31. Among the relevant publications, see *Sinba* (Rio de Janeiro), *Jornegro* (São Paulo), *O Saci* (São Paulo), *Afro-Chamber* (São Paulo), *Ébano* (São Paulo), and *Tição* (Porto Alegre); and in the 1920s and 1930s, *O Getulino* (Campinas), *O Clarim d'Alvorado* (São Paulo), and *Voz da Raça* (São Paulo).

32. See, "Quando todos se dispersam: Os homens de côr formam a Frente Negra da Bahia," *A Tarde*, 24 November 1932; also, "Frentes Negras: Um problema novo: A Bahia e os problemas artificiais," *A Tarde*, 6 December 1932.

33. Edvaldo Brito, subsequently became the first Black mayor of Salvador in the last eight months of Governor Roberto Santos's administration. This author was part of the Otum-fuo's party. See "Edvaldo Brito, primeiro negro prefeito da cidade," *Tribuna da Bahia*, 8 August 1978; and "Conterráneio de Castro Alves: católico, filho de Ogum," *Veja*, 23 August 1978.

34. *Afro-Chamber* is published in São Paulo. See *Afro-Chamber* 2(3): 6, 31–32 (1979).

35. *Ibid.*

36. "Nós e África," *Jornegro* 1(4) (September 1978).

37. Sr. Antonio Neder's speech was criticized in Black newspapers and many Black circles. See *Jornegro*, August 1979, 2(6): 28. See also *Sinba* (2): 1 (April 1979). [Arthur de Gobineau (1816–1882) was a racist author whose works, such as *Essai sur l'inegalité des races humaines*, influenced Brazilian thought on race in the nineteenth century.]

38. "The African countries have much to teach the manipulators of Brazilian cultural exports. Here, if Blacks protest they are immediately called racist. You can't get away with this with the government of Angola. The revision of the Brazilian mentality, which many want to see, is pushed forward. Brazil's camouflaged racism did not go over in Africa." *Sinba*, 1978. [editor's translation]

39. *Ibid.*

40. See *Lampião da Esquina* 2(18) (November 1979).

41. See Rubem Confete, "Olga de Alaketo: Objeto de consumo do poder," *Lampião* 2(18); "Pelé continua o mesmo, quem mudou?" *Jornegro*, 1 March 1976. See *Nacões amigas (Revista brasileira especializada em comércio e relacões exteriores)* 1 (1978), in which Carlos Santana, the vice-president of the Intebras company, is quoted as saying, "thanks to the publicity and support given by the appealing figure of Pelé, projected by newspapers and television and broadcast on radio," operation Tamá was able to conquer new markets, especially Nigeria. [editor's translation]

42. Confete, "Olga de Alaketo."

43. Nascimento's visit to Salvador, Bahia, in August 1978 attracted headline coverage because of his criticism of the role of the Centro de Estudos Afro-Orientais and its director at that time, Guilherme Castro Alves. He also criticized George Alakija, who responded in kind. See *Tribuna da Bahia*, *A tarde*, and *Jornal da Bahia*, 1–3 August 1978. "Pretos e brancos," *A tarde*, 3 August 1978; also, "Negro gera polêmica," *Jornal do Brasil*, 2 August 1978. Alakija himself has conceded that his forte is not the study of Black culture in his introduction to a volume of poems by Antonio Vieira.

44. In the heat of the controversy there was, perhaps, a bit of oversimplification on both sides, with Nascimento virtually describing Alakija's presence at FESTAC as a joke, and with the latter in turn accusing Nascimento of hating all things white.

45. Even more remarkable about these opening ceremonies was the presence of a large number of Afro-Bahians, the result of a special barrage of hand-delivered invitations, for opening nights are not traditionally graced with a significant Black presence, even in Bahia.

46. From 1976 to 1977, he was Visiting Professor in the Department of African Languages and Literature at the University of Ife, Nigeria. It was during this time that he participated

in the Festival of Black Arts and Culture held in Lagos and Kaduna, Nigeria. His *Racial Democracy in Brazil: Myth or Reality?* (Ibadan, Nigeria: Sketch Publishing, 1977) is the paper "presented to and rejected by" the official colloquium at FESTAC. It had been serialized by the *Daily Times* (Lagos), and the *Daily Sketch* (Ibadan) in January 1977. See also, "The Plight of Blacks in Brazil," *Nigerian Observer*, 28 January 1977. The colloquium topic was "Black Civilization and Philosophy."

47. "The sole fact of being African does not necessarily make it good. We see perfectly, within our own country, supposed Afro-Brazilian brothers, who play the game of the oppressing classes. The classes which utterly exploit Blacks even on the African continent itself." Abdias do Nascimento, "Etnia afro-brasileira e política internacional," in *Quilombismo* (Petrópolis: Editôra Vozes, 1980), 155–208. [editor's translation]
48. J. Michael Turner, *Les brésilians.*
49. Edson Nunes da Silva (Bahia), Sebastião Rodrigues Alves (Rio), and Dra. Sebastiana Arruda (Rio) are among them. Before the move of diplomatic representations to Brasília, Ghana, Nigeria, Senegal, and Ivory Coast had embassies in Rio de Janeiro in the early 1970s. By 1978, Senegal and Ivory Coast had consulates in Rio, both of which were subsequently closed. A new Nigerian consulate will soon reestablish an official African presence in Rio. Ghana, Senegal, Nigeria, Ivory Coast, Zaire, Gabon, and Togo have resident ambassadors in Brasília.
50. Dzidzienyo, "A África — Vista do Brasil," *Afro-Asia* (1970).
51. On the "Sítio do Pica Pau Amarelo" incident of 1978, see "O sítio racista," *Jornegro* 2(6): 5 (1979); see also *Sinba* (1979).
52. See Ofuatey-Kodjoe, "The Ideological Triangle," especially notes 1–10.
53. See Amilcar Alencastre in *Senhor*, January 1981, as well as articles by Fred Aflabo and Mirna Grzich.
54. Alencastre, *Senhor*, January 1981.
55. See Roy Lashley, "Brazil and Cuba Court Africa," *South: The Third World Magazine* (2): 15–18 (November 1980).
56. See *Africa Confidential* 22(3), 11 February 1981.
57. The chairman of Ambras, the Brazilian subsidiary of Anglo-American, is Mario Ferreira of Portugal. In 1973 Indústria Química Contiqueira (IQM) negotiated with Imperial Chemical Industries (ICI) to attract needed capital for expansion. ICI, meanwhile, co-owns African Explosives Company International (AECI) in the Southern Hemisphere. IQM sold to EMPAR, the Brazilian subsidiary of SOFIN, which has prepared to sell 30 percent of new holdings to Anglo-American; the remaining 20 percent of its shares were sold to BRASEX, AECI's Brazilian subsidiary in 1979. Rumors were about that SOFIN was willing to surrender its 50 percent share of IQM to AECI for an acceptable price, which would greatly strengthen Anglo-American's position in the Brazilian mining industry.
58. In *Senhor*, January 1981.
59. "The creation of new conditions of life on the mother-continent holds a special significance for us descendents of Africans scattered through the Americas. Therefore, we must take advantage of the positive lessons of African liberation, to learn to work better to meet the necessities of here and now." From "Nós e a Africa," *Jornegro* 1 (4): 1. [editor's translation]

ABBREVIATIONS

ABC	Region around the city of São Paulo
ACBB	Christian Charitable Association of Brazil
AECI	African Explosives Company International
AHSA	African Heritage Studies Association (U.S. organization)
ANPOCS	National Association for Postgraduate Studies and Research in the Social Sciences
ARENA	National Renovation Alliance (party of the military government)
BRASEX	Brazilian subsidiary of African Explosives Company International
CEAA	Center for Afro-Asian Studies (Candido Mendes University, Rio de Janeiro)
CECAN	Center for the Study of Black Culture and Art
CEN	National Executive Commission (MNU)
CLs	Centros de Luta (Centers of Struggle, MNU)
CMs	Municipal Coordinating Committees (MNU)
CNBB	National Conference of Brazilian Bishops
FAFERJ	Federation of Associations of Favela Dwellers of the State of Rio de Janeiro
FESTAC	Festival of Black Arts and Culture (Nigeria)
FNB	Brazilian Negro Front, or Black Brazilian Front (Frente Negra Brasileira)
IBEA	Brazilian Institute of Africanist Studies
IBGE	Brazilian Institute of Geography and Statistics
ICI	Imperial Chemical Industries
IPCN	Institute for Research on Black Cultures (Rio de Janeiro)

IQM   Indústria Química Contiqueira (Contiqueira Chemical
            Industry)
IUPERJ   University Research Institute of Rio de Janeiro (Candido
            Mendes University)

MDB   Movimento Democrático Brasileiro (Brazilian Democratic
            Movement)
MNU   Movimento Negro Unificado (shortened form of
            MNUCDR)
MNUCDR   Movimento Negro Unificado Contra Discriminação
            Racial (Unified Black Movement against Racial
            Discrimination)
MPLA   Popular Movement for the Liberation of Angola

PCB   Brazilian Communist Party
PC do B   Communist Party of Brazil
PDS   Social Democratic Party (government)
PDT   Partido Democrático Trabalhista (Democratic Labor
            Party)
PMDB   Party of the Brazilian Democratic Movement
PNAD   National Household Sample Research
PP   Partido Popular (Popular Party)
PT   Partido Trabalhista (Workers Party)

RJ   Rio de Janeiro

SBPC   Brazilian Society for the Progress of Science
SCEAM   Simpósio da Conferencia Episcopal Africana e de
            Madagascar (Symposium of the African and Madagascan
            Episcopal Conference)
SECNEB   Society for the Study of Black Culture in Brazil (Bahia)
SNI   National Information Service
SP   São Paulo

TEN   Teatro Experimentál do Negro (Negro Experimental
            Theater)

USP   University of São Paulo

GLOSSARY

abertura: Literally the act or effect of opening; abertura, or *abertura democrática*, refers to the process of "redemocratization" in Brazil (see chapter 7).

abre-fecha: Open-shut; used in reference to the uncertain process of *abertura*.

afoxé: Afro-Brazilian cultural and religious club that forms a *bloco* for carnaval and sings *candomblé* songs in Nagô or Yoruba. Once outlawed by the government afoxés (pronounced ah-foh-shay) were reestablished circa 1978.

amarelo(s): Literally "yellow," a colloquial term for Asians.

aproximação: The process of getting closer.

bairro(s): Administrative district(s).

bloco(s): Group(s) of activists; carnaval cortege(s).

cabo eleitoral: Precinct captain, or person who gathers votes for a political candidate.

capoeira: A martial art developed by Africans in Brazil during slavery which is played by pairs of *capoeiristas* within a circle to traditional music performed on the berimbau and other instruments; often performed as a dance; practiced in schools and academies throughout Brazil.

candomblé: Afro-Brazilian religion, primarily practiced in Salvador da Bahia; worships *orixás*, or deities; has great similarities to Yoruba practices of worship in West Africa. Once persecuted—*orixás* were "syncretized," or associated with saints so that they could be worshipped under the guise of embracing Catholicism—candomblé is now proudly referred to as evidence of Brazil's "Africanity," both by Blacks and by the government that would exploit it.

cassação: The act of depriving a person of political rights.

cassado: Deprived of political rights.

Castelista: Follower of Humberto Castelo Branco; supporter of *abertura*.
centros de luta: Centers of struggle; name given by the MNU to their community organizations; now renamed "Action Groups" (see chapter 8).
cordialidade: Hospitality; claimed by Brazilians to be a national trait.

distensão: Détente.

empreguismo: "Jobbism," or struggle for political appointments.
escolas de samba: Samba schools; groups that form corteges composed of samba and frevo dancers, composers, musicians, and others, who promote festivals, spectacles, and parades, especially at carnaval. This term also refers to the schools themselves, where the groups rehearse year-round for the fierce song, music, and costume competition of carnaval.
espaço de ninguem: No-man's-land.
Estado Nôvo: "New State"; name given to the period of the dictatorship of Getúlio Dórtico Vargas (1937–1945).
estatização: "Statism"; the policy of forming state-owned corporations, such as Petrobrás.

favela(s): Squatter settlements, or shantytowns, that have sprung up on the outskirts of urban areas. The term is most frequently used in Rio de Janeiro, where favelas perch precariously on the *morros*, often bordering on the most affluent areas of the city.
favelado(a): Favela dweller.
fazendeiro: Owner of a *fazenda* (plantation, ranch, or farm); generally a large-scale planter, farmer, or rancher.
Frente Negra Brasileira: Brazilian Black Front, a Black movement of the 1920s and 1930s (see chapters 2 and 8).

gaúcho: From Rio Grande do Sul, the southernmost state of Brazil, which is geographically and culturally contiguous to Argentina and Uruguay. Derives from "gaucho," the cowboy of the Southern Cone.
golpe de estado: Coup d'etat.
grupão: "Big group"; term given by the MNU to meetings of its Coordinating Committees (see chapter 8).
Guarda Nacional: National Guard; a vehicle for mulatto social mobility in nineteenth-century Brazil.

ialorixá: Yoruba for "priestess"; refers to a priestess of *candomblé*.
institutos: Institutes; formed by Geisel to oversee commerce.
irmandades: Brotherhoods; refers to Black brotherhoods (see chapter 5).

jogo: Game.

latifúndio(s): Large rural estate(s); generally associated with agriculture and the exploitation of cheap manual labor.

macumba: Afro-Brazilian religion (see *candomblé* and *umbanda*).
mãe-de-santo: Afro-Brazilian priestess of *macumba* or *candomblé*.
mestiço: Person of mixed racial origin.
mestre: Master; title of respect for a teacher or elder.
moreno: Brown; one of the many terms used to identify Afro-Brazilians.
morro(s): Steep hill(s); usual location of *favelas*, especially in Rio de Janeiro.
Movimento Negro Unificado: Unified Black Movement (see chapter 8).
mulato, mulata: Man, woman, of mixed African and Caucasian heritage, or having a Black and white parent; light- or brown-skinned Black.

negro: Black; phenotypically African and dark-skinned.

pacote: Package (e.g. "Pacote de Abril," or "April Package").
pardo: Brown-skinned.
pastoral, pastorais (pl.): Pastorale(s); in this case, a dramatic religious presentation (see chapter 5).
povo: The people.
preconceito de marca: Prejudice based on physical appearance.
preconceito racial de origem: Prejudice based on racial origin, or consanguinity.
preto: Black.

Quilombismo: Movement begun by Abdias do Nascimento for promoting Black consciousness. Based on the premise that Blacks today are escaping racism by entering activist movements just as they escaped slavery to join *quilombos*.
quilombo: Settlement of escaped slaves. The quilombos, some of which maintained their independence until Abolition, were formed primarily in the wilds of the state of Alagoas. The *quilombolas* organized the quilombos as miniature African states. The most famous such settlement was the Quilombo dos Palmares, whose leader Zumbi has become a heroic figure in Afro-Brazilian history. Black activists have made the anniversary of his death, November 20, 1695, a day for the celebration of their African heritage.
quilombola: Person who lived in a quilombo; quilombola science is the scientific application of Quilombismo's ideology.

Semanas Afro-Brasileiras: Afro-Brazilian Weeks; weekly series of cultural events sponsored by the CEAA and SECNEB in 1974.
suplente: Substitute; used here to mean substitute senators.

telenovela(s): Soap opera(s), or serial dramas; a popular form of entertainment in Brazil.
terreiros: Places of worship, or temples, for Afro-Brazilian religions.
trabalhista: Labor (adj.).

umbanda: Formerly an Afro-Brazilian religion, this primarily Rio-based faith has blended African religious elements with "urban spiritism."
umbandistas: Practitioners of *umbanda*.

Zona Norte: Northern Zone; the poorer section of Rio de Janeiro.

CAAS Special Publication Series

Previous, unnumbered, volumes in the series include:

Dances of Haiti by Katherine Dunham, 1983, 78pp. + xxv
   ISBN 0-934934-17-7 (cloth) $22.50
   ISBN 0-934934-11-8 (pbk.) $14.50

Walter Rodney, Revolutionary and Scholar: A Tribute, Edward A. Alpers and
Pierre-Michel Fontaine, eds., 1983, 200pp.
   ISBN 0-934934-09-6 (cloth) $17.95
   ISBN 0-934934-08-8 (pbk.) $10.95

Nightstar 1973-1978 by Mari Evans, 1981, 78pp.
   ISBN 0-934934-07-X (pbk.) $5.25

*Graduate Research in Afro-American Studies: A Bibliography of Doctoral Disser-
tations and Master's Theses Completed at the University of California, Los
Angeles, from 1942 to 1980*, Nathaniel Davies, ed., 1981, 48pp.
   ISBN 0-934934-12-6 (pbk.) $1.95

Minorities in the Labor Market, Paul Bullock, ed., 1977, 119pp.
   ISBN 0-89215-095-5 $5.50

Ethnic Serials (compiled by Ethnic Materials Librarians at the UCLA Chicano,
Asian-American, American Indian, and Afro-American Studies Centers), 1977,
368pp., $5.50

These and other UCLA Center for Afro-American Studies publications may be
ordered from CAAS Publications, Publishers Services, P.O. Box 2510, Novato,
CA 94948.